Fort Worth

Fort Worth's Enterprises by Kathryn Jones

Produced in cooperation with The City of Fort Worth

Windsor Publications, Inc.
Chatsworth, California

Fort Worth

NEW FRONTIERS IN EXCELLENCE

A Contemporary Portrait by Mike Patterson

Windsor Publications, Inc.—Book Division
Managing Editor: Karen Story
Design Director: Alexander D'Anca
Photo Director: Susan L. Wells
Executive Editor: Pamela Schroeder

Staff for *Fort Worth: New Frontiers in Excellence*
Senior Manuscript Editor: Jerry Mosher
Photo Editor: Larry Molmud
Senior Editor, Corporate Profiles: Jeffrey Reeves
Production Editor, Corporate Profiles: Justin Scupine
Proofreaders: Mary Jo Scharf, Michael Moore
Customer Service Manager: Phyllis Feldman-Schroeder
Editorial Assistants: Elizabeth Anderson, Dominique
    Jones, Kim Kievman, Michael Nugwynne, Kathy B.
    Peyser, Theresa J. Solis
Publisher's Representative, Corporate Profiles: Marcus
    Black
Designer: Thomas McTighe
Art Director: Ellen Ifrah
Layout Artist, Editorial: Tanya Maiboroda
Layout Artist, Corporate Profiles: Sue Hartman

Windsor Publications, Inc.
Elliot Martin, Chairman of the Board
James L. Fish III, Chief Operating Officer
Michele Sylvestro, Vice President/Sales-Marketing
Mac Buhler, Vice President/Acquisitions

Library of Congress Cataloging-in-Publication Data
Patterson, Mike.   Fort Worth, new frontiers in
    excellence : a contemporary portrait / by Mike Pat-
    terson. — 1st ed.
p. 192 cm. 23 x 31
"Produced in cooperation with the City of Fort
    Worth." Includes bibliographic references and
    index. ISBN: 0-89781-355-3
1. Fort Worth (Tex.)—Civilization. 2. Fort Worth
    (Tex.)—Description—Views. 3. Fort Worth
    (Tex.)—Economic conditions. 4. Fort Worth
    (Tex.)—Industries. I. Title
F394.F7P38 1990
976.4'5315—dc20   90-40964
                                              CIP

**Frontispiece: The city of Fort Worth—
"Where the West Begins." Photo by
James Blank**

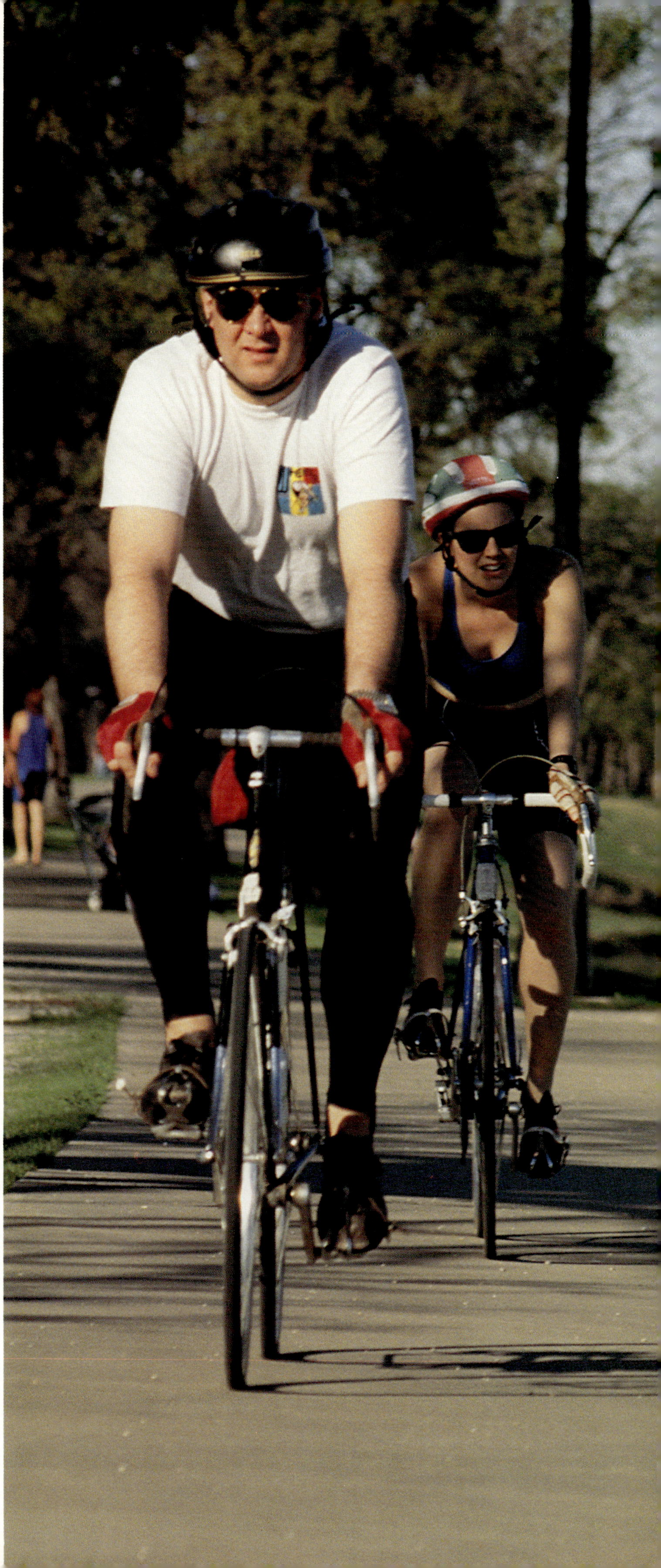

**Right: Cyclists pedal along the Trinity
Park bike trail. Photo by Michael
Lyon/ TexaStock**

Contents

Acknowledgments

A book of this undertaking is never the product of only one person, nor of only one year of writing and research. What is presented here is the result of a decade of observations, either as an outside spectator or inside participant in Fort Worth.

For this reason, I am deeply indebted to a number of people who have directly or indirectly contributed to my work and helped me form the themes that are woven through these pages.

I wish to thank Mayor Bob Bolen and former City Manager Doug Harman. These men radiate a contagious enthusiasm for Fort Worth and willingly shared their time and resources. Doug's abiding appreciation for Fort Worth's frontier heritage will serve him well in his new position as executive director of the Fort Worth Convention and Visitors Bureau.

The entire Fort Worth City Council is owed my gratitude as well. Their debates over city issues offered me insights into the complexity of problems that a government must grapple with.

Tom Higgins, the city's economic development director, and Pat Svacina, assistant to the city manager and public information officer, served as liaisons between the publisher and the city. They were extremely helpful during the course of this project, and Pat provided me with more detailed background data than any writer could hope for. His excellent FYI bulletins should be on the weekly reading list of anyone interested in current events at City Hall.

Bruce McClendon, director of planning and growth management, is due a special note of thanks for first mentioning this project to me.

At the Fort Worth Chamber of Commerce, Vicki Dietmeyer, vice president/economic development, and Michael S. Rosa, director of research, were especially invaluable in offering insights and research on business and the economy.

Quentin McGown IV, my colleague on the city's Historic and Cultural Landmark Commission, made his rare reference material available to me and reviewed the chapter on Fort Worth's history.

Finally, I must express my appreciation to all my friends in the Fairmount Association. They have taught me that good neighbors are the best part of living in Fort Worth.

Mike Patterson

At Fort Worth Water Garden, visitors can descend 38 feet below ground level and experience 1,000 gallons of water a minute rushing down a 710-foot wall into the Active Water Pool. Photo by Jane Stader/TexaStock

A luminescent cityscape brightens
the night sky above downtown.
Photo by Bob Rowan/Progressive
Image Photography

CHAPTER ONE

COMMERCE ON THE PRAIRIE

A volley of rifle shots fired by the Second Dragoons, Company F, saluted the U.S. flag as it was raised over the muggy floodplain of the Trinity River on June 6, 1849, and marked the founding of Camp Worth.

The post was so isolated that Brevet Major Ripley A. Arnold, the 32-year-old garrison commander, had his mail sent to "Dallas, Dallas County, Texas, a town about thirty-five miles east of me."

Located at the confluence of the river's Clear and West forks, the site was selected by Arnold during a reconnaissance mission in May. The West Point graduate was pleased with the site's nearby spring, its strategic position, and an offer by landowner Middleton Tate Johnson to donate the property to the U.S. Army.

The countryside was thick with hardwood timbers and prairie grasslands, and teemed with wild mustangs, deer, antelopes, buffaloes, wolves, prairie chickens, turkeys, geese, and partridges. "I thought it the most beautiful and grand country that the sun ever shone on," recalled Simon B. Farrar, a Texas Ranger who joined Arnold and Johnson in choosing the site.

Camp Worth was serving as the northern link in a chain of eight forts stretching to the Rio Grande. The federal government developed the cordon to protect the Texas frontier, newly annexed to the U.S., from the Comanches and Kiowas.

Arnold, commanded by Major General William Jenkins Worth, had established Fort Graham in Hill County on April 17 and was now executing the second part of his orders from Worth by founding another post 50 miles north on the Trinity River.

Arnold named the new camp in honor of Worth, commander of the U.S. military forces in Texas and New Mexico. Worth, however, contracted cholera and died in San Antonio before hearing about the honor or visiting the camp.

Authorized for three officers and 86 enlisted men, Arnold had only three sergeants and 25 privates fit for duty to defend a 200-mile section of frontier. "My company is so small that I cannot keep up my scouting parties," he informed his superiors.

The soldiers were hardly useful, anyway. By the time the federal government set up the 1849 defensive line, the frontier had already advanced westward. Arnold's outpost was never attacked. Within months after the establishment of the forts, military planners were developing a second defense line closer to the action.

Nearly a decade earlier, numerous expeditions, including a sweep led by militia General Edward H. Tarrant, had dissipated the major Indian threat in North Texas and cracked open the gate to settlement. When the troops arrived, Dallas already had a population of 300 and Birdville, a settlement east of the camp, had a population of 50. Other settlements and farms dotted the region.

Thus Arnold had more trouble with the Trinity than with the Indians. Rainstorms sent the river spilling over its banks in July, creating a ravenous flock of malaria-carrying mosquitoes. In August, Arnold decided to move the post to a bluff overlooking the river. Here he found Press Farmer and his family living in a tent about where Arnold wanted to put his parade grounds.

Farmer traded 22 acres for a team of mules and an appointment as the post's sutler. As a sutler, Farmer could only sell supplies to troops. This created an opportunity for Henry Daggett and Archibald F. Leonard to open a trading post for civilians about a mile northeast of the military camp.

Despite the scorching summer heat and exposure to winter northers, the new site proved adequate and on November 14, 1849, the U.S. Army elevated Camp Worth to "Fort Worth." And on December 20, Governor George T. Wood signed legislation creating Tarrant County and designating Birdville as the county seat.

Arnold and his troops were eventually relieved on August 13, 1852, to return to Fort Graham. A year later, on September 6, the young major was shot to death during an argument with the post surgeon whom Arnold had ordered arrested for "drunkenness and falsifying."

Telegram **compositors were captured in action in this 1904 photograph. When Amon Carter purchased the** *Telegram,* **he combined it with his** *Ft. Worth Star* **and began publishing the** *Fort Worth Star-Telegram* **in 1909. Photo by Bryant Studio. Courtesy, Fort Worth Public Library**

In 1849 Uncle Sam ordered Major General William Jenkins Worth to erect a series of forts in Texas. In June of that year, Brevet Major Ripley A. Arnold, who had distinguished himself under Worth's command, established Fort Worth (actually Camp Worth) on a site about 35 miles west of Dallas, naming it for the general. Before hearing that his name would remain part of Texas history forever, however, Worth died of cholera. Lithograph by Charles Fenderick. Courtesy, Amon G. Carter Museum, Fort Worth

SETTLEMENT

About two weeks after Arnold's death, on September 17, 1853, Fort Worth was ordered abandoned and the remaining troops moved west to Fort Belknap.

The settlers moved in. Ephraim M. Daggett, Henry's brother, started the town's first hotel in the army stable, while Henry Daggett and Leonard moved their mercantile store to the barracks, competing with Julian B. Feild, who operated his store in the officers' quarters. In 1854, John Peter Smith, a future mayor, arrived and started a school, an endeavor he soon gave up for surveying and law.

Then came the matter of the county seat. Some folks felt they should unseat Birdville of the honor and move it to Fort Worth. Eph Daggett even paid to build the first county jail in Fort Worth, on land donated by Middleton Tate Johnson.

Under intense lobbying by Daggett and Johnson, the state legislature eventually consented to calling a special election in November 1856 to settle the question.

The balloting was close. When it looked in the final hours like Fort Worth could lose, 15 voters rode into town. They cast their ballots in favor of Fort Worth, pushing it to victory. Election officials didn't bother to ask where the men lived. Good thing. They were from neighboring Wise County and legally ineligible to vote in Tarrant County.

Although Birdville lost the county seat, the rivalry didn't subside; sometimes it ended in bloodshed. The state legislature finally set a new election for April 1860. Determined to keep the county seat in Fort Worth, 38 civic leaders pledged $2,700 to build a courthouse if their side won. Birdville lost the election, and its momentum. Today, the town no longer exists.

What can be said of the next half-dozen years is that Fort Worth simply endured the hardships of the Civil War. Tarrant County's population had risen to 6,020 in 1860 from 599 only a decade earlier. It dropped twice as fast. Men left to fight for the South. Families fled elsewhere to avoid possible Indian attacks. By war's end, less than 1,000 lived in Tarrant County. Fort Worth's population had dwindled to a mere 250.

Only a couple of businesses were still open. There wasn't even a saloon. The new two-story courthouse stood half-finished. Houses were empty.

THE CHISHOLM TRAIL

Fort Worth's salvation rested with 3.5 million Texas longhorns that had spent the war grazing in South Texas.

After the war, the North faced a beef shortage. Cattle rounded up in Texas could fetch $20 a head in Kansas. By a geographical fluke, Fort Worth was directly between the cattle ranges and the Abilene, Kansas, railhead. The route to market was called the Chisholm Trail.

In 1867, some 35,000 longhorns were driven over the Chisholm Trail. In 1869, it was 350,000 head. By 1871, 700,000 head of cattle were driven north in herds of 2,000 to 3,000.

"The trail is swarming with cattle," reported the *Fort Worth Democrat*.

The Chisholm Trail was Fort Worth's first stable industry. Tarrant County's population jumped from 5,788 in 1870 to 24,761 a decade later.

Because it was the last town before the Oklahoma Indian Territory, cattlemen stocked up in Fort Worth. Merchants supplied them with rifles, ammunition, flour, coffee, and beans. Others supplied whiskey and women.

Fort Worth featured gunfights, knifefights, fistfights, dog fights, and cock fights. Gambling, drinking, and prostitution were rampant. The worst section was known as Hell's Half Acre, a bawdy downtown section where outlaws like

Sam Bass, Butch Cassidy, and the Sundance Kid could hang out without being pestered by the law.

RAILROADS AND PROSPERITY

At the height of the cattle drives in 1871, the U.S. Congress chartered a transcontinental railroad, later known as the Texas and Pacific. In 1872, Thomas A. Scott, owner of the Texas and Pacific, and John W. Forney, editor of the *Philadelphia Chronicle*, visited Texas to find a suitable western terminus for the line, which would eventually run to San Diego, California.

Civic leaders K.M. Van Zandt, E.M. Daggett, Thomas J. Jennings, and H.G. Hendricks signed a pledge guaranteeing the railroad 320 acres of land south of town for a depot and yard if Fort Worth were selected as the site. Scott quickly accepted the offer. The state legislature also promised a land grant to the railroad of 16 sections per mile if the line were completed from Marshall, Texas, to Fort Worth by January 1, 1874. The prospect of the railroad coming to town created another boom in Fort Worth. The population doubled to 4,000. Land prices escalated. Cattle buyers moved to Fort Worth. Unfortunately, Scott ran into problems. Construction ran behind schedule and anticipated funding did not materialize. Then came the economic crash of 1873. European money backers pulled out. Construction stopped less than 30 miles from Fort Worth. The population of Fort Worth plummeted to less than a thousand. One wag wrote to the *Dallas Times Herald* that Fort Worth was so sleepy that he saw a panther dozing in the middle of town. Fort Worth became known as "Panther City."

Economic prosperity slowly started to return in 1874, however. B.B. Paddock, editor of the *Democrat,* printed the "Tarantula Map," and depicted nine railroads radiating out of Fort Worth like the legs of a spider. He wrote that there was no reason why Fort Worth could not be the heart of such a transportation network.

The legislature granted two extensions to the original deadline. Its final deadline was the close of the legislative session in 1876, anticipated in July. Desperately seeing the need for a railroad in Fort Worth, Van Zandt and other businessmen formed the Tarrant Construction Company to grade the final miles into town. Threatened with losing a 15-million-acre land grant, the Texas and Pacific sent 300 teams of mules and 1,000 workers to lay ties and track.

The line got closer to Fort Worth, but the legislature also got closer to adjourning. The city rallied to the challenge. Businesses turned their employees out to help lay track. Women brought food and coffee to the men who worked around

Against highly improbable odds, the first Texas and Pacific train arrived in Fort Worth in July 1876, making it the city's first railroad. This photograph of the railroad's public buildings probably dates from around the turn of the century. Courtesy, Fort Worth Public Library

This 1889 poster advertises Fort Worth's imposing Spring Palace, built that year to facilitate a trade fair organized to display the state's produce. The palace, constructed of Texas lumber and agricultural products, was located between Galveston and Jennings facing Railroad (Vickery) Street. In May 1890 this 225-foot by 375-foot structure with its 150-foot-diameter dome was destroyed by fire. Courtesy, Fort Worth Public Library

the clock racing to finish the line before the legislature finished passing bills.

Finally, at 11:23 a.m. on July 19, 1876, steam engine No. 20 slowly rolled into town to cheers and a 12-piece cornet band.

REFORM

Hell's Half Acre continued to flourish night and day. "Long Hair" Jim Courtright, one of the fastest draws in the West, was elected town marshal in 1876. But Courtright soon learned that he was not hired to clean up, but merely to keep a little bit of the peace.

In 1878, a reform slate won the city election on a platform of cleaning up the gambling and prostitution. With their election, Courtright had a mandate to fill the jails every night. Word of this quickly spread along the Chisholm Trail.

On April 18, 1879, a newspaper advertisement placed by businessmen and citizens complained that "the stringent enforcement of the law closing all places

Though founded as a private banking establishment in 1873, this financial institution was renamed the Fort Worth National Bank in 1884. Its growth has consistently paralleled that of the city whose name it shares. Courtesy, Mrs. Laura H. Portwood

of amusement" was causing the cowpokes to stay in camp and was hurting business throughout the town.

The reformers backtracked and settled for ordinances regulating street salesmen and loose hogs. Courtright resigned, left the city for a period, and returned in time to start a detective agency. He was later shot to death during a Main Street gunfight with saloon owner Luke Short in 1887.

The *Democrat* trumpeted: "The dance halls are in full blast again." Merchants rode out to greet the cattle drives with bottles of whiskey and boxes of cigars. Cowpokes soon resumed tearing through the town on horseback, firing their pistols.

In 1878, the Yuma Stage Line made Fort Worth its eastern terminus to Yuma, Arizona, creating a 1,560-mile, dust-choked route. Thus, passengers could take the railroad to Fort Worth and catch a stage to western destinations not yet served by the railroad.

Other railroads soon brought service to Fort Worth. The Missouri-Kansas and Texas (Katy) made Fort Worth its Texas headquarters. The Santa Fe agreed to serve Fort Worth with the donation of right-of-way and a bonus of $75,000 raised by Paddock, Van Zandt, and others during a town meeting.

BUSINESS AND DIVERSIFICATION

The cattle industry and railroad helped Fort Worth continue to grow during the last quarter of the nineteenth century. The number of businesses jumped from 56 in 1876 to 460 by 1879.

K.M. Van Zandt, John Peter Smith, and others restarted their bank that had closed in the depression of the 1870s. In 1884, it became the Fort Worth National Bank (now Team Bank). The First National Bank (now NCNB Texas) had been incorporated in 1877.

William and George Monnig founded Monnig's Dry Goods Store, N.M. Washer started Washer Brothers, and the Sanger brothers started the Cheap Cash Store. Fort Worth Brewing Company in 1890 became the city's first large industry, eventually sending out 3,000 freight cars of beer a year.

St. Joseph's Hospital opened in 1889 and All Saints Hospital opened in 1895. Medical and legal training was offered at the now-defunct Fort Worth University. At the time of its founding in the late 1880s, it was the third medical school in the state.

There was even a short-lived boom in buffalo hides. From 1876 to 1880, Fort Worth shipped out more hides than any other city.

Unlike many towns along the route, Fort Worth continued to grow as the Chisholm Trail era closed in the 1880s. Business and civic leaders had worked hard to diversify the economy to offset the day when the cattle drives ended.

Fort Worth emerged as a major agricultural and ranching center, providing farm supplies, milling, and cotton processing services and developing strong links to West Texas. The Texas Cattle Raisers Association even voted to move its headquarters from Jacksboro to Fort Worth because it felt Fort Worth was destined to be the state's livestock headquarters.

Prominent West Texas ranchers, who had assembled massive spreads during the cattle drive era, built homes and offices in Fort Worth. These included Burk

These horse and mule barns of the Fort Worth Stockyards Company, seen here in 1911, could hold 2,500 head. Though sales fluctuated, they were generally good through the 1930s and it was not until the late 1940s that Fort Worth halted its horse and mule auctions. Courtesy, Fort Worth Public Library

Burnett and W.T. Waggoner. Theater, opera, and social events, often held at the mansions of the cattle barons, were popular.

The city's population jumped from 6,663 in 1880 to 23,076 in 1890.

PROMOTING FORT WORTH

To promote Fort Worth, Paddock suggested sponsoring an "exhibition of the products of the field, forest, orchard and garden" of Texas. The result was the Spring Palace, a two-story domed structure made entirely of Texas lumber and agricultural products. The Palace opened on May 10, 1889.

At a dress ball a year later, it caught fire and was totally destroyed within 11 minutes. Thirty were injured. One man was killed—Alfred S. Hayne. He died of burns suffered while guiding terrified guests to safety.

The combination of cattle and railroads led to several fledgling attempts to start a meat packing industry in the 1880s and 1890s.

In 1896, a fat stock show was held along Marine Creek north of Fort Worth to coincide with the Cattle Raisers convention in Fort Worth. It grew into the Southwestern Exposition and Livestock Show, and is still held each year. The Marine Creek area would later be the site of the city's massive meat packing industry—a place called the Stockyards.

In 1901, Swift & Co. and Armour & Co. started looking at making an investment in a Fort Worth operation. They indicated that a cash bonus would help them make up their minds. Local citizens raised $100,000 to entice them to locate plants in Fort Worth.

The companies opened packing plants on March 4, 1903, sending the city's population soaring from 26,688 in that year to 73,312 by 1909, and making Fort Worth the state's fourth-largest city. To accommodate livestock shows and rodeos, a huge coliseum was built in 1908. By 1909, the companies were processing 1.2 million cattle and 870,000 hogs a year. During the 12 years preceding World War I, the livestock market contributed $550 million to the Fort Worth economy.

With the arrival of a new century came the arrival of a new promoter—Amon G. Carter. He arrived in 1905 and started the *Fort Worth Star* to compete with the *Telegram*. Three years later, he and a group of investors bought the *Telegram*.

Swift and Company's Fort Worth meat packing facilities are shown here about 1915. By 1938 the city's Swift and Armour meat packing firms were processing 9,400 hogs and refining 457,000 pounds of lard each day. Swift's capacity expanded over time as the flow of livestock increased. Courtesy, North Fort Worth Historical Society

Carter was consumed with building Fort Worth and throughout his life did everything he could to make sure the whole world shared his enthusiasm. He coined the phrase that Fort Worth was "Where the West Begins," a slogan that still appears on the nameplate of the newspaper he created. When Carter died in 1955, a good half of the working population was employed at companies he had helped bring to Fort Worth.

Higher education opportunities expanded in the early 1900s as well. When the Waco campus of Texas Christian University of Disciples of Christ burned in 1910, city leaders offered the school 56 acres and $200,000 if it moved to Fort Worth. It moved. In 1910, the Southwestern Baptist Theological Seminary also left Waco for Fort Worth.

Fort Worth's introduction to its next major industry occurred on October 17, 1911, when C.P. Rodgers flew the first airplane into Fort Worth. Landing south of town in Ryan's Pasture, Rodgers was welcomed by a cheering crowd and Amon G. Carter.

The Armour and Company meat packing plant in Fort Worth, shown here in 1915, was completed in 1903. The packinghouses of both Armour and Swift were located in the middle of nearly 100 acres of stock pens, in part assuring Fort Worth's success as a livestock marketing center. Courtesy, North Fort Worth Historical Society

When World War I started, Canada's Royal Flying Corps selected Tarrant County to build three training bases for pilots. When the U.S. entered the war, the bases were used to train American pilots. In 1917, the army also selected the Arlington Heights area of west Fort Worth as a major training center called Camp Bowie. More than 100,000 troops trained for infantry and artillery duty during the war.

BOOM AND BUST

With the boom of Camp Bowie there came another boom for Fort Worth—oil. Oil was found in Ranger in 1917, in Burkburnett in 1918, and in Desdemona in 1918. As the largest city near the West Texas oil patches, Fort Worth quickly took on the aura of a frontier mining camp.

Known as "wild cat center," Fort Worth was the place to buy and sell oil stock. Millionaires were made while others lost millions in phony transactions. The Westbrook Hotel looked like the trading floor of Wall Street. Oil traders used the lobby to conduct business. Among those making fortunes were Sid Richardson, Clint Murchison, and Amon Carter.

Refineries and pipeline companies built plants in town. Allied companies such as steel producers also expanded. By 1922, Fort Worth had 22 refineries, and a population of over 100,000.

The oil boom also was responsible for the building of the first "skyscrapers" in downtown—the Life of America, Sinclair, and W.T. Waggoner buildings.

Along with the boom, Fort Worth emerged from a gangling adolescent to a mature adult. In 1924, it changed from a mayor-commission form of government to a council-manager form. Through a series of major annexations from 1909 to 1928, the city grew from 16.83 square miles to 61.37 square miles. Areas annexed included Arlington Heights, Niles City, Riverside, and Polytechnic Heights.

By the end of World War I, civic leaders realized the potential that aviation held for the city. In 1925, Mayor H.C. Meacham convinced the Army Air Corps to establish a permanent field in Fort Worth on 100 acres of land donated by the city.

When the army left a year later, control passed to the city and the National Air Transport. The airport was named after Meacham. It was formally opened in 1927 with a landing by Charles Lindbergh.

The National Air Transport offered passenger service to Oklahoma City. Other airlines soon flew into Fort Worth, including Delta, locally owned Braniff, and Texas Air Transport, a forerunner of American Airlines.

Other agricultural industries continued to grow in the 1920s. Universal Mills and Ralston Purina Company built mills and grain elevators. Kay Kimbell, who would later endow the Kimbell Art Museum, brought his grain company to town.

The optimism of the bright future was shattered again with the stock market crash. The city was faced with dire budget shortfalls, requiring it to cut worker salaries and eventually pay employees with warrants that some banks recognized as legal tender. New Deal programs would ultimately spend $15 million in the area on schools, public buildings, a sewer plant, viaducts, overpasses, and an airport terminal.

Fort Worth's cultural affairs took a leap forward during the Depression, however. When the state Centennial Commission failed to give West Texas any money to mark the state's 100th birthday in 1936, Carter hired entertainment promoter Billy Rose to stage Fort Worth's own extravaganza celebration at Casa Manana, an outdoor arena.

Amon Carter, publisher of the *Star-Telegram* and enthusiastic promoter of Fort Worth, described the city he believed in as "Where the West Begins." Carter is pictured here around 1940. Courtesy, Amon G. Carter Museum, Fort Worth

WAR AND RECOVERY

When World War II started, local businesses started returning to life by supplying area military bases.

Consolidated Aircraft Corporation moved to Fort Worth in 1941 after the Chamber of Commerce offered 1,450 acres near Lake Worth. The company finished a 4.9-million-square-foot assembly plant by April 1942 and soon was delivering B-24 bombers to the military. Within two years, 3,000 bomber and transport planes rolled off the assembly line.

The army built Tarrant Field next to the plant to train pilots for the B-24 and B-32. The base was renamed after the war in honor of Major Horace S. Carswell, a Fort Worth native who won the Medal of Honor. The base was also attached to the Strategic Air Command.

Convair was formed by the merger of Consolidated Air Craft Corp. and Vultee Aircraft Inc. and continued to get government contracts to build B-32s and

B-36s. In 1953, General Dynamics Corporation bought Convair and now manufactures supersonic military aircraft.

The war left Fort Worth on the economic upswing. In 1948, $30 million worth of building permits were issued, 4,000 new homes were built, and 871 businesses expanded or opened. Employment was an astonishing 138,000 out of a population of 273,000.

The 1950s saw the beginning of a downtown building frenzy that included the construction of several major office buildings, such as the 28-story Continental National Bank, 15-story Fort Worth National Bank, and 18-story First National Bank. And in 1951, Bell Helicopter Textron, the world's largest manufacturer of helicopters, transferred a division to Fort Worth.

In 1964, the Civil Aeronautics Board told Dallas and Fort Worth to select a joint site for a regional airport. A regional airport board was eventually assembled and 17,500 acres between the two cities were purchased for the airport. The Dallas/Fort Worth Airport formally opened in 1974, playing a role in the continued growth of Fort Worth as significant as the arrival of the railroad.

Changing economics of the cattle business eventually resulted in the closing of the Armour plant in 1962 and the Swift plant in 1971. However, the Stockyards were designated a national historic district while local businesses, with the support of the city, developed the area into a western-style entertainment destination.

DOWNTOWN RENAISSANCE

Meanwhile, a renaissance was starting in downtown Fort Worth, again led by the initiative of one man—Charles Tandy. Tandy had transformed a small leathercraft company into the international Tandy Corporation and Radio Shack chain. When he finally had the chance, he moved the corporate headquarters from Boston to his native Fort Worth and created the twin Tandy Center towers, across the street from the original site of Fort Worth.

Tandy Center was built as other businesses looked for opportunities to leave the deteriorating downtown business district. In addition to cleaning up a depressed section of downtown, Tandy's development was a key force in persuading other businesses to do the same. Tandy Center was the first permanent office Charles Tandy ever had. He enjoyed it one year before his death in 1978 at the age of 60.

Tandy's dream inspired others to develop downtown, most notably the wealthy Bass family. Next to Tandy Center, they re-created and renovated a late nineteenth-century shopping and restaurant district called Sundance Square. They also built the 14-story Americana luxury hotel (now the Worthington), linking it with a pedestrian bridge to Tandy Center.

Other building projects propelled Fort Worth into the 1980s, including another Bass project in Sundance Square—the City Center towers.

Today, on the bluff overlooking the junction of the Clear and West forks of the Trinity River, you can see a cross section of Fort Worth's heritage laid out like an open history book. It is a panorama shaped by the efforts of entrepreneurs and visionaries.

The site of the original fort. A taste of the majestic countryside that Simon B. Farrar saw in 1849. The grasslands where the longhorns rested on the Chisholm Trail. The Stockyards. The Paddock Viaduct, named after a crusading newspaper editor. Modern office buildings beside beautifully restored old ones.

There is also a sculpture of Charles Tandy on the bluff, behind the Tarrant County Courthouse. He is looking north, beyond the horizon and into the future, with confidence and anticipation.

In celebration of the 1936 Texas Centennial, Amon Carter invited New York showman Billy Rose (fourth from left) to produce the Show of Shows in Fort Worth. A spectacular cafe-theater called Casa Manana was erected, and it entertained audiences until the beginning of World War II. Twenty-two years later, a new Casa Manana Musicals Theatre, in the tradition of its predecessor, opened to national theatrical headlines. It continues to bring Fort Worth the best of the Broadway musicals. Courtesy, North Fort Worth Historical Society

CHAPTER
TWO

A DIVERSE ECONOMY

mon G. Carter, the late publisher of the *Fort Worth Star-Telegram*, said that Fort Worth is "Where the West Begins."

That phrase rings as true today as it did when cowboys drove rambling herds of Texas longhorns down dirt-packed Fort Worth streets. "Where the West Begins" is not just a place, it's a way of life.

It's a place where business executives can accent their pinstripe suits with a grey Stetson and lizard-skin cowboy boots made in Fort Worth, of course, by the Justin Boot Co.

It's a way of life that blends modern corporate executive savvy with the straight-talk of a cowhand. A city that values substance over glitz. The pace is slower than in other cities, perhaps because there are few rush hour bottlenecks to grate on people's nerves.

And it's a place and way of life that can be deceptive to the uninitiated. Fort Worth's appeal has captured for a lifetime many an executive who planned to do a short stint here before moving to the next assignment. And the slow-talking western charm often beguiles those who underestimate the talents of Fort Worth business people. Their acumen is as sharp as a prickly pear.

EXPANSION

By the end of the 1980s, Fort Worth's down-home style was turning out to be a hot item. "Where the West Begins" was even a phrase picked up by *Newsweek* magazine in February 1989 when it named Fort Worth as one of the top 10 cities in America in which to work and live.

". . . A funny thing happened on the way through Texas's recession: Fort Worth came through the hard times in better shape than Dallas, Austin or Houston," *Newsweek* said. "Although more folks are still out of jobs than the national average, Fort Worth added 20,000 jobs in 1987. Area manufacturers won $3.6 billion in new defense contracts. Fort Worth beat out 83 competitors for the only U.S. currency plant outside Washington, and nearby Waxahachie was selected as the site of the coveted supercollider."

The *Newsweek* recognition was earned through the hard work and efforts of the entire community to make it through the rocky period of the late 1980s.

Texas, and Fort Worth, had enjoyed a prosperous time in the early 1980s, with the rise in the price of oil and the desire of corporations to escape the tax burdens and deteriorating infrastructure of the northern states. Hardly a week or month passed without word of another company moving to Texas or another southern or southwestern state.

Although Fort Worth did not enjoy the building frenzy that was going on in Dallas, Houston, or Austin, it chalked up some significant successes.

American Airlines moved its corporate headquarters to Fort Worth in 1979—a homecoming, actually, since it had roots at Fort Worth Meacham Airport. In 1984, the Burlington Northern Railroad Company moved to downtown Fort Worth. (Pleased with what it found here, Burlington Northern Inc. joined its subsidiary in late 1988.)

Downtown was also expanding. The twin-towered Tandy Center, Americana Hotel (now the Worthington), and Sundance Square retail and restaurant center reversed the trend of deterioration and sparked a move for business to return to the central core. Other new office buildings included Continental Plaza, InterFirst Bank, and City Center Towers.

Fort Worth is "selling a corporate home with all the amenities and none of the problems of a big city," the *Dallas Times Herald* reported in 1982. "They're selling a downtown with ultramodern offices and plenty of space between people and between cars. They're selling an office only 10 minutes by highway from mansions and country clubs. They're selling Texas with all the economic advantages and none of the social negatives of a Houston or Dallas."

Fort Worth, considered the most Texan of Texas's cities, has evolved from a heritage of cowboys, cattle drives, and oil booms into a city with a diverse economy. Here the owner of Finchers Western Wear and his nephew pose in front of the family-owned store. Photo by Bob Rowan/ Progressive Image Photography

WHITE FRONT
ERN
WE A
JUSTIN B

RECESSION

The Texas economy was moving at a brisk pace until 1985, when a major recession hit the state, sparked by a collapse in the price of oil and overspeculation in the real estate market.

Although Fort Worth was not the oil production center that it was at the turn of the century, it was slugged by the economic downturn, primarily in the real estate sector. Many of Texas's and Fort Worth's largest banks and savings and loans institutions, burned by non-performing real estate investments and loans, declared bankruptcy and were taken over by federal regulators or new owners. The name and ownership changes became so frequent that the *Fort Worth Star-Telegram* ran a contest to see who could match the new name with the original institution.

But it could have been worse. Fort Worth fared better than other cities. At its worst, the unemployment rate hovered just over 7 percent.

In hindsight, the recession's economic bark was worse than its bite.

What saved Fort Worth from greater economic hardships was the diversity of the economy. In 1988 the employment in the Fort Worth metropolitan area was 517,500. Of this, nearly 23 percent of the jobs were in manufacturing, 25.7 percent in trades, 22.5 percent in services and miscellaneous, and 13.2 percent in government.

In fact, between 1980 and 1987, Tarrant County witnessed a 25.5 percent increase in employment, rising to 514,400 from 410,000. Retail trade, another barometer of economic conditions, increased 62.1 percent during the same period.

Fort Worth's population also grew from 385,141 in 1980 to a projected population of 465,000 in 1990—the highest 10-year gain recorded since the baby boom era of 1940-1950. Annexations raised Fort Worth to the nation's 13th-largest city in total land area—289.4 square miles.

And despite the depressed economy, the value of new building construction during 1980-1987 was nearly $3 billion—the highest for any previous eight-year period in Fort Worth's history. Of this amount, 57 percent was in residential construction.

"I feel that there is no real reason why Fort Worth and Tarrant County should be as bad off as the rest of the state, mainly because of the strong manufacturing sector here," said Mike Norman, business editor of the *Fort Worth Star-Telegram*.

Toward the end of 1989, the community's economic problem was focused on the instability of financial institutions and the large amounts of foreclosed property awaiting disposition by federal regulators.

"The problem in the financial industry here in Texas has caused both a real business impact from lack of capital to finance growth and a terrible psychological impact. The sooner we get all that out of our minds the better off we'll be," Norman said.

DALLAS/FORT WORTH INTERNATIONAL AIRPORT

Like the railroad that helped Fort Worth change from a cattle drive economy to a transportation center, the economic factor that kept the city moving toward the future was the Dallas/Fort Worth International Airport, located between Fort Worth and Dallas.

Spread a ruler across a map of the southern tier of the United States and you'll see why the airport plays such a critical role.

There, just over the halfway point between California and Georgia, is the D/FW Airport, a sprawling transportation hub that links Fort Worth business and industry with the rest of the world.

D/FW Airport—only 17 freeway miles from downtown—puts state, national, and international markets within a few hours striking distance of Fort Worth executives and manufacturers. Los Angeles is 2:58 hours away. New York, 3:08 hours. Chicago, a mere 1:58-hour flight. Paris, 9 hours. Tokyo, 14:25 hours.

In total, D/FW International—the world's third-largest airport—is served by 23 airlines that provide flights to 150 cities in the U.S. and 29 cities abroad.

Local development experts agree that the one economic factor that has influenced the economy the most has been D/FW Airport. The airport has put Fort Worth/Dallas on the map.

D/FW Airport handles 675,000 landings and takeoffs a year. Airport officials were planning to add two new runways in the 1990s that would boost the number of landings and takeoffs to 950,000 a year by 2000. Moreover, American Airlines was examining the feasibility of building a new terminal at D/FW.

With an annual economic impact of $5 billion a year in the late 1980s, the

In the 1980s Fort Worth's downtown was expanding with new office buildings and retail centers. Photo by Bob Rowan/Progressive Image Photography

The Tandy Center, with its restaurants and shops, also features an ice rink. Photo by Bob Rowan/ Progressive Image Photography

airport was expected to increase its impact on the Fort Worth/Dallas area to $9.3 billion when the expansion is completed.

Fourteen miles north of downtown Fort Worth, a totally new concept in industrial development was occurring on the rolling Texas prairie—the Alliance International Centre and Alliance Airport, named in honor of the public-private partnership effort that created and developed the mammoth undertaking.

Spearheading the project was The Perot Group, headed by Ross Perot, Jr., scion of billionaire Dallas entrepreneur H. Ross Perot. Built in cooperation with the City of Fort Worth, the Federal Aviation Administration, neighboring communities, and other agencies, the Alliance project is an industrial airport and business center.

Opened in December 1989, Alliance Airport is located on a 380-acre tract of land donated to the city by The Perot Group. The airport, part of a 5,619-acre annexation in 1987, is designed to accommodate the largest of industrial aircraft on a 9,600-foot runway, including 727s, C-5s, 747s, and DC-10s. While owned by the City of Fort Worth, the airport is managed by Perot's Pinnacle Air Service.

The Perot Group is developing and managing the 2,500-acre Alliance International Centre, a major business and industrial complex on the Perot properties surrounding the airport.

The concept behind the project is to provide industrial and business users the convenience of an airport at their doorstep. The project was suited for small and large users, including manufacturing and distributing facilities, aircraft manufacturers and industrial aviation companies, and general corporate and business users. A unique Airport Overlay District provides appropriate height limits and restricts zoning to protect against non-compatible uses.

The U.S. Drug Enforcement Administration will be among the first users. In May 1989, the DEA announced it was building a $10.8-million aircraft maintenance and administration center at Alliance as a headquarters for fighting drug smugglers. American Airlines also announced plans to build a major aircraft maintenance base at Alliance, which would employ 4,500 people by 1992.

Adjacent to the project is a 3,500-acre mixed use development with two residential communities. Plans called for the development of a regional shopping mall, 200 acres of greenbelt and park systems, and neighborhood schools.

In addition to D/FW Airport and Alliance, Fort Worth is also served by the city-owned Fort Worth Meacham Airport, a corporate and general aviation complex located four miles north of downtown. In 1988, the city dedicated a second

Old and new Fort Worth coexist in this photo of downtown. Photo by Bob Rowan/ Progressive Image Photography

municipal airport, Spinks Airport in South Fort Worth, to offer flight training, a corporate aircraft port, and general aviation services.

But air transportation alone is not enough to provide Fort Worth with the trade links it needs to other cities. It is also served by seven main rail lines, Amtrak, and dozens of trucking freight lines serving the local, intrastate, and interstate markets. Overnight trucking service links Fort Worth with most major cities in Texas and adjacent states, and second morning service reaches cities as far away as Kansas City, Missouri, and Jackson, Mississippi.

A SPIRIT OF COOPERATION

Behind the amenities of being centrally located and having accessible transportation, there is a western spirit that permeates Fort Worth's civic, business, and government community—that same civic spirit that was shared by the early leaders who helped turn Fort Worth from a raw frontier town to an elegant city.

Air traffic controllers at Dallas/Fort Worth International Airport direct 675,000 landings and takeoffs a year. Photo by Bob Rowan/ Progressive Image Photography

The spirit is evident in the cooperation and partnership between the public and private sectors in the community.

The City of Fort Worth assumed a major role in the process when it created an Economic Development Office.

The office works with the Chamber of Commerce and other local development entities to identify the proper roles of the various agencies and eliminate duplication of efforts. At the same time, the office helps trade information and explore new alternatives.

"Here, [Fort Worth] Mayor Bob Bolen hears a rumor of a prospective company. He gets on the phone and calls the Chamber of Commerce. He says, 'Let's get together and figure out how to get this company down here.' The city has a lot of vision. There's a real belief in excellence," said Vicki Dietmeyer, economic development vice president of the Fort Worth Chamber of Commerce.

The public-private partnership was visible in November 1986 when the *Fort Worth Star-Telegram* proclaimed: "We got it. By George, we got it!"

"It" referred to the first U.S. Treasury Department currency printing facility to be located outside Washington—and it was coming to Fort Worth.

The Western Currency Production Facility was expected to generate about 1,200 permanent jobs and $100 million in local services annually, and attract up to 500,000 visitors to the National Currency Museum at the plant.

In selecting the site, the Treasury Department's Bureau of Engraving and Printing asked for proposals from 83 southwestern and western cities. Bureau officials visited 21 before narrowing the list to 11.

Meeting the requirements of the Treasury's proposal request required considerable cooperation between the City of Fort Worth, private business, the county, and the State of Texas. Even the City of Dallas endorsed the project after it was eliminated from consideration.

The value of the bid submitted by the city was more than $15 million. This included a 100-acre site donated to the government by William Y. Harvey and

A futuristic-looking Airtrans vehicle travels high above the ground, skirting the sky. Photo by Bob Rowan/ Progressive Image Photography

Associates of Fort Worth. The building, land, property improvements, utilities, and city services were provided free of charge. Construction of the 288,000-square-foot facility was funded with about $7.5 million in cash contributions raised from the private sector.

When completed, the total value of the complex was estimated at $40 million.

THE CHOICE OF CORPORATIONS

The currency facility was only one of many major economic announcements to come during the 1980s. Other companies opening or expanding facilities in Fort Worth included Holt, Rinehart & Winston College Publishing, Uniden Corp., Alcon Laboratories, Inc., Mattel, Mercedes Benz, Volkswagen of America, Affiliated Foods, Inc., Keebler, and Albertson's Inc.

American Airlines, the city's largest non-manufacturing employer and the world's largest and most profitable airline, was planning to add about 42 planes a year to its fleet and increase its aircraft inventory from nearly 478 planes in 1989 to as many as 782 by the early 1990s.

In addition, the airline company was making plans to expand its Fort Worth headquarters operations, which it established a decade earlier. About 32.1 percent—21,400—of all American employees worked at the airline's operations at the Dallas/Fort Worth International Airport or the airline's cluster of corporate headquarters. American was adding an addition to its headquarters building to hold 1,800 employees.

Fort Worth was also expected to benefit from the selection of nearby Ellis County as the site for the Superconducting Super Collider atomic research project.

Despite the diversity, the defense and aerospace giants of General Dynamics and Bell Helicopter-Textron are still dominant economic forces. Together, they employ 39,000 workers.

The city's largest employer is General Dynamics, which employs 32,000 workers in the design, development, and manufacture of military aircraft. It had an annual payroll of one billion dollars in 1988.

With a diverse product and service line, General Dynamics generated more than $3 billion a year in sales. Major activities included the production of the F-16 Fighting Falcon, the F-111 Tactical Fighter-Bomber, Advanced Tactical Fighters, ground electronic simulators, and command, control, and communications systems. GD also provided worldwide logistics service and management and aircraft modification service, and was teamed with McDonnell Douglas Corp. in developing the Navy's A-12 attack plane. Moreover, GD was working with Japan to develop a new fighter plane, the FSX, based on GD's F-16.

In 1988, General Dynamics opened an expanded facility known as G.D. West

AMR Corp./ American Airlines' corporate headquarters is located in the Centreport development. Photo by Bob Rowan/ Progressive Image Photography

that housed about 3,000 technical, administrative, and clerical people. The company was planning an additional million-square-foot facility.

"The biggest feeling of recovery or moving on is General Dynamics," Mike Norman said. "They've got several very big projects in the works out there. It's kind of mind-boggling that they've grown so much and can grow even more."

Fort Worth is also home to Bell Helicopter-Textron, the nation's largest helicopter manufacturer. Employing 7,196, the company was developing the V-22 Osprey for the U.S. Navy, Marine Corps, and Air Force. The Osprey was a new generation of helicopter, lifting like a helicopter but flying like an airplane due to rotors that can tilt 90 degrees.

Closely related to the defense manufacturing industry was defense itself. Fort Worth is home of Carswell Air Force Base, a unit of the Strategic Air Command that employs 8,828 people.

In addition to the corporate giants, Fort Worth also has mid-sized manufacturers and corporations that have a worldwide presence. For example, Delta Airlines Inc. employs 5,600 in Fort Worth. A sample of others include Justin Industries, Inc., manufacturer of leather goods and bricks; Williamson-Dickie Manufacturing Co., apparel products; Paul R. Ray & Company, Inc., executive search consultant; Panhandle Slim, western wear; M.L. Leddy's Boot & Saddlery, boots and saddles; Mrs. Baird's Bakeries, Inc., bread and cake products; Fort Worth Star-Telegram newspaper, winner of Pulitzer Prizes for photography and public service reporting;

Nearly 9,000 civilian and military workers are employed by Carswell Air Force Base, a unit of the Strategic Air Command. Photo by Bob Rowan/ Progressive Image Photography

The Treasury Department's Bureau of Engraving and Printing selected Fort Worth from a field of 83 southwestern and western cities as the site for its 288,000-square-foot Western Currency Production Facility. Photo by Bob Rowan/ Progressive Image Photography

Volkswagen of America has chosen Fort Worth as an assembly site. Photo by Kolvoord/TexaStock

and Pier 1 Imports, retail products.

Moreover, Fort Worth-based executives such as Robert M. Bass are considered among the nation's major stockholders, investors, and entrepreneurs.

In short, Fort Worth companies cover the entire gamut of American enterprise. And new ones keep emerging every year.

"When we started the *Tarrant Business* section in 1988 we had the opportunity to do stories about people we've never done stories about before," Norman said. "I have been continually amazed at the new companies we discover that we never knew were out there. And they're just going strong."

One example is in the export industries. A study cosponsored by Arthur Anderson & Co. and the *Fort Worth Star-Telegram* found that "small and mid-sized companies in Tarrant County and outlying communities are selling their products to international customers as never before," shipping everything from Teflon plastic tubing to toner cartridges used in personal computers and laser printers.

Of the 40 fastest-growing companies responding to the survey, the newspaper reported that more than half had fewer than 100 employees and 75 percent had fewer than 200 employees. The 40 export companies had sales growth rates as high as 1,847 percent in 1988.

ROOM TO GROW

Another of Fort Worth's advantages as a business and industrial center is the availability of land. There are more than 128 industrial parks covering over 30,000 acres of land and 132.7 million square feet of space. Unabsorbed industrial land totals more than 5,500 acres within a five-mile radius of downtown and 15,800 acres within a 10-mile radius. Nearly all have easy accessibility to rail service, major highways, and existing utility service.

Countywide, there was a 25.3 percent vacancy rate, with lease rates from $10 to $12.50 a square foot.

In 1988, Fort Worth received state approval to create two enterprise zones to encourage business investment and job creation under the Texas Enterprise Zone Act. With the approval of the 14.4-square-mile North Enterprise Zone and 14.5-square-mile South Enterprise Zone, the city was able to devise strategies to attract new business investment through incentives and certain types of regulatory relief.

Although development was occurring in all areas of the city, perhaps the one with the most visibility was North Fort Worth—a 122,300-acre tract that spread from near downtown to the City of Justin in Denton County. Parts of the area fell in the North Enterprise Zone.

Adding 191 square miles to the city limits, North Fort Worth development projects are expected to add an estimated 180,000 jobs by the year 2010 and up to an additional 200,000 residents. The area is described as "one of the most sensitively planned and developed areas of the world." At the northern tip of the area is the new Alliance Airport and Centre project. Anchored at the southern end is the Fort Worth Stockyards, a tourist destination area and light industrial and manufacturing area.

In the Stockyards area, the city and private enterprise are combining efforts to stimulate redevelopment of the historic meat packing district.

There are several first-class industrial and business parks located through the area, along the Interstate 35 corridor. Mercantile Center, located east of Meacham Airport, is a 1,250-acre business and industrial park that is already the home of the Coors Distributing Company, Keebler Company snack plant, and others.

Woodbine Development Corporation created the Fossil Creek area along the I-35 corridor, just north of Loop 820, which encircles the entire city and provides easy linkages with the Dallas/Fort Worth International Airport. Fossil Creek features clients such as Motorola and Coca-Cola, plus prime residential areas and an Arnold Palmer-designed golf course.

In East Fort Worth, Centre Development Co. of Dallas purchased the site of the former Greater Southwest International Airport in 1980 and began a project known as Centreport. "An abandoned airfield turned into a real economic flagship," said Tom Higgins, Fort Worth's economic development director.

Originally 1,300 acres, the site now has about 770 acres remaining for development at the southern end of the Dallas/Fort Worth International Airport. During the 10-year period, the development has attracted 5.6 million square feet of offices, warehouses, and apartments, 25 companies, and 4,000 jobs.

Centreport clients read like a Who's Who of American industry. They include AMR Corp./American Airlines (corporate headquarters); Mattel, Inc. (500,000-square-foot distribution center); Panasonic (250,000-square-foot regional sales and distribution center); Uniden of America (240,000-square-foot U.S. headquarters and distribution center); Keebler Co. (211,000-square-foot distribution center); and Mercedes-Benz of North America (128,000-square-foot parts distribution center).

The historic meat packing district in the Stockyards area is the target of redevelopment by public and private enterprise. Photo by Bob Rowan/ Progressive Image Photography

The 1894 Tarrant County Courthouse underwent a $9-million restoration in 1983. Photo by James Blank

Additional development activities were occurring in the south and southwest sections of the city, including the Carter Industrial Park—home of distribution facilities for Albertson's Inc. retail food sales and Ben E. Keith food and beverage distributor.

One of the problems Fort Worth is having in attracting new manufacturers is that there is very little existing manufacturing space left in the market. That's good and bad. It's good because companies are either expanding or moving into buildings that are empty. It's bad because there isn't an available inventory of space to put new prospects in.

But the heart of the city remains downtown. The north end is anchored by the renovated Tarrant County Courthouse, government complex, and public safety building. The south end is anchored by the Fort Worth/Tarrant County Convention Center—built atop the infamous Hell's Half Acre section of cowboy days.

They are linked by wide landscaped bus spines and brick-paved Main Street. The downtown area is included in a special use district administered by Downtown Fort Worth, Inc.

With a small tax charged to downtown property owners, Downtown Fort Worth, Inc., promotes the downtown area and pays for additional clean up, police patrols, and maintenance.

Except for the completion of a new city-county jail and expansion, there was little major new construction for nearly a decade in the downtown area. But at the dawn of the 1990s, there were two major developments under way.

Developer Ed Bass, brother of Robert M. Bass, built a $25-million, 12-story apartment building in the Bass-owned Sundance Square area. The project, the first downtown housing in decades, contains shops and a multiscreen cinema. The project was made possible by a 13-year tax abatement approved by the City Council.

And the Tandy Corp. built a new development called Technology Square west of the existing Tandy Center complex. The Square consists of a seven-story, 240,000-square-foot office and laboratory building and a six-story parking garage. The complex houses up to 600 employees and adds 200 to 300 new jobs.

In early 1989, Tandy Advanced Products, a division of Tandy Corp., completed a 216,000-square-foot manufacturing facility in North Fort Worth to produce Tandy's 1000 line of computers and Panasonic computers. It also announced plans to build a 500,000-square-foot warehouse, pending voter approval of a business tax exemption.

The continued growth of the Tandy Corp. was indicative of the increasing role of high-technology in Fort Worth's economy.

At the close of the 1980s, Fort Worth had the third-largest concentration of high-technology industry in the United States.

This was most apparent in 1988 when the Automation and Robotics Research Institute in the River Bend Industrial Park was opened.

The Robotics Institute is a 48,000-square-foot, three-level complex that contains classrooms, laboratories, and two large workshops. A combined project of the University of Texas at Arlington and the Fort Worth Chamber of Commerce, the Institute is expected to offer technology that will help draw high-tech manufacturers to the area.

Kenneth and David Newell donated the 18-acre site for the facility, while 20 companies donated $1.5 million in equipment. Other businesses, foundations, and individuals contributed $10 million to build the institute. The State of Texas provides the annual operating budget, administered by the University of Texas at Arlington.

"Automation is critical to the future competitiveness of the country," Tandy Corp. Chairman John Roach said at the dedication of the facility. "We need to be better, smarter, faster and more economical than the rest of the world."

It is a lesson that is not lost on Fort Worth's business and civic leaders. As they look to the future, they see a need to continue to diversify the Fort Worth economy, perhaps to one even less reliant on the defense and aerospace industry and more on high-technology, telecommunications, and other future-oriented industries.

To help reach this goal, the Fort Worth Chamber of Commerce in May 1989 unveiled a multimillion-dollar, four-year effort to lure more industry to Fort Worth, and to encourage the retention and expansion of existing industries. In a Fort Worth tradition, the project is being funded by local businesses.

Robert Herchert, chairman of the Chamber of Commerce, said the plan represented a doubling of resources for economic development. Projects in the plan include developing national marketing and advertising programs; developing incentives for local businesses to expand; helping businesspeople become more knowledgeable about how to make their operations profitable; and serving as a resource on where to obtain financial assistance.

Thus, Fort Worth was preparing for a new future in the 1990s. Like Fort Worth's founders who saw the value of a railroad, business leaders in 1990 understood that they would not grow by standing still. They saw what transportation had done to build the city. And they understood what potential awaited them on the frontiers of high-technology.

Mayor Bolen best summed it up: "We're going to have a city that will be the envy of the world."

And that's "Where the West Begins."

The city's stately post office building serves as an imposing backdrop for a candid portrait of a Fort Worth resident. Photo by Bob Rowan/ Progressive Image Photography

BUSINESS: APPLY HERE

Fort Worth's local government is rooted in the traditions of the past. The city's logo is a Texas longhorn. Police officers wearing cowboy hats still patrol downtown and the Fort Worth Stockyards National Historic District on horseback. Even the mayor and council members are frequently spotted wearing Stetsons and cowboy boots—which are also favorite gifts presented to visiting dignitaries.

Doug Harman, executive director of the Fort Worth Convention and Visitors Bureau and a former city manager, is apt to don a pair of boots, western cut slacks, and cowboy hat, and show off his collection of Fort Worth memorabilia—post cards, photographs, buttons, pins, Casa Manana programs—which adorn his office and den at home.

These are the surface signs of Fort Worth's heritage. Business executives who have worked with the local government know that beneath the surface is a tradition of responsiveness to their concerns and needs.

INCENTIVES FOR BUSINESS

From its earliest days as a frontier town to today's metropolis, local government has worked closely with business and civic leaders to give Fort Worth the competitive edge it needs to attract new industry to town. Although the policy of providing tax and other financial incentives to stimulate selected projects is criticized by some, it is a development tool that dates to the 1840s when the Republic of Texas parceled out free land to anyone willing to settle the Fort Worth frontier. Other examples include:

• In 1872, before the city was incorporated, community leaders donated 320 acres of land to entice the Texas & Pacific Railroad to make Fort Worth its western terminus, an action that resulted in building the city into a major transportation hub.

• In 1901, community leaders held a rally at City Hall and raised $100,000 as a bonus for the Swift and Armour companies to build packing plants in an unincorporated area north of Fort Worth. The area was initially left outside of the Fort Worth city limits to avoid subjecting new businesses to city taxes—although the city would reap many economic benefits rippling off any new enterprises there.

• In 1910, city leaders offered 56 acres of land, $200,000, and guaranteed utilities and street car service to bring Texas Christian University to Fort Worth. Today, the university continues as a major educational institution.

• In 1925, the city purchased a 100-acre site for Meacham Field as a way to entice the Air Corps to make Fort Worth an airmail stop. Today, Fort Worth Meacham Airport is a prominent industrial and business aviation airport.

• In 1941, the City Council bought a vast acreage in West Fort Worth, cleared the land, and built roads to it. Constructed on the property was the forerunner to General Dynamics and Carswell Air Force Base. Together, they generate a multi-million-dollar economic impact on the city.

This tradition continues today as well. In 1986, the city spearheaded an effort to assemble a $15-million package of public and private contributions to win the bid for the new Western Currency Production Facility. And in 1989, the city provided funding to help develop the infrastructure at the new Alliance International Centre and city-owned Alliance Airport.

Despite the criticism that the city should not offer financial incentives to developers, elected leaders and city administrators long ago realized that this was a tradition that had built Fort Worth into the success it is today—but it is also necessary to attract new business and to keep existing businesses from moving elsewhere.

Abatements and incentives "seem to be necessary because that's what everybody expects nowadays," said Mike Norman, business editor of the *Fort Worth Star-Telegram*.

While some Fort Worth police officers still patrol on horseback, these officers perform their duties on bicycles. Photo by Brad Crooks

**The Texas Electric Power Plant is sil-
houetted against the early morning
sky. Photo by Bob Rowan/
Progressive Image Photography**

Looking at Fort Worth's history, city and community leaders could see that short-term incentives paid off in long-term benefits for the entire city.

"Our City Council is business oriented," explained Mayor Bob Bolen. "We don't apologize for that because we think that's job oriented. We think the best way for anybody to get out of poverty and to enhance their lives is to have a productive job and opportunities to advance.

"We also have a council that is generally understanding of the business community, working with the chambers, the business community, and the larger employers in the city," he said.

The result is that Fort Worth has earned a reputation as a city government that is sensitive to the needs of businesses and willing to work with them to achieve a win-win situation for both the public and private sectors.

GOVERNMENT IN FORT WORTH

One key reason for this attitude is the composition of the Fort Worth City Council. The council is made up of nine elected officials: eight members representing specific districts, and one member—the mayor—elected at-large. Throughout its history, Fort Worth has traditionally elected council members with strong business or professional backgrounds. This gives them first-hand experience in not only knowing how to manage budgets, but also in seeing issues from the perspective of the business community.

"It adds a great deal to the environment that they're dedicated to donating their services," Bolen said. "Most of us do this as our duty to our community, rather than as a stepping stone to other areas in politics. That's unusual in the country. In cities this size, it's rare."

The strong pro-business point of view is sometimes grating to representatives of the black and Hispanic communities, which make up about 40 percent of Fort Worth's population. They believe that the council tends to avoid addressing social problems, such as drug addiction, minority joblessness, and a shortage of decent, affordable housing.

"Bob [Bolen] says the right things, but he and the council as a whole haven't been very sensitive to these issues," Councilman Louis Zapata told the *Fort Worth Star-Telegram*. "He talks about running the city like a business. My God, we end up talking about cutting free dental care for people who won't get it any other way and then blow a bunch of money for a development project that might give us some tax money down the line."

Although dominated by business interests, city government generally flows smoothly and without the political rift that often marks other cities. This is because council members are generally elected on a nonpartisan basis.

"We're supportive of each other, even if we differ on specific issues. But we're not archenemies over Republican or Democratic labels. We're each trying to do what we think is in the best interests of the city," Bolen said.

As an independent, for example, Bolen has spent time with Phil Gramm, the Republican U.S. senator from Texas, and Republican Governor Bill Clements. "Our delegation has been very supportive of Fort Worth and I've tried to be equally supportive of them on issues that pertain to us," he said.

Despite its nonpartisan airs, Fort Worth was believed the first city in U.S. history to be home to speakers of both the Texas State Legislature and the U.S. Congress, and on districts that generally overlapped each other.

Bolen said former U.S. Speaker of the House Jim Wright and Texas Speaker of the House Gib Lewis can be credited with "elevating the community to being well-known around the world."

The two powerful leaders ensured that Fort Worth got its share of funding for air-

Charles D. Tandy has been memorialized with this statue set amid the greenery of the county courthouse. Photo by Bob Rowan/Progressive Image Photography

Even with numerous road construction projects underway, most of the time drivers can travel throughout the Fort Worth-Arlington-Mid-Cities area at a brisk pace. Photos by Michael Lyon/TexaStock

Circling Fort Worth is Loop 820, by far the best method of crossing or circumventing downtown. Photo by Jane Stader/TexaStock

port, highway, and water projects, and they could often get things done simply with a telephone call. They also gave Fort Worth "visibility that you wouldn't have had."

Wright resigned his seat in 1989 to avoid a protracted fight to defend himself against alleged ethical violations. Pete Geren, Jr., a Fort Worth attorney, was elected to fill his seat. During his 35 years in Congress, however, Wright was credited with fighting for the interests of his constituents in Tarrant County, which was one of the top U.S. urban areas in the receipt of federal funds on a per capita basis. According to an analysis by the *Dallas Morning News*, Tarrant County received $9.9 billion in government funding in 1986 and 1987.

Although Wright did have an impact on Fort Worth and Tarrant County, the leadership void was not expected to be devastating, considering the weight that other Texans carried at the national level, including President George Bush, a Texan.

Fort Worth achieved another significant milestone when Mayor Bolen assumed the presidency of the National League of Cities, giving him—and Fort Worth—still another nationwide platform to air issues affecting his constituents.

Yet the City of Fort Worth is not the sole government entity that has an impact on the community.

The Fort Worth Independent School District is a separate jurisdiction from the city, although the district's and city's boundaries generally overlap. The school district does incorporate some communities or areas outside of the Fort Worth city limits. An elected board—similar to the City Council—ensures that the final authority for the district rests in the hands of citizens. A superintendent oversees the day-to-day operation of the district and reports to the board.

Fort Worth is the county seat for Tarrant County, which is administered by elected county commissioners and a county judge. The title is misleading, for the

position is not a judicial one. The county judge is generally the chief administrator for county government. Unlike the school board and City Council, these are paid positions and partisan.

County government covers a more regional area and is responsible for running the county and district court system, registering and running elections, issuing vehicle license plates, operating the county jail system, providing human service assistance, maintaining all state records such as deeds, assumed names, and court suits, and maintaining roads that are outside of cities.

Least visible is the state government, which provides human services, driver's license renewals, state highway construction and maintenance, and often interstate highway construction.

Federal agencies provide a number of services in Fort Worth, including agricultural services, local watershed management by the Corps of Engineers, weather forecasting, federal courts, public safety, housing and human services assistance, Social Security services, postal service, and veteran's assistance.

There are also special districts to provide specialized services, such as the Hospital District, the Tarrant County Junior College District, and the Metropolitan Transit Authority, which operates the city bus line, The T.

TAXES AND UTILITIES

Despite the various layers of government, tax rates in Fort Worth are favorable. There is no state property tax, corporate income tax, personal income tax, general use tax, or payroll tax, other than unemployment compensation.

Electric service is provided by TU Electric. In 1987, the service had a capacity of 19,500 MW with a planned capacity in 1990 of 21,570 MW. In 1990 it was beginning operation of the Comanche Peak nuclear power plant.

Electrical industrial rates vary with electrical load requirements and are among the lowest in Texas.

Natural gas service is provided by Lone Star Gas Company, which in 1987 had a peak demand of 290,510 MCF a day. The capacity is about 398,515 MCF a day.

Tree-shaded areas furnished with benches make for a people-friendly environment outside the Fritz G. Lanham Federal Building. Photo by Bob Rowan/ Progressive Image Photography

About 14 telephone companies serve the area.

Fort Worth purchases its water from the Tarrant County Water Control & Improvement District Number One. The water district completed a new lake in the late 1980s, which will provide Fort Worth's water needs well into the next century. In addition to the new Richland-Chambers Reservoir in East Texas, the district will continue to provide water to Fort Worth customers from several older reservoirs, including Bridgeport, Eagle Mountain, Marine Creek, and Cedar Creek. An example of Fort Worth's planning for ample water supplies occurred when a blistering drought struck Texas in the 1950s. Unlike Dallas, Fort Worth had sufficient water resources to meet the needs of its customers without rationing.

And to ensure that the water purchased can reach customers, the City of Fort Worth will open in 1992 a new water treatment plant to serve North Fort Worth.

CITY OPERATIONS

Despite these other vital government jurisdictions, people continue to have the most contact with representatives of the City of Fort Worth, including police officers, firefighters, and a wide range of other civil servants managing the day-to-day operations of the city.

The day-to-day function of the city is the responsibility of City Manager David Ivory, who reports directly to the City Council. He and his staff provide recommendations and input on matters to the council and execute their directions on major policy matters and actions.

The annual operating budget for the city in 1989-1990 was more than $365 million. There were 5,440 full-time city employees in 1988. City operations include fire and police protection, traffic courts, local street construction and maintenance, water service, garbage pickup, parks, recreation facilities, libraries, local airport services, housing assistance and zoning, job assistance, and building standards enforcement.

Private citizens also take a major part in the functioning of City Hall by serving as volunteers on any of the nearly three dozen boards and commissions. Working closely with city staff, these panels serve as advisory bodies to the City Council, as vehicles for providing public input on matters affecting the city, and as liaisons with other government entities. Examples of boards and commissions include the Art Commission, Aviation Advisory Board, Citizen's Cable Board, City Plan Commission, Civil Service Commission, Historic and Cultural Landmark Commission, Library Advisory Board, and Park and Recreation Advisory Board.

A few boards, such as the Zoning Board of Adjustment, are empowered to make the final decision on specialized issues.

The boards are designed to make the democratic system run as effectively and quickly as possible, while still giving citizens an opportunity to present their views. In most cases, the process enables adherents of different points of view to resolve their concerns before the matters are ever taken to the council for a final decision.

For example, the Zoning Commission may instruct neighborhood groups and developers to try to reach a compromise on a building project before actually voting to approve or deny the zoning request.

CITY PLANNING

Critical to the success of economic development is careful planning, a process that functions in Fort Worth with the full involvement of private citizens, government officials, and business leaders.

"Fort Worth is not an accidental city," City Planning Director Bruce McClendon told the Conservation Foundation in June 1988. "It hasn't been an accidental city, and won't be an accidental city. We know how Fort Worth is going to develop. We have a vision, and we have people committed to that vision. Fort Worth is probably one of the shining monuments on the hill. Fort Worth has been a well-planned community."

Fort Worth has achieved nationwide recognition for its planning process that not only offers possible solutions to specific problems, but also outlines long-term planning concepts to help the city grow in an orderly fashion.

In 1970 and 1980, for example, the city developed a series of Sector Plans through the input of citizens. These plans identified specific goals and objectives for each area of Fort Worth. These included strategies for solving problems and development plans to ensure the conservation of neighborhoods while encouraging the growth of business.

In concert with other departments, the planning staff has developed additional development strategies for other areas of Fort Worth, including inner city neighborhoods, the Stockyards area, and the Polytechnic Heights Main Street area. These projects are intended to offer more specific planning and problem solving tools than the broader Sector Plans. In several cases, the Planning Department even helps individual neighborhoods establish task forces that bring in the expertise of appropriate city departments to meet on a regular basis with citizens, civic leaders, and businesspeople to tackle specific projects.

One example of where the planning process is having an impact is in the Cultural District. Here, a cross section of city officials and community leaders serve on the Cultural District Committee, a 22-member panel that meets regularly to discuss how the city's Cultural District should be developed. Included in the district are the Amon Carter Museum, Kimbell Art Museum, Modern Art Museum of Fort Worth, Will Rogers Memorial Center, Trinity Park, and Botanic Gardens.

The city has set aside 24 percent of the nearly $3 million in taxes collected on hotel and motel revenues to promote the cultural facilities in the 500-acre district located west of downtown.

A full-time planning director coordinates plans for the institutions in the district. The committee is following a five-year master plan for the area. The objective is to make the outstanding cultural entities that are concentrated in the Cultural District a cohesive unit and provide visitors with the finest museums, theaters, parks, and gardens in a convenient and attractive setting.

Although the district can claim to

Trains converge in Fort Worth's railroad yard. Photo by Bob Rowan/ Progressive Image Photography

The Will Rogers Memorial pays homage to the great American humorist and entertainer. Photo by Brad Crooks

be home of some of the nation's most highly respected art museums, it is also the home of the most modern livestock facilities in the world.

The Will Rogers Memorial Complex features meeting and convention space as well as the new Will Rogers Equestrian Center, an $18-million investment by the city to build the finest horse facility anywhere. More than two million people attended functions at the complex during the 1987-1988 fiscal year.

"We want to make sure Fort Worth was *the* place to bring horses," said Harman, the former city manager.

Covering 12 acres, the Will Rogers Equestrian Center hosts many national and international equestrian events, including the National Cutting Horse Association, Texas Quarter Horse Association, International Arabian Horse Association, Southwest Peruvian Horse Club, American Miniature Horse Association, Texas Longhorn Association, American Paint Horse Association, and Appaloosa Horse Club.

In mid-1989, the Southwestern Exposition and Livestock Show, a major user of the livestock facilities, unveiled proposed plans for renovating the 50-year-old Will Rogers Coliseum. The plan included restoration of the facility, while increasing the seating capacity from 5,700 to 6,300.

These giant cranes mark the site of only some of the commercial construction progressing in the city. Photo by Bob Rowan/ Progressive Image Photography

PUBLIC SAFETY

Public safety, however, is the backbone of the services provided by the City of Fort Worth.

The Police Department was having success reducing the overall crime rate through a combination of programs—decentralization of forces, neighborhood crime watches, increased street patrols, and a crackdown on narcotic trafficking.

Police patrols were being increased through the addition of patrol officers. Innovative programs were also having success, such as using bicycles to patrol apartment complexes. (The Police Department first used bicycle patrols in 1913 because officers could quickly sneak up on burglars without being heard.)

The Fort Worth Fire Department, selected by the Federal Emergency Management Agency as one of three exemplary departments in the nation, added three new stations in 1987-1988 to respond to additional growth in the city. And in an example of public-private partnership, the department received two vehicles donated by the *Fort Worth Star-Telegram* to serve as on-site canteen and rehabilitation. Mrs. Baird's Bakery donated a van that carries specialized rescue equipment to scenes of cave-ins and building collapses.

Emergency medical service is operated by the Fort Worth Ambulance Authority, which contracts with a private firm to actually staff and manage the ambulances. The service in Fort Worth is called MedStar, which also provides emergency ambulance service to 14 neighboring communities. The authority is managed by a 14-member board appointed by the City Council. The board includes the medical director of each hospital with an emergency room in Fort Worth, and five other physicians who are trained in emergency pre-hospital care medicine.

The Emergency Physicians Advisory Board—one of the city's newest commissions—sets medical standards by which emergency ambulances operate in Fort Worth. Before it was established, there were no uniform standards for ambulances in Fort Worth, other than state standards.

CITY DEPARTMENTS

Other Fort Worth city departments are recognized around the country for their achievements.

In 1988, for example, the Environmental Protection Agency recognized Fort Worth's Village Creek Wastewater Treatment Plant as the best operated in the country. The award came less than 10 years after the EPA scrutinized the plant for not meeting its permit and for producing bad odors.

The city's Employment and Training Department—The Working Connection—was recognized in 1988 as one of the most effective programs in the nation and received the National Association of Counties Job Training Partnership Act Award for Excellence and the U.S. Department of Labor Outstanding Performance Award.

The city's Budget Office was one of 14 local government offices chosen to receive the award of merit for outstanding achievement in local government records management from the Texas Library and Archives Commission, while the Housing and Human Services Department was recognized by the U.S. Department of Housing and Urban Development for its rental rehabilitation program.

To meet the growing demands of ground transportation in the rapidly growing Southwest and North Fort Worth areas, new freeways are being planned to link them with downtown. The North Pass Freeway will connect Alliance Airport to Texas 114, while the North Tarrant County Freeway will link Interstate 35W with the Dallas/Fort Worth International Airport. The Southwest Beltway will

tie the Southwest section of Fort Worth with downtown and the D/FW International Airport.

A Principal Arterial Street System program will ensure that Fort Worth will receive about $30.3 million in state funding for urban street construction.

A master thoroughfare plan is kept updated with current growth trends and sets priorities for future highway and road needs. It envisions an outer loop as well as a freeway along the Trinity River corridor to provide an additional link to Dallas in the future.

The social needs of its citizens are also addressed by the city. The Housing and Human Services Department and Public Health Department offer a wide variety of programs. These include the Urban Homesteading Program to provide homes for families who could not otherwise afford one, the Job Development Project to place homeless people in jobs, the Summer Food Service to provide lunches to children, and breast screening clinics and campaigns to reduce infant mortality.

GROWTH AND THE FUTURE

By the end of the decade of the 1980s, Fort Worth had established a solid municipality that was struggling to meet the demands of growth, mixed with budget shortfalls caused by a statewide economic recession in the real estate and financial communities.

While devoting resources to help new businesses get established, it was at the same time hard-pressed to maintain even the status quo in many city departments, including the police and fire departments.

This was sparking a debate in the community over how much Fort Worth should grow and how fast. The business community and most council members favored continuing to provide incentives to attract new business and thus generate more tax revenues. This would enable more of the tax burden to be taken up by business, rather than homeowners, who had traditionally carried a large tax load. Others in the city wanted Fort Worth to slow the growth, to avoid becoming like Dallas or Houston, which they perceived to be busy, impersonal cities.

"There's no question that we have grown enormously in size," Bolen said.

There are an estimated 1.3 million people living in Tarrant County, with about 430,000 calling Fort Worth home. Photo by Bob Rowan/ Progressive Image Photography

"That takes a tremendous battle with your budget. A lot of people don't want to grow or annex."

This attitude, some city leaders contend, helped create the budget constraints that Fort Worth faced in the late 1980s. Fort Worth, for example, is surrounded by smaller communities whose shopping malls would compose 5 percent of Fort Worth's budget if they were only located literally across the street in the Fort Worth city limits.

"We wouldn't have had budget problems if we had made different decisions years ago," Bolen said.

To begin planning for the future, City Council members assembled in the spring of 1989 to discuss the challenges that awaited the city as it entered a new decade.

Council members heard a wide range of speakers discuss trends that would affect Fort Worth in the future. Speakers included former San Antonio Mayor Henry Cisneros, Social Sciences Dean Royce Hanson of the University of Texas at Dallas, and John Roach, CEO of the Tandy Corp.

The *Fort Worth Star-Telegram* described the session as "nothing less than a Socratic exercise in vision-making . . ."

A recurring theme was the need for a well-trained and educated work force that can meet the demands of a changing economy.

"You need a trained and trainable labor force," McClendon told the council members. "You need kids to stay in school. You need excellence in education." Environmental authorities also told the council that cities in the future will likely be forced to deal with increased environmental regulations.

Based on the retreat, the city now faces a set of challenges that it must address as it enters a new decade. These include:
• Competing effectively for new business.
• Upgrading and enhancing education and training opportunities.
• Diminishing the threat of crime.
• Enhancing recreational and cultural amenities.
• Projecting an attractive picture of Fort Worth and attracting more visitors as a revenue source.
• Conforming to federal and state environmental regulations.

"Meeting these challenges will require generating new sources of revenue because of the declining level of federal and state assistance to local communities," a *Star-Telegram* editorial said.

"This will mean cutting across the traditional boundaries of local government jurisdictions and establishing new vehicles of cooperation between the public and private sectors."

At the conclusion of the two-day retreat, Bolen said he would appoint a task force composed of a cross-section of the community to look at the issues facing Fort Worth and develop a long-range plan on how to address them.

Bolen has his own vision of the future, one bright with promise:

I want to see a city that is based on education facilities that are second to none. The University of North Texas on one side. The University of Texas at Arlington on the other. Texas Christian University, the Southwestern Baptist Theological Seminary, Texas Wesleyan University and Tarrant County Junior College in Fort Worth. This way we can produce people to fill outstanding jobs and have a great job creation ability. High tech jobs. Good paying jobs. Clean industry, clean water. Opportunities for our people to grow.

A solitary fisherman tries his luck in the Trinity River in the Tarrant County Water District and Heritage Park area. Photo by Bob Rowan/ Progressive Image Photography

CHAPTER FOUR

A GOOD PLACE TO CALL HOME

Fort Worth is spread over a gentle, warm land; in turn, it produces a gentle, warm people. People who live with a sense of humor and with respect for their fellow man. A people who are always willing to extend their hand in friendship or to a friend in need.

An almost ideal climate produces a home and business life-style that is less aggressive than in most other cities. For one thing, there are hardly any rush hour traffic jams to set your nerves on edge. Drivers can be most anywhere in Fort Worth in 15 minutes or less.

The coldest month is January, when the low averages 35 degrees and the high averages 55 degrees. August is the hottest month, with highs averaging 95 degrees and lows averaging 74 degrees. On an annual basis, the temperature averages a high of 76 and a low of 55.

In an average year, it freezes only 35 days. Extreme fluctuations in temperatures are rare and short-lived. Rainfall is an ample 32.88 inches a year, making for plenty of sun-filled days for outdoor activities.

Fort Worth represents a diversity of cultures and life-styles. Its estimated population in 1990 of 446,300 was composed of about 68.9 percent white, 22.7 percent black, 12.6 percent Spanish-speaking heritage, and 8.4 percent other.

This combination provides Fort Worth with a rich, unique mixture of heritage, which in turn contributes to the total quality of life through business, cultural, dining, and festive activities.

Strongly blue-collar, the 1985 per capita income was $10,515.

At the same time, the cost of living was right at the national average. In 1987, the cost of living index for all items in Fort Worth was 101.7, compared to a national average of 100.

In the first quarter of 1989, the average home in Fort Worth was $81,005, a slight drop from the year before because of several economic factors, including overbuilding and the large number of foreclosures on the market resulting from the slumping Texas economy. Housing experts, however, expected house prices to rebound.

Fort Worth, in fact, was considered to offer the most affordable housing in Texas over the last decade.

"Houses in Fort Worth that are on the market for $300,000 would cost $1 million in places like Washington, D.C.," said Dr. Michael Sumichrast, an economist and consultant to the National Association of Home Builders. The average price of a home in the Fort Worth/Dallas area was 27 percent less than the average price nationwide.

PRESERVING NEIGHBORHOODS

But the quality of life is most reflected in Fort Worth's neighborhoods.

Hemmed in by the Trinity River and a high bluff, Fort Worth initially grew to the south. Here is where old-house lovers can find gracious tree-lined neighborhoods, the suburbs of the early 1900s.

Among these are the Fairmount/Southside National Historic District, Ryan Place, Berkeley, and Mistletoe Heights. Ryan Place is the home of Elizabeth Boulevard, a shaded street lined with stately mansions, which is also listed on the National Register of Historic Places.

Later developments include the Arlington Heights area in West Fort Worth, site of the World War I training base, Camp Bowie. To the far south are the newer Candleridge and Mira Vista, an exclusive neighborhood developed at the end of the 1980s.

Farther east, Fort Worth swallowed whole communities whose only identity today is the name of their neighborhood, such as Polytechnic Heights and Stop Six.

The 1980s were a period when neighborhood associations grew strong in Fort Worth. Many banded together to address common concerns through the League of Neighborhoods.

The casual, relaxed life-style that pervades Fort Worth is evident in its residents' preference for comfortable, informal eateries such as the Star Cafe. Photo by Bob Rowan/ Progressive Image Photography

GENUINE
GENUINE
Budweiser
LIGHT

Thistle Hill, located on Pennsylvania Avenue and built in 1903 by W.T. Waggoner as a wedding gift for his daughter, is Fort Worth's last remaining mansion built when cattle was king and cattle barons such as Waggoner lived in high style. Photo by Bob Rowan/ Progressive Image Photography

They grew strong and influential, capturing the attention of City Hall and their elected representatives. As a whole, the community leaders worked to preserve neighborhoods from undue or insensitive commercial encroachment and to ensure that streets were repaired, codes were enforced, and the overall community improved.

Former City Manager Doug Harman and his staff displayed a willing ear to listen to their concerns and to work with neighborhood organizations in attacking local problems.

In addition to neighborhood preservation, there is a strong interest among many citizens in preserving the history and culture of Fort Worth through its buildings, houses, and other man-made structures.

A historical resources survey sponsored by the Historic Preservation Council for Tarrant County identified more than 100,000 potential local, state, and national landmarks scattered throughout Tarrant County, including Fort Worth. These landmarks ranged from individual houses of historic significance to entire neighborhoods.

One example is the Fairmount neighborhood on the Southside. Considered one of the biggest, intact turn-of-the-century neighborhoods left in the nation, the 110-square-block neighborhood in 1990 was entered onto the National Register of Historic Places—the largest district in Texas, next to the King Ranch.

The City of Fort Worth has a historic preservation officer on staff, who works with individuals and organizations on questions and issues affecting historic properties. In addition, the city-affiliated Historic and Cultural Landmark Commission acts as the official review body for matters involving historic districts, historical zoning, partial tax exemptions on historic property, and other related issues.

Through historic preservation activities, citizens today can glimpse life at the turn of the century on the Summit Avenue "Silk Stocking Row" at the Eddleman-McFarland House, built in 1898 and one of only a handful of Victorian mansions still standing in the city. Thistle Hill, built in 1903 as a wedding gift from cattle baron W.T. Waggoner to his daughter, is an imposing Neoclassical home that is the sole survivor of what was once a gentry neighborhood dominated by similar houses.

Efforts were also being made to preserve the Mission-style Livestock Exchange Building in the Stockyards National Historic District. The city in the mid-1980s renovated the nearby 1908 Coliseum, home of the world's first indoor rodeo.

The Central Business District is dotted with examples of earlier architecture. Among the most notable are the Flatiron Building, a triangular structure built in 1907; the W.T. Waggoner Building (1919), carefully renovated as a bank and office building; Saint Patrick's Cathedral (1892); and Saint Ignatius Academy (1889).

The Sundance Square area of downtown also creates the atmosphere of early Fort Worth.

CULTURAL EVENTS

History is also the theme of many of the festivals and events held throughout the year.

The largest western heritage festival is Pioneer Days, held each fall in the Stockyards. Pioneer Days re-creates the Stockyards history from the days of the

Civil War to its rise as a meat processing center. The event features plenty of mock gunfights, cowboys, music, and Texas cookery.

In June, the Chisholm Trail Round-Up salutes the cattle drives that tramped through Fort Worth a century earlier. It features Indians, cowboys, western entertainment, arts and crafts, an all-day trail ride, and a county fair. In the fall, Fort Worth celebrates its own version of a German festival at Oktoberfest. And it marks its own rites of spring in May with Mayfest, held outdoors in Trinity Park. In addition, Fort Worth residents celebrate Cinco De Mayo in April, in honor of Mexico's independence from France; Cowtown Goes Green in March, the local version of a St. Patrick's Day; and the Parade of Lights in November, when horses and carriages draped in twinkling lights parade down Main Street.

The largest event is the Main Street Arts Festival. In 1989, some 400,000 people thronged Main Street to listen to live music, eat, and shop for leather goods, pottery, paintings, and other handmade crafts produced by artists and artisans from throughout the Southwest.

Fort Worth's decades-old institutions and organizations span the spectrum of visual and performing arts. Here, casually attired Fort Worth residents gather in the Texas sun for the Main Street Arts Festival. Photo by Michael Lyon/TexaStock

Among the events that take place during the annual Southwestern Exposition and Livestock Show is a parade through the city. Photo by Kevin Vandivier/TexaStock

MEDICAL CARE

A central core of the quality of life is the availability of medical care. Fort Worth is served by 1,924 doctors, 428 dentists, 30 hospitals, and a total of 5,133 hospital beds.

While these are spread across the city, the one-square-mile Hospital District south of downtown is home for the city's major hospitals, clinics, doctor offices, and medical supply firms. These include John Peter Smith Hospital, the tax-supported county hospital; Saint Josephs Hospital, Fort Worth's oldest hospital; All Saints Episcopal Hospital; Harris Methodist Hospital Fort Worth; Cook-Fort Worth Children's Medical Center; Care Unit Hospital; and the Psychiatric Institute of Fort Worth.

The most nationally recognized of all is Cook-Fort Worth CMC, the largest independent pediatric medical center in the country. The hospital offers specialized pediatric care in emergency medicine, surgery, and trauma.

More than 400 physicians are on staff, including 75 subspecialists representing 27 specialties of medical care. Ninety-seven percent of the nurses are registered nurses.

Cook-Fort Worth was the product of a merger between Fort Worth Children's Hospital and Cook Children's Hospital. In 1989, Cook-Fort Worth moved into a new $53-million, six-story facility in the heart of the Medical District.

The building is unique in that its architectural style is more reminiscent of a fairy tale castle than a hospital—exactly the feeling that the hospital executives wanted to create for the children.

The driving force behind the new facility was Fort Worth financier Robert M. Bass and his wife, Anne. Bass served as chairman of the hospital and helped raise funds to build the new facility.

Across the street is Harris Methodist Fort Worth, the city's largest hospital, which has branches in several other areas of the county. Harris, a nonprofit institution sponsored by the Methodist Church, conducts open-heart surgery and kidney transplants, provides rehabilitation programs for head and spinal cord injuries, operates a full-time emergency room, and offers CareFlite, an emergency helicopter service. It has 628 beds.

Saint Joseph Hospital was founded 11 years after members of the Congregation of the Sisters of Charity of the Incarnate Word arrived from San Antonio in 1885 to take over the Missouri-Pacific Railroad infirmary. When the infirmary burned in

1885, the nuns bought 15 acres on a hilltop, the site of the present-day 475-bed facility.

Saint Joseph offers psychiatric programs, chemotherapy, hospice programs, cardiac services, physical therapy, wellness programs, and general surgery.

Next door to Saint Joseph is John Peter Smith, named after one of Fort Worth's early founders. The 429-bed hospital is run by the Tarrant County Hospital District. Inpatient services include medical and surgical care, obstetrics, pediatrics, psychiatry, intensive care, orthopedics, physical and occupational therapy, and maxillofacial surgery.

A master facility renovation scheduled for completion in 1991 includes expansion of the trauma center and the radiology, laboratory, intensive care, obstetrics, and psychiatry areas, and will increase the bed capacity to 653.

John Peter Smith has been involved in general practice training since the turn of the century, but in 1973, a three-year Family Practice Residency was fully approved and affiliated with the University of Texas Southwestern Medical School. It is one of the largest family practice residencies on one campus in the country.

All Saints Episcopal Hospital is another major medical facility located in the district, offering general hospital services. Adjacent to the hospital is the Moncrief Radiation Center, one of the largest freestanding centers in the nation for the treatment of cancer.

Other medical facilities in the district include Care Unit, an 83-bed hospital treating adults and adolescents with alcoholism, drug dependencies, anorexia, and bulimia; Psychiatric Institute, a 118-bed psychiatric hospital for preadolescents, adolescents, and adults; and Tarrant County Psychiatric Center, a 56-bed psychiatric hospital operated by the Tarrant County Mental Health-Mental Retardation Services.

Other medical centers in Fort Worth include Osteopathic Medical Center of Texas and Huguley Memorial Hospital, an acute care facility affiliated with the Adventist Health Systems.

The 60-bed Harris Methodist Southwest Hospital on Harris Parkway provides general emergency services, surgery, obstetrical/gynecological care, occupational therapy, orthopedics, and pediatrics. Photo by Michael Lyon/TexaStock

John Peter Smith Hospital, a 414-bed facility located on South Main Street in central Fort Worth, is a Tarrant County Hospital District teaching hospital. Photo by Bob Rowan/ Progressive Image Photography

Saint Joseph Hospital on South Main provides the community with 475 hospital beds, surgery, cancer treatment, cardiac rehabilitation, gynecology, hospice, kidney dialysis, occupational therapy, open-heart surgery, and orthopedics. It also offers treatment for chemical dependency, psychiatric and general emergency room services, and a psychiatric unit. Photo by Bob Rowan/ Progressive Image Photography

SOCIAL NEEDS

In addition to medical care, Fort Worth citizens also work together to address the social needs of the city. The dominant umbrella organization is the United Way of Metropolitan Tarrant County, which provides financial support to 56 agencies and services at 322 local sites.

Supported by contributions from individuals and corporations, the United Way agencies serve thousands of residents struggling with problems of day-care, teenage pregnancy, substance abuse, aging, and parenting.

Among the organizations that are members of the United Way are the American Red Cross, Boy Scouts of America-Longhorn Council, the Bridge Association of Fort Worth (emergency shelter and counseling for youths), Catholic Social Services, Child Study Center (diagnostic, treatment, and rehabilitation services for children with physical, developmental, learning, sensory, behavioral, or emotional problems), Family Service (family, personal, parent/child, sex and physical abuse, alcohol and drug abuse counseling), First Call for Help referral link, Parenting Guidance Center, Senior Citizen Services, Women's Center of Tarrant County, and Women's Haven of Tarrant County.

Moreover, Fort Worth offers citizens the services of the Tarrant Council on Alcoholism and Drug Abuse, Tarrant County Area Agency on Aging, Tarrant County Association for the Blind, Tarrant County Cancer Society, Tarrant County Multiple Sclerosis Association, United Cerebral Palsy of Tarrant County, and Sickle Cell Anemia Association of Texas.

And Fort Worth is also home of the nationally renowned Edna Gladney Center, which provides medical, housing, educational, counseling, and adoption placement services for unwed mothers. The Lena Pope Home is an intensive res-

The 72-bed All Saints Hospital Cityview on Oakmont in southwest Fort Worth provides major trauma emergency services, surgery, cancer treatment, cardiac rehabilitation, obstetrics/gynecology, occupational therapy, orthopedics, and pediatrics. Photo by Michael Lyon/TexaStock

idential treatment facility offering structured family-home life and an educational plan for emotionally disturbed adolescents.

In addition, Fort Worth is the home of 127 foundations with assets totaling
more than $700 million. These foundations, often established with the fortunes
made by Fort Worth families and individuals, devote considerable sums of money
to addressing social problems, improving education, and supporting arts and culture in the community. Among the largest are the Sid Richardson, Amon G.
Carter, and Anne Burnett and Charles Tandy foundations.

RELIGION

Religion plays an important role in the fabric of lives of Fort Worth residents.

Since the First Christian Church established the first church in Fort Worth in
1855, the number of denominations has blossomed to fill the many needs of residents.
The Tarrant Area Community of Churches has 161 member organizations, including
mainline Protestant, Catholic, and Orthodox groups. In total, there are 914 churches
in the area, representing 72 denominations.

The largest denomination is Baptist. The Tarrant Baptist Association reports
172 Southern Baptist churches in the county, plus 119 mission congregations. In
addition, there are 100 independent or fundamental Baptist congregations in
Fort Worth.

First United Methodist Church in downtown Fort Worth has a membership of
9,500 and is the third-largest United Methodist congregation in the United States.

The Catholic Diocese of Fort Worth has more than 30 churches in Tarrant
County. Congregation Ahavath Shalom, a traditional synagogue, and Beth-El Congregation, a part of the Reform movement, provide services for the Jewish faith.

**Cook/Fort Worth Children's Medical
Center on Seventh Avenue contains
169 beds and offers these pediatric
services: surgery, cancer treatment,
diabetic unit, neonatal ICU,
occupational therapy, orthopedics,
pediatric ICU, drug overdose, and
general emergency room services. It
also operates a Poison Information
Center. Photo by Bob Rowan/ Progressive Image Photography**

PARKS AND RECREATION

Newsweek magazine has saluted Fort Worth's "network of parks with total acreage second only to Chicago's . . ." Maintained by the Fort Worth Park and Recreation Department, this encompasses 171 city parks with a total acreage of 9,026, ranging from developed downtown greenspaces to nature preserves. Twenty-one of those parks have been adopted by civic groups, who help stretch budget dollars by working to maintain them.

Perhaps the most unique park in Fort Worth is the Japanese Gardens, where an old gravel pit has been transformed into Asian splendor.

Shaded pathways through the six-acre park wind among the Meditation Garden, Teahouse, Pagoda, waterfalls, and water pools stocked with imperial carp. The park was designed by architect Kingsley Wu of Denton, Texas.

Adjacent to the Japanese Gardens is the Botanic Gardens, a 114-acre tract of meadows, woods, roses, and aromatic gardens for the blind built in 1933-1935 by more than 750 relief laborers working for two dollars a day, paid in meal tickets. A $4-million conservatory houses exotic plants and flowers.

In 1988, a conservatory was added to the Gardens to feature additional exotic plants in a glass-enclosed setting. The conservatory also provides community meeting space.

Downtown, near the site of Hell's Half Acre of Fort Worth's rowdier frontier days, is the world-famous water park, the Fort Worth Water Garden.

Designed by architect Philip Johnson, the five-acre urban park was opened in 1974 and features waterfalls, fountains, and sunken pools of moving water. The

The First Methodist Church stands in all its majestic splendor in downtown Fort Worth. Photo by Bob Rowan/Progressive Image Photography

The Masonic Temple, one of the city's historic buildings, is a grand sight to behold on Henderson. Photo by Bob Rowan/ Progressive Image Photography

most spectacular feature is the Active Pool, in which visitors can walk down a stairstepped concrete cliff and find themselves surrounded by cascading waterfalls on all sides. The park was financed by a gift from the Amon G. Carter Foundation.

A half-dozen blocks west is another urban landscaped setting, Burnett Park. The square-block site was donated to the city at the turn of the century by rancher Samuel Burk Burnett and now features concrete gridwalks around pools of water and patches of grass.

One of Fort Worth's major attractions is the Zoo, located southwest of downtown in Forest Park near Texas Christian University.

Situated at the base of limestone bluffs beside a meandering creek, the Zoo is in the process of a long-term expansion and renovation process to replace animal cages with more realistic open habitats, such as an African Savanna and Asian Diorama.

The newest attraction is the 11-acre Texas Exhibit, depicting life in late nineteenth-century Texas. The exhibit features native domestic and wild animals, including bison and Texas longhorns, and nine buildings, including a schoolhouse, barn, saloon, ranch house, and blacksmith shop.

For an even earlier view of Texas, the Log Cabin Village, also located in Forest Park, has seven authentic pioneer log cabins moved to the site from rural areas of Texas. Most were built in the 1850s, when Texas, and Fort Worth, were still the frontier.

Visitors can see period antiques and watch demonstrations in spinning and candlemaking. And it also provides a sample of the rugged life-style faced by the early Fort Worth pioneers.

The Fort Worth Nature Center and Wildlife Refuge, a 3,500-acre park located on the northwest side of Lake Worth, provides visitors with a sample of authentic Texas habitats, including prairie, cross timbers, live oak savanna, marsh, and the Trinity River.

With 20 miles of trail, the park provides opportunities to see native animals such as buffalo, whitetail deer, and prairie dogs in their natural environment.

SOCIAL LIFE

For other tastes, much of Fort Worth's social life revolves around country clubs. Most provide golf courses, swimming, tennis, and dining facilities. Among the most popular and prestigious clubs are the River Crest, Ridglea, Colonial, and the new Mira Vista.

And among the most fashionable events of each year are the presentations of

Visitors to the Fort Worth Botanic Garden may catch a glimpse of three stone monkeys signifying "speak no evil," "see no evil," and "hear no evil." Photo by Jane Stader/TexaStock

debutantes each fall. The Steeplechase Club and the Assembly Club are the two most significant.

The Jewell Charity Ball, a gala function to support Cook-Fort Worth Children's Medical Center, is perhaps the most prestigious general social function of the year.

Fort Worth features plenty of modern shopping facilities and malls, most within 15 minutes of every neighborhood in the city.

The largest mall is Ridgmar, which is located on the West Side near Carswell Air Force Base and General Dynamics. To the south is Hulen Mall with approximately 90 stores.

Fort Worth Town Center is the oldest shopping mall in the area.

Western wear, complete from jeans to boots to cowboy hats, is available in shops throughout the city. But many cowpokes prefer to buy their wares on West Exchange in the Stockyards, where handmade boots, saddles, and chaps are still available. Popular western shops are Leddy's, Ryon's, and Fincher's.

Dining in Fort Worth spans the entire culinary spectrum. While there are excellent French, Italian, and Asian restaurants, home cooking, steak, barbecue, and Tex-Mex food are the standard dishes native to Texas.

Home cooking, a perennial Fort Worth favorite, consists of chicken-fried steak (steak fried in batter), squash, fried okra, black-eyed peas, and biscuits. The Paris Coffee Shop and Massey's, both located on the Southside, are two old-time favorites in this category.

More than 2,000 species of plants are represented in the 114-acre Fort Worth Botanic Gardens, which was put together as part of a Depression-era work relief project. Photo by Bob Rowan/ Progressive Image Photography

Following the tradition of cattle drives and cowboys comes steak and barbecue. While the cattle of the trail drive days were grass fed and offered tough, stringy beef, today's feedlot cattle make for tender, juicy cuts, best prepared when grilled over mesquite chips. Although steaks are a staple at most restaurants, the Cattleman's in the Stockyards is among the best known, largely due to the ambiance of its location in the historic meat packing district.

Slow-cooked, smoked beef coated with spicy sauce is known as barbecue—a featured attraction at home cook-outs and neighborhood restaurants. All types of meats respond well to the sweet taste of barbecue, including ribs, sausage, briskets, and even bologna. A popular place to find it in Fort Worth is Angelo's.

Tex-Mex is an Anglo variation of the Mexican staples of beans, rice, and tortillas—flat corn or flour meal disks. Usually highly spiced, Tex-Mex dishes include tacos, enchiladas, tamales, and most recently, fajitas. Although Joe T. Garcia's is perhaps the best known of Tex-Mex restaurants in Fort Worth, the strong Hispanic heritage in the city has spawned many excellent Tex-Mex establishments.

Executives of the city's leading companies are generally found at the private Petroleum Club or Fort Worth Club, both graceful establishments in downtown office buildings.

SISTER CITIES

Fort Worth's quality of life is also enhanced by its relationship with other cities, especially those in other nations.

The International Sister Cities Association of Fort Worth provides ways for citizens to expand their horizons culturally and civically and form lasting friendships with citizens of other countries.

A member of Sister Cities International, Sister Cities Fort Worth has established Sister Cities with Reggio Emilia, Italy, Trier, West Germany, and Nagaoka, Japan. In 1987, the local chapter hosted the Sister Cities International Annual Conference, an affair that brought in visitors from around the world.

In 1989, Sister Cities Fort Worth won one of nine awards presented by the international organization for its community service. Fort Worth was honored for a membership drive that boosted the number of members to 550, for signing ceremonies with Trier and Nagaoka, for its youth organization, and for its broad-based community support.

CIVIC COMMITMENT

But the secret to the quality of life in a city is not just its neighborhoods, restaurants, social services, and medical facilities. The people set the tone.

Fort Worth is blessed with strong civic commitment that starts at the very top of the social and economic scales. As witnessed throughout its history, the city has reaped the benefits of benefactors who not only gave their money, but also gave their time and personal energy to the city.

Fort Worth is a city that tends to envelop its residents, to make them want to give something back in return for what it gives them. Corporate executives newly arriving in the city soon find that their talents are in high demand in various civic and social causes. And they soon find themselves captured by the desire to help out, even though they are stretched to find enough hours in the day to keep their own businesses running smoothly.

The leadership and love of Fort Worth is something you don't see in a lot of towns across the United States.

The City of Fort Worth sponsored an evening picnic called Neighborhood USA in General Worth Square. Photo by Bob Rowan/ Progressive Image Photography

EDUCATING FOR THE FUTURE

The future of Fort Worth lies in the hands of its children. These youngsters were photographed at the Cowtown Coliseum. Photo by Bob Rowan/ Progressive Image Photography

T he employee we hire today must do more reading, more math, and must know how to operate a computer terminal. The days of Rosie the Riveter are long gone. The worker on the floor is riveting by operating a computer terminal."

These are the words of Edward M. Petruska, vice president of General Dynamics, Fort Worth's largest employer. His remarks came in March 1989 when he addressed the Fort Worth City Council, city staff, and about 100 citizens gathered in a retreat to forge a long-range plan for the city.

Petruska was one of many corporate executives, national leaders, and urban experts who drove home the message that the community must invest in education to ensure that Fort Worth can offer employers a well-trained and educated work force in the future.

The message delivered at the City Council retreat was one that made sense to the business community. Representatives of the City of Fort Worth and large and small businesses are major backers of a strong education system in Fort Worth, from the public school district to local universities.

Examples of their support are evident in the Stay In School Task Force and reactivation of the chamber's education committee.

The 85-member task force was formed in 1989 to help find ways to address the school dropout problem. The group, composed of a cross-section of community leaders, educators, and businesspeople, hoped to determine which dropout programs work in Fort Worth and elsewhere, and support them.

"The chamber has focused a lot on economic development, and a key piece of that is trying to be supportive, trying to find out what role we can play, in having an educated work force," said Paul R. Ray, Jr., chairman of an education committee and president of Paul R. Ray & Company, a Fort Worth-based executive search firm.

PUBLIC SCHOOLS

The backbone of the education system is the Fort Worth Independent School District. The district, with an enrollment of 67,984 pupils, has 64 elementary schools, 19 middle schools, 12 high schools, and 7 special schools. In December 1985, voters approved an extensive five-year, $111-million bond program to finance the construction of six new schools and dozens of additions and upgrades to existing schools.

The public schools were originally operated by the City of Fort Worth when they were founded in 1882. In 1925, the Texas Legislature removed the city's authority and created the Fort Worth Independent School District.

Today, the FWISD is controlled locally through a Board of Education selected by voters from seven single-member districts. The board president and vice president are elected at-large. They serve without pay.

A superintendent hired by the board is responsible for the day-to-day management of the district and its nearly 7,250 employees.

Of the teachers, 2,030 have at least 10 years experience and 1,297 have a master's degree.

The 1988-1989 budget was nearly $247 million. Court-ordered busing has ended in the Fort Worth school district, although bus transportation is provided for students living more than two miles from their schools. Transportation is also provided for magnet students and special education students.

While test scores in years past were below average, the Fort Worth school district, under the leadership of Superintendent Don Roberts, was taking long strides in providing pupils with a quality education.

"We have the fourth-lowest tax rate of 75 ISDs in the state," said board president Gary Manny. "We spend less per child. But we get good returns for what we spend."

For example, one-third of the 1,469 seniors who took the Scholastic Aptitude Test (SAT) in 1989 scored above the national average of 903; 11 percent scored

above 1100 (1600 is a perfect score). Districtwide, the SAT average was 844 in 1989, reflecting a gain of 14 points over three years.

Another example is that more seventh-graders in the Fort Worth school district passed all sections of the Texas Educational Assessment of Minimum Skills (TEAMS) in 1989 than in any of the state's seven urban school districts, including Dallas, Houston, San Antonio, Austin, El Paso, and Ysleta (also in El Paso). The test is given to third, fifth, seventh, ninth, and eleventh graders to measure their mastery of essential learning skills.

The FWISD provides a rich variety of programs that can be tailored to fit the needs of most any student in the district.

Magnet programs offer specialized academic training in Montessori, language immersion, and accelerated and enriched curriculums in science, math, communications, finance, college readiness, and the medical professions. There is also a pre-international baccalaureate program that includes history, English, computer science, calculus, chemistry, and physics.

Depending on their needs, gifted students are offered group and individualized instruction in their classrooms, accelerated pacing, and enrichment activities. Almost all of the district's high schools have students enrolled concurrently in college courses. Academically talented seniors were offered nearly $5 million in scholarships in 1988. The FWISD has fielded 126 National Merit Finalists since 1977-1978.

Students with special needs are given the help they require. The Special Education Department offers programs for the hearing impaired, visually impaired, physically handicapped, learning disabled, mentally challenged, emotionally disturbed, and autistic. Vocation education programs are available in home economics, vocational office, trade and industrial, technology education, marketing education, and health occupations.

Bilingual and English as a Second Language programs serve more than 7,700 students with limited proficiency in English. While most of these are Spanish-speaking, the program also serves students who speak Laotian, Cambodian, Vietnamese, and 47 other languages.

The support of the business and civic community is most apparent in the district's nationally recognized Adopt-A-School program. In this public-private partnership, 112 companies or organizations have volunteered 100,000 hours and have adopted 72 schools in the district.

They provide attendance and achievement incentives, tutors, mentors, pen pals, guest speakers, fine arts programs, and special seminars for teachers and parents.

PTAs and PTOs contribute through fund-raisers for school bus stop arms, campaigns promoting educational issues, and special events to raise money to buy equipment and instructional materials. Parents, teachers, and community leaders also serve as advisors to school principals as members of school management teams.

And the Volunteer Services Offices matches the skills of parents, grandparents, and community leaders with the needs of schools and students. Some 5,000 volunteers have provided 196,630 hours of time to the schools.

PRIVATE SCHOOLS

For parents looking for alternatives to a public school education for their children, the Fort Worth area has 30 parochial schools with a total enrollment of 5,800. There are also three private schools offering grades K through 12 with an enrollment of 2,084. And there are an additional 19 other private schools, including those for special learning disabilities, for a total enrollment of 1,284.

Two of the most prominent private schools are Fort Worth Country Day School in Southwest Fort Worth and Trinity Valley School in Far South Fort Worth. Both schools—Country Day, founded in 1962, and Trinity Valley, founded in 1959—are considered college preparatory and have selective admission policies.

Among the others are All Saints Episcopal School for preschool through 12th grade; All Saints Catholic School for kindergarten through eighth grade; St. Andrew's Catholic School for preschool through eighth; and Nolan High School, a Catholic school for the seventh to 12th grades.

The Hill School offers kindergarten through eighth grade, teaching children with average or above-average intelligence who have learning difficulties.

TEXAS CHRISTIAN UNIVERSITY

Within Fort Worth, there are two universities, a theological seminary, a medical school, and a junior college system. Within 50 miles, there are 29 colleges and universities, with a total enrollment of 178,207 students.

Texas Christian University, situated on a shaded campus southwest of downtown, is the largest institution of higher education in Fort Worth, with an enrollment of 7,105 students. The university moved to the site in 1910 when city leaders offered it 56 acres of grazing land and $200,000 after its Waco campus burned.

The move was actually a homecoming. Texas Christian University had its genesis in 1869 when a group of Fort Worth citizens invited Addision and Randolph Clark to establish a private school in the frontier town. The brothers came and started holding classes in a church.

They soon discovered that the disreputable Hell's Half Acre next to the church was incompatible with the morals taught at their academy. In 1873, they moved to a community west of Fort Worth called Thorp Spring and founded the AddRan Male and Female College. In 1889, they affiliated with the Christian Churches of Texas and in 1895 moved to an abandoned college campus in Waco. The name was changed to Texas Christian University in 1902 when it had an enrollment of 302 students.

Fort Worth Technical School is but one such school in the area. Others include American Trades Institute, ITT Technical Institute in Arlington, DeVry Institute of Technology in Irving, and Lincoln Technical Institute in Dallas. Photo by Bob Rowan/Progressive Image Photography

Today, Texas Christian has grown into a 237-acre campus with 60 buildings. One of the newest is the state-of-the-art Tandy Hall, housing the M.J. Neeley School of Business. It is named after Charles Tandy, a TCU alumnus and founder of the Fort Worth-based Tandy Corp.

The university is independent and coeducational, with colleges and schools of arts and sciences, business, education, fine arts and communications, nursing, and theology. Degree programs run through the Ph.D. level.

Of the 1,150 entering freshmen in 1987, about 20 percent are from Fort Worth, 40 percent from elsewhere in Texas, 35 percent from other states, and 5 percent from other countries. Most graduate in the top quarter of their high school class. The 385 faculty members hold their highest

degree from more than 125 different institutions, and 86 percent of the full-time faculty have earned doctorate or other terminal credentials in their field.

Student to faculty ratio is 14.6 to 1. More than half of the classes have fewer than 20 students in them.

In 1988, the university initiated a new core curriculum that comprises 40 percent of every baccalaureate program. Unique to the program are its extension into the junior and senior years of writing emphasis courses in all disciplines and the requirement of at least one upper-level critical inquiry class to enhance clear thinking and good writing.

Although TCU offers a wide spectrum of majors, among its more unique is its undergraduate degree offering in ballet and modern dance. TCU was the first university in the nation to offer an academic degree program in ballet.

TCU also offers the only four-year nursing degree program in Fort Worth through the Harris College of Nursing. And it prepares students for the ministry at the Brite Divinity School.

As a member of the prestigious Southwest Athletic Conference, TCU athletes compete with students from other major universities in Texas, Arkansas, and Oklahoma.

Fall is the season of purple and white in Fort Worth. That's when Coach Jim Wacker leads his Horned Frogs against football powerhouses such as Texas, Texas A&M, and Arkansas at Amon G. Carter Stadium.

TEXAS WESLEYAN UNIVERSITY

Across town in the Polytechnic Heights neighborhood is Texas Wesleyan University, the oldest institution of higher education continuously located in Tarrant County.

The school was founded in 1890 by the Methodist Episcopal Church South, on a hilltop four miles east of Fort Worth.

It was first called Polytechnic College, meaning "many arts and sciences."

The J.M. Moudy Building for Visual Arts and Communications is located on the campus of Texas Christian University. Photo by Bob Rowan/ Progressive Image Photography

The city of Polytechnic Heights soon grew around the school and was later incorporated into the Fort Worth city limits.

In 1914, Polytechnic College became the women's college of the Methodist Church in Texas and was renamed Texas Woman's College. In 1934, it was made coeducational again and called Texas Wesleyan College. In 1989, the name was changed to Texas Wesleyan University, "an official acknowledgment that Texas Wesleyan is more accurately described by the term 'university' than by the term 'college,' " according to President Jerry G. Bawcom.

Affiliated with the five Texas conferences of the United Methodist Church, Texas Wesleyan integrates liberal studies with professional and career preparation in four schools: business, education, fine arts, and science and humanities. Undergraduate degrees are offered in 56 areas. The two graduate programs are education and nurse anesthesia—the only nurse anesthesia program in the Fort Worth/Dallas area.

With an enrollment average of 1,500, the university stresses the development of students to their full potential as individuals and members of society. The 14:1 student-to-faculty ratio enables teachers to provide students with personal attention.

All undergraduates are required to complete 52 hours of liberal arts studies to provide them with a foundation for entrance into professional careers or graduate study.

Graduates of the Pre-Professional Program experience a 94 percent acceptance rate to the medical, dental, law, theology, or graduate schools of their choice.

Texas Wesleyan graduates taking the Certified Public Accountants examination for the first time average a 23.1 percent pass rate. The national pass rate is 20.8 percent. The Texas rate is 18.6 percent.

The School of Fine Arts has produced musicals annually since 1955. And many alumni have gone on to theater work in both New York and California, including award-winning television actress Joy Garrett and former Miss Texas Terri Eoff.

Male and female athletes have achieved national recognition for various sports. In 1988, two men golfers made the National Association of Intercollegiate Ath-

Texas Wesleyan University is a small, private college founded in 1890 by the Methodist Episcopal Church. Photo by Bob Rowan/ Progressive Image Photography

letics Academic All-America team. In 1987, four Texas Wesleyan students made the team out of only 20 chosen nationwide. And again in 1987, the women's volleyball team ranked third nationally in the NAIA.

U.S. News and World Report in 1988 named Texas Wesleyan as one of the top five small comprehensive colleges in the United States in terms of resources.

The cornerstone for a multi-year master plan development effort on the historic campus was the dedication in late 1988 of the $10-million, 90,000-square-foot Eunice and James L. West Library.

SOUTHWESTERN BAPTIST THEOLOGICAL SEMINARY

Another church-affiliated college in Fort Worth is the Southwestern Baptist Theological Seminary, the largest theological seminary in the world.

And like its neighbor—Texas Christian University—the seminary was brought to Fort Worth through the efforts of citizens.

Southwestern had its origins in 1901 in the theological department of Baylor University in Waco. Four years later the department evolved into the Baylor Theological Seminary, which was formed into the Southwestern Baptist Theological Seminary by the Baptist General Convention in 1907.

Chartered in 1908, Southwestern operated on the Baylor University campus until 1910 when Fort Worth citizens, competing against other Texas cities, wooed the seminary with the offer of a campus site and funds to construct its first building. By the end of the 1980s, it had grown to 200 acres and 14 major buildings.

In 1925, the Southern Baptist Convention became the controlling entity for the seminary—one of six affiliated with the convention. Southwestern has expanded to four off-campus centers: Houston; San Antonio; Garland, Texas; and Shawnee, Oklahoma. And in 1982, Southwestern merged with the Mexican Baptist Theological Seminary to form the Hispanic Baptist Theological Seminary in San Antonio.

Today, 4,800 students are enrolled at the seminary in a wide variety of subject areas. Primarily oriented toward the graduate levels, the seminary offers master's and doctorate-level degrees from the School of Theology, School of Religious Education, and School of Church Music.

Nearly half of the seminary-trained missionaries now serving with the Southern Baptist Convention's Foreign and Home Mission Boards are former Southwestern students. Every year Southwestern graduates three times the number of students enrolled in the average seminary.

And since its founding in 1908, Southwestern has enrolled some 52,000 students and graduated nearly 30,000.

The programs are designed to prepare students for work in fields such as the ministry and leadership positions in missions, evangelism, teaching, preaching, philosophy of religion, ethics, historical studies, administration, counseling, and church music.

A continuing education program for the ministry provides conferences and workshops for updating and cultivating education for the ministry.

Students are supported in their studies by the A. Webb Roberts Library, one of the largest research centers in the nation, with more than 700,000 items housed on 25 miles of shelves.

TEXAS COLLEGE OF OSTEOPATHIC MEDICINE

Located on a hill in the Cultural District on the city's West Side is Fort Worth's own medical school—the Texas College of Osteopathic Medicine.

TCOM was founded as a private school in 1970 to meet the needs for more family doctors in Texas. Five years later, it became a state-supported school when it affiliated with the University of North Texas, located 35 miles north in Denton, and placed under the direction of its board of regents.

About 400 students are enrolled in the four-year curriculum. By state law, 90 percent of each class originates in Texas. About 70 percent of TCOM's graduates elect to stay in the state and nearly 75 percent are family or primary care physicians. Some 40 percent practice medicine in small towns or rural communities.

Upon earning their degree as a Doctor of Osteopathy, graduates are qualified to be licensed for the unlimited practice of all branches of medicine and surgery in all 50 states. Graduates can also specialize in areas such as anesthesiology, surgery, sports medicine, and pediatrics.

As part of their training, TCOM students work with experienced physicians in the college's six general and family practice clinics, 13 specialty clinics, and 12 affiliated hospitals.

They are also trained in modern methods of diagnosis and therapy, including laboratory analysis, medications, surgery, and X-rays.

As part of the distinction of osteopathic medicine, students learn how to approach the entire family—not just an individual—in the treatment and prevention of disease.

They also are given extensive instruction in the musculoskeletal system and how its improper functioning can both cause and reflect ill health. In a medical skill unique to the profession, students are taught osteopathic manipulative therapy—using their hands in detecting and treating structural problems.

In 1988, all 93 juniors who took Part I of the National Osteopathic Board Examination—a prerequisite for graduation—passed. Part II is administered during the senior year.

The Texas Board of Medical Examiners reported that all 47 of the 1988 grad-

The Texas College of Osteopathic Medicine is located at 3500 Camp Bowie Boulevard. Photo by Brad Crooks

uates who took the licensing exam passed both Component I (basic science) and Component II (clinical science).

Faculty members conduct research on a wide range of medical problems, including the biochemistry of aging, osteoporosis and arthritis, heart disease, substance abuse, and the link between nutrition and cancer.

TARRANT COUNTY JUNIOR COLLEGE

Fort Worth is also served by Tarrant County Junior College with campuses in Northeast, Northwest, and South Tarrant County.

The junior college district was created in 1965 when voters approved the sale of more than $18 million in bonds for construction, elected a seven-member Board of Trustees, and approved taxes for debt service and operations.

The 158-acre South Fort Worth branch was the first unit completed in the fall of 1967. It was followed in 1968 by the opening of the Northeast branch in nearby Hurst and in 1976 by the Northwest Fort Worth branch, funded with a $20 million bond election, which also provided additional buildings for the other campuses.

In 1983, the May Owen District Center opened across the street from the Water Garden in downtown Fort Worth. It serves primarily as administrative offices, with a small number of classrooms.

Voters in 1985 approved a $50-million bond package for new construction, renovation, and equipment, as well as for the acquisition of future campus sites. In the fall of 1987, the district purchased a 123-acre site in Arlington for a campus there.

Tarrant County Junior College provides a wide range of educational opportunities. These include general academic courses such as English, mathematics, science, and history.

More than 50 occupational or technical-vocational programs are offered, ranging from air conditioning and refrigeration technology to respiratory therapy.

The general courses give students a stepping stone to four-year colleges and universities through an associate in arts degree program. About 85 percent of the associate in arts graduates pursue additional degrees where they do as well or better than students who entered universities as freshmen.

The technical-vocational programs offer students training so that they may enter the job market with an employable skill or transfer to a four-year institution with an associate of applied science degree.

The district works closely with the business community to ensure that TCJC is providing instruction that is parallel to the needs of particular major industries and professions in the area.

TCJC also serves the community through a variety of community services and continuing education programs. Noncredit courses and activities are frequently planned in cooperation with business representatives, educators, individuals, and special interest groups. They are designed to appeal to youth, adults, and senior citizens.

OTHER INSTITUTIONS

The largest four-year institution in Tarrant County is the University of Texas at Arlington. The school offers undergraduate and graduate programs in liberal arts, science, business, engineering, architecture, nursing, and urban studies. The school is a member of the University of Texas System and provides instruction to many students commuting from Fort Worth.

The University of North Texas in Denton, Southern Methodist University and University of Texas (both in Dallas), the University of Dallas in Irving, and others are among the other educational institutions located within an easy commuting distance of Fort Worth.

FULFILLING THE DREAM

Together, Fort Worth's educational institutions are working to help fulfill Mayor Bob Bolen's dream of having a city based on exceptional educational facilities.

Erma Johnson, Human Resource vice president of Tarrant County Junior College, obviously agrees.

"Education and economic development go hand-in-hand," she said during the council retreat. "There is a high correlation between poverty and crime. The education system undergirds everything."

The economy of the city of Arlington benefits greatly from the University of Texas at Arlington. The university's engineering building is pictured here. Photo by Brad Crooks

ARTS AND CULTURE— COWTOWN STYLE

Fort Worth is a fusion of unsophisticated cowpokes and high brows. A place that can cradle the rambunctiousness of an Amon Carter with the psychological insights of a Katherine Anne Porter, who lived in Fort Worth in 1917.

Like all frontier towns, Fort Worth was starved for entertainment in its early days. Folks turned out to enjoy any touring dance, music, or theater troupes that performed in town.

Given this background, Fort Worth's culture today might well resemble that of Dallas—good, proper, yet with all the wit of a corporate boardroom during a takeover battle.

"FORT WORTH FOR FUN"

Amon G. Carter and Billy Rose changed Fort Worth's direction while it still had a chance to develop its own style. After the two master showmen teamed up for a uniquely Fort Worth-style spectacle in 1936, nothing was too brash, nothing was too impossible for Fort Worth again.

"Wild and Whoo-pee," the neon sign flickered in Dallas. "45 minutes west."

That's what Amon Carter, owner of the *Fort Worth Star-Telegram*, promised Dallasites after the State Centennial Commission gave money to their city for the 1936 Texas Centennial Celebration, yet gave nothing to Fort Worth or West Texas.

Heck, thought Amon, he'd throw his own celebration. And he did.

Carter hired Broadway producer Billy Rose to come to Fort Worth for $1,000 a day to produce a show that would gladden any Depression-era heart.

"You people stick with me," Rose said, "and I'll make a big state out of Texas."

To stage his production, Rose built an outdoor arena with a revolving stage called Casa Manana—"House of Tomorrow" —and billed it as the "largest cafe-theater in the universe." It was built in the shadows of the new Will Rogers Auditorium and Coliseum.

He enlisted a lineup of stars that would brighten any county fair midway: a mind reading dog, frog circus, monkey mountain, Indians, cowboys, and 500 semi-nude dancing girls.

Anticipating problems with the church-going crowd, Rose met beforehand with J. Frank Norris, the fiery Baptist preacher who led the Cowtown moral brigade.

Rose told Norris that "we've got this Centennial show and some nude girls, and we're going to sell liquor." Rose thought this might be a good time for Norris to see the rest of the country, rather than be around so much sinning. Norris thought this was a gem of an idea and left on a 2,700-mile long revival tour.

When the show finally opened, Amon Carter declared: "Dallas does have something Fort Worth doesn't have—a real city 30 miles away."

As a slap at the erudite Centennial celebration in its rival city, signs were erected that advertised "Dallas for education; Fort Worth for fun."

And the crowds came in droves.

The acknowledged star was Sally Rand, who performed nude on the Casa stage behind a few strategically held balloons and a feathered fan. The city showed its appreciation for her talents by naming November 6 "Sally Rand Day"; she was thanked for finally bringing "culture and progress to Tarrant County."

With the city's cultural standards forever defined by Sally Rand, Fort Worth was released to nourish the arts and culture with a flair for the unexpected, a taste for wit, and a sense that culture should be enjoyed. Where but Fort Worth could you find opera star Enrico Caruso or rocker Elvis Presley performing in a rodeo barn?

THE BUSINESS OF ART

Today, culture flourishes in Fort Worth—art museums, ballet, music, theater. In large measure, Fort Worth is able to field such a wide variety of activities because

The Fort Worth Museum of Science and History contains the Noble Planetarium, one of the country's best. Photo by Bob Rowan/Progressive Image Photography

Casa Manana, a domed musical arena-theater rebuilt in 1958, offers a full summer season and features national touring groups as well as productions headlining local performers. Photo by Bob Rowan/ Progressive Image Photography

it receives generous support from local citizens, foundations, and corporations.

Though the recession of the late 1980s caused some cutback in contributions, the arts managed to survive and even grow.

"This is a city that has always pulled itself up by the bootstraps. And I don't believe this community will allow its arts programs to suffer," Bob J. Crow, executive director of the Amon G. Carter Foundation, told the *Business Press*.

The quality and scope of art is used as a selling point to attract corporations and executives to Fort Worth.

The Arts Council of Fort Worth and Tarrant County deserves credit for ensuring that the arts are supported and nourished.

Founded in 1963, the council provides leadership, funding support, and marketing activities to stimulate and advance the arts throughout Tarrant County.

In addition to making a project grants pool available to a wide variety of arts groups throughout the county, the council specifically assists eight organizations: Fort Worth Ballet, Fort Worth Opera, Fort Worth Symphony Orchestra, Fort Worth Theatre, Hip Pocket Theatre, Schola Cantorum of Texas, Texas Boys Choir, and Van Cliburn Foundation.

Together, these organizations are responsible for 500 full- and part-time jobs and a payroll of more than $3.5 million. They make a $10-million impact on the local economy.

They also promote Fort Worth and Tarrant County on regional, national, and international tours. For example, the Fort Worth Symphony Orchestra has performed in China; the Hip Pocket Theatre has performed in Scotland; the Schola Cantorum has toured Europe; and the Van Cliburn draws applications from around the world. The broad community support given the arts is evident by the composition of the Arts Council board of directors and volunteers—a veritable Who's Who of Fort Worth corporate, social, and civic life.

In 1989, the council launched an ambitious campaign to raise $7 million over a three-year period. Funding was earmarked for direct support of its eight organizations; arts enrichment programs for children; enrichment for family and community life; and financial support for other arts organizations in Tarrant County.

THE CULTURAL DISTRICT

While the Arts Council may be the collective mind of the arts in Fort Worth, the Cultural District is its heart.

Located on the 1936 Centennial grounds west of downtown, the Cultural District is home of the Kimbell Art Museum, Amon G. Carter Museum of Western Art, Modern Art Museum of Fort Worth, Fort Worth Museum of Science and History, Will Rogers Auditorium and Coliseum, Amon G. Carter, Jr. Exhibits Hall, Will Rogers Equestrian Center, and Botanic Gardens.

The city-owned land is so special that there is a full-time director to coordinate planning for the district and a 22-member blue-ribbon committee of civic leaders charged with developing and implementing a master plan to make the 500-acre area a cohesive unit.

"One has to look far and wide to find an American city that can boast of having such a rich variety of cultural, educational and entertainment amenities concentrated in one convenient location," the *Fort Worth Star-Telegram* bragged.

The first permanent structures to rise in the Cultural District were the Will Rogers Auditorium and Coliseum and Pioneer Tower, which were completed in 1936 with the help of federal funds and a friend in Washington. When Amon Carter was rebuffed in his efforts to obtain funding for the project, he appealed to his pal, James Farley, then postmaster general. When Farley told President

The Amon G. Carter, Jr. Exhibits Hall is part of the Will Rogers Complex in Fort Worth's Cultural District. Photo by Bob Rowan/ Progressive Image Photography

Hundreds of thousands of Texas longhorns were driven over the Chisholm Trail until the railroads and wire fencing made the route impassable. Richard Haas' mural depicting the trail appears on the side of a Fort Worth building. Photo by Bob Rowan/ Progressive Image Photography

Roosevelt that "Amon wants to build a cowshed," the project was approved.

After Billy Rose staged his Centennial celebration, the area was forever staked out as the cultural and entertainment center of Fort Worth. During World War II, Carter even convinced the Fat Stock Show to move its annual show to the Coliseum.

The only buildings that remain from the Centennial are in the Will Rogers complex. The original Casa Manana was torn down and rebuilt in 1958 based on the geodesic dome design popularized by Buckminster Fuller.

The 1,800-seat theater-in-the-round is now the home of the popular Summer Musical series, featuring classic Broadway hits like *Oklahoma* and *The King and I*, as well as a children's theater series.

Next door to the complex is the Museum of Science and History, which contains exhibits on anthropology, geology, history, natural science, and wildlife. The uniform and other personal effects of General William Jenkins Worth are on display in a glass case.

The museum contains the Noble Planetarium, one of the country's best, and the Omni Theater, featuring an 80-foot-wide domed screen and 70mm film, which envelops viewers in a sea of sound and sights.

KIMBELL ART MUSEUM

A block northeast of Casa Manana is the world-renowned masterpiece of the Fort Worth Cultural District—the Kimbell Art Museum. The museum is housed in a building that is widely recognized as a work of art in its own right.

Like many Fort Worth attributes, the Kimbell grew from the inspired dreams of a publicity-shy philanthropist and art lover.

Born in 1886, Kay Kimbell dropped out of school at age 13 and went on to assemble a fortune in agriculture, oil, and business. During the 1930s, his wife, Velma, convinced him to attend an exhibition in downtown Fort Worth hosted by the Art Association. He fell in love with an eighteenth-century English painting. Although it wasn't for sale, he managed to buy it anyway.

From that point, Kimbell was hooked on art. He began to assemble eighteenth-century British portraits and works of the late European Renaissance. He collected so much art that he had no place to keep it all, so he loaned out works.

When Kimbell died in 1964, he had no children. He left his entire estate, valued at an estimated $100 million, to an art foundation charged with building "a museum of the first class in the city of Fort Worth."

Richard Fargo Brown was selected as the founding director of the museum and began a seven-year worldwide quest to assemble a collection worthy of Kimbell's wishes. In the meantime, Louis I. Kahn was commissioned to design and oversee construction of a $7.5-million building.

When the Kimbell Art Museum opened in 1972, it stunned the art world with two masterpieces—the collection assembled by Brown, and the building itself.

Kahn today is recognized as one of America's greatest architects, in the same league as Frank Lloyd Wright and Louis Sullivan. The Kimbell was his last project, and perhaps his best.

Filled with natural light, the Kimbell is particularly distinguished by the U-shaped cycloidal vaults, which support the building with minimum interior supports to disrupt the galleries. The entrance courtyard is graced with small lagoons and a grove of yaupons. In 1975, the Kimbell received the Honor Award for architectural excellence from the American Institute of Architects.

The galleries were filled with Gainsboroughs, Rembrandts, El Grecos, Picassos, Matisses, and Goyas. Brown had also located *Madonna and Child,* a Bellini painting that had been owned by Napoleon III and that had disappeared a century earlier.

"For its size, the Kimbell probably has a higher percentage of discovered or

The Fort Worth Museum of Science and History, located on Montgomery, offers visitors this hands-on, IBM-sponsored computer exhibit. Photo by Bob Rowan/ Progressive Image Photography

rediscovered pieces of art than any museum in the country," Brown wrote.

With an annual acquisition budget estimated at more than $7 million, the Kimbell is dedicated to enhancing its already impressive collection, now under the direction of Edmund Pillsbury. In 1987, for example, the Kimbell made international news when it paid some $15 million for Caravaggio's "The Card Sharps," which is perhaps the museum's most important acquisition.

Today, the Kimbell boasts a permanent collection of European, Asian, and pre-Columbian art, and frequently hosts exhibitions of popular and well-known works from around the world. In 1989, the Kimbell announced an $8-million, privately funded expansion plan that would add wings on the north and south sides and double the gallery space. Several months after the preliminary plans were unveiled, criticism began to surface from the media and prominent architects around the country, who stated that the expansion would disrupt a classically balanced design and spoil a masterpiece. The expansion plans were then put on an indefinite hold.

AMON G. CARTER MUSEUM OF WESTERN ART

On a hilltop overlooking the Kimbell, the Amon G. Carter Museum of Western Art provides a majestic view of downtown and an excellent collection of Ameri-

Among the Fort Worth Museum of Science and History's most interesting exhibits is this experimental four-million-chip memory showing circuit lines on a single IBM computer chip. Photo by Bob Rowan/ Progressive Image Photography

can painting, photography, and sculpture. The museum had its origins in 1935, when Will Rogers introduced the Fort Worth newspaper publisher to Charles Russell. A lover of the West and cowboys, Carter bought a few of Russell's water-colors, and later acquired Frederick Remington's pieces.

Carter and his friend, oilman Sid Richardson, were locked in a rivalry over who could collect the most Russell and Remington western and cowboy art.

Their fun eventually resulted in the establishment of two fine museums—the Carter and the smaller Sid Richardson Collection of Western Art in downtown's Sundance Square.

The Amon Carter Museum was built of Texas shellstone from a design by Philip Johnson—the same architect who designed the Fort Worth Water Garden. Five segmented arches on tapered columns form an expansive porch overlooking garden terraces, graced by a Henry Moore sculpture. A glass wall opens the building to the city, while providing a peaceful bronze and teak interior.

Carter Director Jan Muhlert oversees a permanent collection of 200 Russell and Remington paintings, 60 Russell bronzes, and 14 Remington bronzes. Carter's original collection has expanded to include works by other noted nineteenth- and twentieth-century artists, including Georgia O'Keeffe and Winslow Homer, as well as a schedule of changing exhibitions.

The film projection area of the Omni Theater is quite a sight in itself. Photo by Bob Rowan/ Progressive Image Photography

World-class, yet surprisingly inviting, the Kimbell Art Museum was opened in 1972 thanks to Fort Worth industrialist Kay Kimbell, who had established a private foundation to build a museum to house his private collection. Photo by Bob Rowan/ Progressive Image Photography

MODERN ART MUSEUM

One of the Southwest's best collections of twentieth-century art is located across the street from the Carter in the Modern Art Museum of Fort Worth—under the leadership of Director E.A. Carmean since the mid-1980s.

The Modern Art Museum is an outgrowth of the Fort Worth Art Association's activities and the city's municipal art museum, once located on the second floor of the Carnegie Library in downtown. The existing building was constructed in 1954, with additions added later. It is adjacent to the 500-seat William Edrington Scott Theater, home of the Fort Worth Theatre.

The museum's permanent collection includes works by Pablo Picasso, David Hockney, Mark Rothko, Frank Stella, Andy Warhol, and Robert Rauschenberg. During the first five years of his tenure as director, Carmean acquired 135 works of art, mainly a mix of European and American masters, and presented 44 exhibitions.

The art museums also benefit from the work performed by the InterCultura of Fort Worth, a nonprofit organization that arranges museum exchanges in order to increase international understanding between nations and people. In late 1989, the organization announced that it was bringing prized Russian works of art on a tour of U.S. museums, including the Modern Art Museum and Amon Carter.

VAN CLIBURN COMPETITION

Fort Worth also draws worldwide acclaim from the quadrennial Van Cliburn International Piano Competition. It is also the home of Van Cliburn himself, who lives in the Kay Kimbell mansion in the exclusive Westover Hills enclave.

The competition was originated after the lanky six-foot, four-inch tall East Texas native dazzled the world by winning first prize in the Tchaikovsky International Piano Competition in the Soviet Union. After the competition, Cliburn was honored at a dinner in Fort Worth. Dr. Irl Allison of Austin announced during the program that he was making a $10,000 gift to establish a Van Cliburn piano competition in Texas.

Speculation focused on Austin, Dallas, or Houston as the site. Instead, Fort Worth was selected for the competition, which has emerged as one of the premier music events of the world, attracting international press, television, and radio coverage. Hosted by Texas Christian University, the Van Cliburn is also one of the major social events of the city. More than 600 volunteers donate one million dollars' worth of time to make the celebration a success.

In 1989, the eighth competition attracted some 35 pianists who performed solo recitals, chamber concerts with the Tokyo String Quartet, and concerts with the Fort Worth Chamber and Symphony orchestras. Alexei Sultanov, a 19-year-old Soviet artist, defeated the world's most brilliant piano performers to win the gold medal in 1989. He also won $200,000 in prizes, a Carnegie Hall debut, concert tour, recording contract, and $15,000 cash.

The Van Cliburn Foundation also presents an ongoing series of concert tours of medalists, piano institutes, and other education programs.

At the conclusion of the eighth competition in 1989, Cliburn captured the world's attention again at age 55 by resuming concert performances to critical acclaim after an 11-year hiatus. He even performed in Moscow and Leningrad at the invitation of Mikhail and Raisa Gorbachev. "Van is an international ambassador for our city," brags Mayor Bob Bolen.

MUSIC AND DANCE

Although they provide the accompaniment for the Cliburn performers, musicians in the Fort Worth Symphony Orchestra Association are capable in their own right of taking center stage.

Formed in 1925, the association has featured Kiri Te Kanawa, Isaac Stern, James Galway, and world premieres of commissioned works.

Under the music direction of John Giordano, the Fort Worth Symphony Orchestra Association offers a variety of concert series throughout the year to appeal to a cross-section of tastes. Lighter selections and show tunes are performed by the Fort Worth Symphony Pops, often in conjunction with a visiting celebrity, such as Mel Torme or Doc Severinsen; classical masterpieces are performed by the Symphony Orchestra; and pianists, violinists, and other soloists are the star of the Fort Worth Chamber Orchestra's Virtuoso Series.

The 35-piece Chamber Orchestra is an ensemble styled after the compact orchestras of Mozart's day. Drawn from the principal players of the symphony, the group was the first chamber orchestra to tour China.

Designed by Philip Johnson and built of Texas shellstone, the Amon G. Carter Museum of Western Art houses a fine collection of American paintings, drawings, photographs, and sculptures. Photo by Bob Rowan/ Progressive Image Photography

There is no shortage of vocalists, either. Fort Worth is the home of the Texas Boys Choir, an internationally renowned organization that has performed at Carnegie Hall, traveled over one million miles, including tours of Japan and Australia, and won Grammys and International Film Festival awards.

Started in 1946, the Boys Choir provides a private school for its performers that offers a full academic curriculum designed around the rigors of a professional schedule.

Fort Worth is also home to the Texas Girls Choir, which has trained some 8,000 girls during its 25-year history. Composed of five choral and two bell choirs, the girls have performed in concerts at local, national, and international festivals, nursing homes, and churches.

The Museum of Science and History's Hall of Medicine "In Your Body" exhibit uses human skeletons to teach about the workings of the human body. Photo by Bob Rowan/ Progressive Image Photography

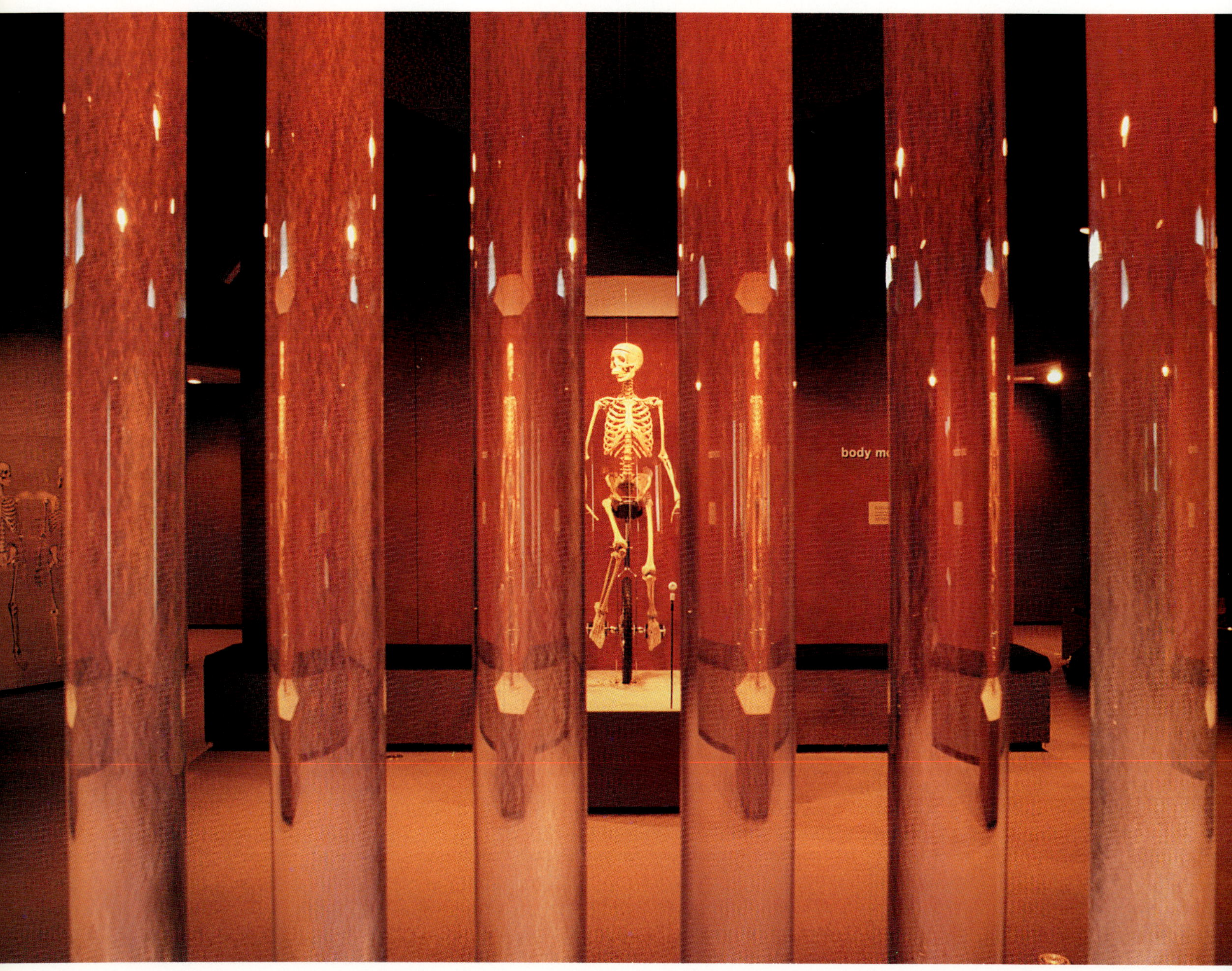

Dancers with the Ballet Folklorico Azteca perform a crowd-pleasing *Jarabe Tapatio*, Mexico's national dance. Photo by Mike Boroff/TexaStock

The state's longest continuing opera company is the Fort Worth Opera Association. Founded in 1946 by former opera singer Eloise Snyder and Broadway singer Betty Spain, the company performs three operas a year, with each receiving two to six performances. A subsidiary organization, the Southwestern Opera Theater, introduces opera to local schoolchildren.

The Fort Worth Ballet Association is under the artistic direction of Paul Mejia, a protégé of the late George Balanchine. A native of Peru, Mejia is married to Suzanne Farrell, a former ballerina under Balanchine.

With the demise of the Dallas Ballet, the 25-member Fort Worth Ballet is positioning itself as the major professional ballet company for the entire Fort Worth/Dallas Metroplex area. Performing in the Balanchine tradition, the company offers five productions each year at the Tarrant County Convention Center.

The company also gains visibility by venturing to try the unusual, such as casting former Dallas Cowboy running back Herschel Walker in a dancer's role in a short piece.

In 1989, the company went to Japan on its first international tour with 14 performances of Prokofiev's *Cinderella*. The production was originally created by Mejia when he was associate artistic director and choreographer of the Chicago City Ballet. The overseas production required the training of 600 Japanese children, who performed with the ballet.

Members of the Ballet Folklorico Azteca take the stage. Photo by Smiley/TexaStock

The Ballet Folklorico Azteca is a popular local company that draws on the rich, colorful Mexican heritage for its material. The 18 young dancers perform folk dances at various celebrations, including Cinco de Mayo and Diez y Seis de Septiembre.

Lions bask in the sun at the Fort Worth Zoological Park. More than 850 species of animals are housed in this, one of the best and most progressive zoos in the country. Photo by Brad Crooks

THEATER

Fort Worth's diverse cultural heritage is also represented in the theater.

The Sojourner Truth Players is Fort Worth's first minority community theater, which performs productions ranging from *for colored girls who have considered suicide when the rainbow is enuf* to *On Golden Pond*.

The Jubilee Theatre provides a stage for works by blacks and other minorities, ranging from drama to satire, such as James Baldwin's *The Amen Corner* to *Negroes in Space*. The Jubilee operates out of its own permanent theater in the historic Polytechnic Heights neighborhood in East Fort Worth.

Avant-garde theater and jazz is found at Ed Bass' Caravan of Dreams Performing Arts Center in Sundance Square. The Caravan has featured experimental theater, as well as performances by Wynton and Branford Marsalis, Eartha Kitt, Maynard Ferguson, Dizzy Gillespie, and Fort Worth native Ornette Coleman.

The oldest live theater in the Fort Worth/Dallas area is the Fort Worth Theatre. Staging six productions a year in the Scott Theater, the company uses local actors and guest artists in a variety of pieces, from the classics to current comedies and new works. William Garber has served as theater director for more than 32 years.

The Stage West Theater, located in a redeveloping arts district south of downtown, was formed in 1979 and features classic and new works by American and European playwrights. The Circle Theatre, housed in a renovated Masonic Lodge building, stages productions by contemporary artists. Several productions are performed at the Circle, before going on to rave reviews on the East Coast.

Everyone gets into the Texas spirit at the Main Street Arts Festival. Photo by Michael Lyon/TexaStock

Started in 1977 as a pilot project of Casa Manana, Shakespeare in the Park has emerged as an extremely popular outdoor summer activity. Held outside in Trinity Park, the season has grown from one play to two, and from nine performances per season to 16. The free performances are held in association with the city's Park and Recreation Department and Texas Christian University.

The Hip Pocket Theatre is one of the most unique in the country. In fact, a performance at the Hip Pocket is a pleasantly off-the-wall experience like nothing else in American theater.

Supported, in part, by grants from the Texas Commission on the Arts and the National Endowment for the Arts, the Pocket's summer season is played outside at the Oak Acres Amphitheatre. The winter season is held in the Stockyards district Upstairs at the White Elephant.

Founded in 1976, the Hip Pocket performs original avant-garde works such as *Lake Worth Monster* and *Attack of the B-Girls* by director Johnny Simons and composer Douglas Balentine. It also stages adaptations by noted playwrights, such as Sam Shepard and Thornton Wilder.

In 1983, the Hip Pocket was the first Texas theater company to perform at Scotland's Edinburgh Festival Fringe and London's Queen Elizabeth Hall.

A HERITAGE OF BEAUTY

Dotted throughout the city is other artistic evidence of the city's heritage, its lifeblood, its appreciation for the beautiful.

Richard Haas' dramatic mural of the Chisholm Trail spread across a downtown building wall. A Matisse in Burnett Park. A sprawling Calder Eagle. And bronzes: Will Rogers riding into the sunset in the Cultural District. A lone cowboy driving a herd of thundering longhorns in the Stockyards. A bucking bronc tossing a rider in front of the Amon G. Carter, Jr. Exhibits Hall.

Or the individual artists who make Fort Worth their home. Don Edwards, who continues to entertain with his authentic western ballads and campfire tales. Leonard Sanders, a novelist who has written dramatic accounts of Fort Worth's development.

Fort Worth is a city that can love both a zany comedy at the Hip Pocket or the dramatic staging of a Shakespearean tragedy.

Fort Worth shows that art can be great, and fun. Thank you, Sally Rand.

FUN FOR ALL SEASONS

Although Fort Worth doesn't have a professional ball club, the North Texas area has most major sports represented.

Fort Worth fans have adopted the Dallas Cowboys professional football team as their favorites. The Cowboys play at Texas Stadium in Irving, between Dallas and the D/FW International Airport.

The Dallas Mavericks are the resident NBA basketball franchise, the Dallas Sidekicks the local soccer club. And the Texas Rangers play baseball next door in Arlington.

Fort Worth itself has sports events that match its personality, the type of sports that lonesome cowhands along the Chisholm Trail might have picked. Entrepreneurial. Tough. Resourceful. Unique.

This is the city of the individual competitor, the man or woman who thrives on single-handedly putting their skills and talents to the utmost test.

Going helmet-to-helmet with a defensive end for the Dallas Cowboys is *nothing* compared to busting your tailbone on a bucking bronco. We're talking pure guts to get on and stay on a firebreathing stallion.

THE STOCK SHOW

There's no better place to watch cowboys and cowgirls test their mettle than the Southwestern Exposition and Livestock Show, held annually in late January and early February.

"The Stock Show" was started in 1896 to coincide with the Texas Cattle Raisers meeting in the burgeoning meat packing district along Marine Creek. As the event quickly evolved, it would be known in its early years as the Texas Fat Stock Show, Fort Worth Fat Stock Show, National Feeders and Breeders Show, and the Southwestern Exposition and Fat Stock Show. The "fat" was changed to "livestock" in the 1980s.

In 1908, the show moved to the newly constructed North Side (now Cowtown) Coliseum, home of the world's first indoor rodeo. The show quickly rose in prominence and gained stature among the city's elite. Today, the exposition is one of the top social events of the season.

The Stock Show enjoyed its residency at the Coliseum, where it shared a calendar of events that included appearances by opera tenor Enrico Caruso, Comanche Chief Quanah Parker, and President Theodore Roosevelt.

In 1944, the stock show organizers moved the event to the Will Rogers Coliseum, located in the heart of what is now the Cultural District. It has grown from a handful of cattle to a show that features over 17,000 animals, representing most every kind of barnyard animal imaginable, including exotic cattle breeds, rabbits, horses, pigs, chickens, goats, lambs, and hogs.

Ranchers and farmers, young and old, from across Texas and the nation, bring their families and their livestock to the show each year to compete in the Stock Show Rodeo, various riding events, and judging. Nearly 750,000 people attend the show each year.

Operated as an incorporated nonprofit civic and educational enterprise, the Stock Show supports 4-H Clubs and Future Farmers of America with scholarship programs and the Ranch Management Program at Texas Christian University.

Recognizing the $88.5-million economic impact that the Southwestern Exposition and Livestock Show makes on Fort Worth each year, city officials and civic leaders began in the early 1980s to formulate plans for attracting even more western-oriented activities to the Will Rogers Complex.

WILL ROGERS EQUESTRIAN CENTER

The solution was construction of the Will Rogers Equestrian Center, a sprawling maze of 900 horse stalls, the 2,000-seat John Justin Arena, and a 700-seat multipurpose arena—all designed to provide contestants in national and international

Cyclists race toward the finish line at the Fort Worth Stockyards. Photo by Brad Crooks

FORT WORTH STOCK YARDS
WHITE ELEPHANT SALOON
WHITE ELEPHANT BEER GARDEN
Budweiser
BUD LIGHT

horse shows with the most modern facilities available.

The Equestrian Center was built for a price of $18 million, of which $3.4 million was private contributions rounded up by two local horse lovers and civic leaders—John S. Justin, Jr., chairman of Justin Industries (manufacturer of Justin boots), and Bob Watt, Jr., president and manager of the Southwestern Exposition and Livestock Show. The balance was funded through city bond sales and additional private donations.

Success was immediate.

Before the center opened in January 1988, four annual quarter horse shows in Dallas signed up to move their events to the Will Rogers Equestrian Center. Other horse shows in Abilene, Waco, and Albuquerque joined the stampede to the center. A long-term contract was secured with the Fort Worth-based National Cutting Horse Association, ensuring its continued $37-million economic impact from the World Championship Futurity and two other championship events held at the Will Rogers Complex.

The futurity is one of the premier Fort Worth events each fall, featuring gala dinners, parades, and concerts.

Promoters predicted the center alone would eventually generate an annual $90-million economic impact from the events held there.

National and international organizations using the new facilities include the

Livestock exhibitions offer much fun and excitement, both for the professional and casual observer. Photo by Bob Rowan/Progressive Image Photography

Texas Quarter Horse Association, International Arabian Horse Association, Southwest Peruvian Horse Club, American Miniature Horse Association, Texas Longhorn Breeders Association, American Paint Horse Association, and Appaloosa Horse Club.

FORT WORTH IS FOR HORSES

An estimated 30,000 to 35,000 horses are stabled in Tarrant County, while the horse population in the Fort Worth/Dallas Metroplex was estimated at more than 200,000.

If you can't wait for the next horse show to roll around at the Will Rogers, the Professional Rodeo Cowboys Association features the Fort Worth Championship Rodeo each weekend during the summer at the Cowtown Coliseum in the Stockyards area. There you can watch bull and bucking bronco riding, barrel racing, and bulldogging—a sport invented in Fort Worth by cowboy Bill Pickett. Pickett roped a steer, wrestled it to its knees, and bit its lip.

There was also the prospect to see the emergence of horse racing in Fort Worth after Texas voters approved the legalization of wagering.

Although the rodeos, horse shows, and livestock exhibitions offer fun and excitement, a visit to the Cattleman's Museum, sponsored by the Texas and Southwestern Cattle Raisers Foundation, provides a realistic look at ranch life and the historical background for the modern livestock and horse industry.

The museum features life-sized men and women dressed in period clothing, as well as longhorn cattle. The museum also has exhibits on ranch women, cattle and horse breeds, cowboys and cattle barons, branding irons, chaps, barbed wire, and chuckwagon utensils.

Fort Worth's Cattleman's Museum chronicles the century-old Texas and Southwestern Cattle Raisers Association, as well as the livestock industry in Texas. Photo by Brad Crooks

A lone rider makes his way through the Main Street Stockyards area. Photo by Bob Rowan/Progressive Image Photography

A SPORTING PLACE

Fort Worth is more than just rodeo and livestock shows. It's also home of one of the major stops on the PGA Tour—the Southwestern Bell Colonial Golf Tournament. Held in mid-May, the nationally televised tournament attracts the nation's top golfers to the prestigious Colonial Country Club and par 70 course.

The tournament has grown from $15,000 in prize money when it started in 1946 to its current one-million-dollar purse.

Two of golfing's most famous pros got their start in Fort Worth—"Lord" Byron Nelson and Ben Hogan. Both started as caddies at the Glen Garden Country Club and turned pro in the mid-1930s.

But you don't have to be a pro to find a place to play. Tarrant County has some two dozen public and private courses that are designed to test any handicap. Five of the courses are owned by the City of Fort Worth.

Although Fort Worth currently does not have a professional sports team in residence, this has not always been the case. In 1895 it fielded a pro baseball team, and during the 1940s and 1950s the Fort Worth Cats of the Texas League supplied players to the Brooklyn Dodgers.

And Fort Worth and Dallas did work together to lure the Washington Senators to Arlington, where they now play baseball Texas Ranger-style under the partial ownership of the President's son, George W. Bush.

While the Dallas Cowboys fill the bill for a regional NFL team, the Texas Christian University Horned Frogs play rough-and-tumble Southwest Conference football at Amon Carter Stadium.

Football started at TCU in 1896, when the institution was located in Waco and known as AddRan College.

Admitted to the the fledgling Southwest Athletic Conference in 1923, TCU has gone on to win eight conference titles.

Coach of the Purple Frogs is Jim Wacker, who arrived at TCU in 1982 as NCAA Division II Coach of the Year for his work at Southwest Texas State University. At Southwest, he guided the Bobcats to a two-year record of 27-1.

When he arrived, the Frogs had posted a 3-8 season. In 1983, Wacker had a modest 1-8-2 slate. But in 1984, he achieved one of the most dramatic turnarounds in the Southwest Conference, guiding the Frogs to an 8-3 record and the team's first bowl appearance since 1965. Led by All-American running back Kenneth Davis, the Frogs set a Southwest Conference record of 5,109 total yards and broke 38 school records.

Wacker achieved widespread recognition for his feat. He was named Coach of the Year by United Press International, ESPN, and the *Sporting News*, and was a unanimous choice as Southwest Conference Coach of the Year.

TCU also fields a strong Southwest Conference basketball team under Coach Moe Iba and competes in golf, tennis, track, swimming, and baseball.

Texas Wesleyan University plays basketball under the National Association of Intercollegiate Athletics and has exceptional golf, tennis, and baseball teams.

Although the Virginia Slims of Dallas professional tennis tournament is held annually in Dallas, Martina Navratilova, one of the all-time great women players, resides in Fort Worth.

Professional race car driver Johnny Rutherford also makes his home in Fort Worth.

For the footloose, Fort Worth has one of the most grueling marathons in the U.S.—the Cowtown. Held each February, the race attracts thousands of runners from around the world. The race starts in the historic Stockyards District, winds through downtown, and meanders through parks and neighborhoods before finishing at the Stockyards. The course is noted for its steep hills and inclines.

Water sports are popular, especially during the warm spring, summer, and fall months. The City of Fort Worth owns Lake Worth, located on the northwest side of town. Other area lakes, such as Eagle Mountain, Benbrook, Arlington, and Grapevine, are dotted around the county. There are also several boating and sailing clubs.

For an exciting spectacle, Fort Worth celebrates its links to the aviation and defense industry each fall with the Fort Worth Air Show at Meacham Airport. The event features aerobatics and wingwalking, and military, civilian, and experimental aircraft. The 1989 show featured the Aviation Heritage Association reenacting the attack on Pearl Harbor, complete with Japanese Zeros.

STOCKYARDS NATIONAL HISTORIC DISTRICT

Nowhere is Fort Worth's heritage more celebrated on a year-round basis than in the Stockyards National Historic District. This 20-acre district is an eclectic

Fort Worth resident J.W. Brown handcrafts Old West-style wagons and carriages. Photos by Kevin Vandivier/TexaStock

FOLLOWING PAGE: The Fort Worth skyline as viewed from the north side of the Trinity River reveals an eclectic collection of buildings—historic and modern, low-profile and high-rise, stone, brick, and glass-and-steel. Photo by Bob Rowan/ Progressive Image Photography

Kilt-clad marchers in the St. Patrick's Day Parade pipe their way through the Stockyards area. Photo by Brad Crooks

cowboy stew of history, honky-tonks, and hootenannies.

The Stockyards are the leftovers from the days when the area was a sprawling meat packing and livestock processing center. The remnants of the vast maze of livestock pens offer only a token glimpse of the magnitude of the once-massive operation.

Today, the North Fort Worth Historical Society is leading a valiant struggle to preserve the area's heritage, while also spurring redevelopment.

There is some progress. The Swift & Co. headquarters has been turned into a restaurant on a high bluff overlooking the stockpens. The Livestock Exchange Building houses shops, a museum, and agribusiness offices. The Cowtown Coliseum, renovated by the City of Fort Worth, continues to attract a variety of western-oriented and miscellaneous events. The Stockyards Hotel, once a dilapidated flophouse and stopping place for gangsters Bonnie and Clyde, has been eloquently renovated and decorated with a cattle baron motif.

The heart of the district is Main and Exchange. Jutting out like spokes on a wagon wheel are tourist shops featuring mounted longhorns, authentic Texas foods, rugs, quilts, and folk art, bars serving up frosty mugs of cold beer, steak houses, and western wear outfitters.

But the biggest attraction of the Stockyards is Billy Bob's Texas, the self-styled "world's largest honky-tonk." Although financial problems forced the club to close briefly, the new operators are working hard to make it a success. Billy Bob's continues to feature big-name country and western stars and other entertainment and remains one of the most popular attractions in North Texas.

In the meantime, another group was trying to build a railroad.

The Tarantula Corp., named after B.B. Paddock's concept in the late 1800s of having rail lines extending out of Fort Worth like a tarantula's legs, proposed linking the Stockyards, Cultural District, Zoo, and Historic Southside with an old-fashioned railway system driven by vintage locomotives.

The company was already having moderate success simply by hauling freight from one Fort Worth company to another on existing lines. However, their proposal called for adding track to the museums and Zoo, a concept that generated both outpourings of support and outcries of protest.

Backed by Fort Worth oilman and industrialist Bill Davis, the Tarantula Corp. fancied the idea that an old-fashioned train ride through Fort Worth, and eventually dinner and excursion rides to outlying towns, might attract more tourists—and revenue—to the city.

As the decade closed, the Tarantula railroad was still a steaming issue, awaiting the results of an outside feasibility study.

At its essence, the controversy was over how far Fort Worth could go in developing and marketing its heritage, while also preserving the life-style of its residents.

An outing in one of Fort Worth's parks can mean taking a paddle boat out for a spin. Myriad opportunities for water recreation exist in the area. Photo by Michael Lyon/TexaStock

CHAPTER EIGHT

EPILOGUE: THE NEXT FRONTIER

When David Ivory, newly appointed as city manager, was asked by the Fort Worth League of Neighborhoods to deliver a "state-of-the-city" address in December 1989, he asked each municipal department to prepare a status report on its area of expertise.

Reviewing the comments for the first time as he was being introduced at Central Bank & Trust, he was taken aback by the aviation department's summary. Its report was two words long: "Wing it."

Ivory was certainly up to his department's challenge. He was the city's point man in developing the new Alliance Airport project from its initial conception.

Speaking barely above a whisper to the representatives of Fort Worth's neighborhoods, Ivory outlined what he saw as the challenges ahead in the future. Chief among these was the "economic health of the community."

From a development standpoint, Ivory told the neighborhood leaders that "cities have now gotten into this sometimes radical crazy competition to attract business" by making too many concessions to them.

Instead, Ivory said, Fort Worth should "look at what is here now, what employees we have now, what neighborhoods we have now," and focus on ensuring the economic health and expansion of existing business.

This comes in the face of an upheaval in Eastern Europe. The impact could be felt in Fort Worth if thawed relations with the Soviet Union created a reduced Defense Department budget.

In this case, Ivory said, Fort Worth's defense contractors, such as Bell Helicopter-Textron and General Dynamics, could see their orders reduced and workers laid off. Large layoffs at these plants could offset any jobs gained by a major relocation to the area.

In other words, Ivory said, new companies may not necessarily result in more jobs and economic growth. While encouraging outside corporations to look at Fort Worth, local companies should also be nourished, encouraged to expand, and supported in their growth through careful use of enterprise zones, tax financing, and tax abatements.

"We've got to protect what we have," he said.

Ivory's reputation as a straight-shooter was apparent as he outlined the less-positive sides to Fort Worth's face. These include serious social challenges, such as the need to lower a high infant mortality rate and providing better housing for its citizens.

"We still have a very, very serious and significant crime problem," he added.

Beyond these issues is the unsolved dilemma of finding ways to address problems with limited financial resources. "The City Council needs to begin to look at non-traditional" ways to address issues, such as attacking the roots of crime instead of the costly approach of putting more police officers on the street.

Yet Fort Worth, in the last decade of the twentieth century, was ready to meet these challenges.

Along Interstate 30 on the western edge of Fort Worth, the land breaks into a rolling prairie. The suburban sprawl has not reached here, and cattle still graze on the grass-covered hills.

Free of the western stores, the rodeos, cowboys hats, and two-steppin' honky-tonks, this is where you can think without distraction, while watching the sun set in a ruddy glow.

This is the place to sort it all out. What is the authentic and genuine Fort Worth? Is it a modern business center, or is it an old-fashioned cowtown?

Peeling back the layers, you will find that Fort Worth is both of these, and everything in between.

Fort Worth does have a claim on a colorful western heritage, and thank goodness folks still pull on a pair of boots and top out with a Stetson. The heritage is reflected in details, as well: the city's longhorn logo, the brick streets in

Man-made symbols of today loom above those of yesterday in this stunning view of downtown. Photo by James Blank

Banking

downtown, Sundance Square and its Chisholm Trail mural, the bronze cattle cast into the Lancaster Street bridge over the Trinity River.

Details. They help set Fort Worth apart from the dozens of other cities molded out of cookie-cutter glass-and-chrome towers.

Fort Worth is a modern pinstriped business city, too. The Alliance Airport, American Airlines, Tandy Corporation, Pier 1 Imports, and scores of other successful enterprises and corporations prove that Fort Worth workers can compete in the world marketplace.

And Fort Worth is everything in between. It's kids in high-topped tennis shoes. Mothers carpooling in their minivans. Blue-collar workers building space-age aircraft. Volunteers contributing their time and energy to help the less fortunate. School teachers. Doctors. Nurses. Secretaries. Attorneys. Bankers.

The vast in-between is what bridges the gap between the corporate and the western. Life in the neighborhoods. Life in the suburbs. Life in the office. Life on the assembly line. It's like any other American city.

What makes Fort Worth unique is its atmosphere—bellowing from the opposing energies of a twenty-first-century fast-paced corporation and a slow-moving nineteenth-century cattle drive.

The result is a business savvy mixed with abundance of goodwill and friendship.

This comes into focus as you look west across the prairie, sharing that sense of adventure that the early pioneers or trail drivers experienced when they crossed here. Yet when you turn back to the east, the entire city is spread before you, the skyline rising out of the empty land.

Fort Worth is trying to maintain this balance between holding onto its roots in the West, while moving forward into new generations of commerce and culture.

Fort Worth is prepared to face the challenges of the twenty-first century. It settled the frontier once before. The lessons learned from its past can guide the way to its next frontier.

Night descends on the city in this view from the east. Photo by Bob Rowan/ Progressive Image Photography

FACING PAGE: Wide-open spaces give much of downtown Fort Worth a comfortable, friendly atmosphere. Photo by Bob Rowan/ Progressive Image Photography

FORT WORTH'S ENTERPRISES

A blue and cloud-strewn Fort Worth sky
is reflected in the First City Bank Tower.
Photo by Jane Stader/TexaStock

C H A P T E R
N I N E

NETWORKS

Fort Worth's role as a modern, thriving metropolitan center is made possible by its network of communication, transportation, and energy providers.

Photo by Bob Rowan/Progressive Image Photography

TU Electric Co.

In the late 1800s Fort Worth was maturing from a rowdy cow town to a bustling center of western commerce. New and larger homes were being built, downtown streets were surfaced, and the Texas & Pacific Railway extended service to Fort Worth, bringing the city's first railroad. Fort Worth was poised for rapid growth, but it lacked one essential element to light its way into the future—electricity.

Four local businessmen decided to fill that void in October 1885, organizing the Fort Worth Electric Light and Power Co. Four months later light began glowing from 85 newly installed electric lamps.

Such was the start of Texas Electric Service Co., or TESCO, now under the giant Texas Utilities Co. holding company umbrella. TESCO has been melded into Texas Utilities' principal operating subsidiary, Texas Utilities Electric Co., or TU Electric.

Today TU Electric provides electricity to 87 counties, 371 incorporated cities, and about 5.2 million people—approximately one-third of the state's population. The company's service area extends 600 miles, from western Texas almost to Louisiana.

TU Electric has a Texas Electric Service division with three regions: the Fort Worth region, covering Tarrant County and small portions of Parker; Johnson County; and Dallas County. The company provides electric service to more than 450,000 people inside Fort Worth's city limits.

TU Electric's present form evolved through several consolidations, acquisitions, and restructurings over the years. TESCO was formed in 1929 by consolidating the Fort Worth Power & Light Co. and first Texas Electric Service Co., which combined the power and light companies in north-central and western Texas.

Texas Utilities, organized in 1945, acquired the holdings of TESCO and Texas Power & Light Co. and the common stock of Dallas Power & Light Co.

The operating companies and Texas Utilities Generating Co. were merged into TU Electric in 1984.

The merger was designed to save money and improve efficiency by eliminating duplicative functions, reducing time in coordinating system activities, operating power plants more efficiently, and streamlining decision making. Texas Electric Service once employed about 3,000 people in Texas; now it employs about 1,900 workers, 1,100 of whom work in Tarrant County.

After the consolidation Fort Worth's three power plants—North Main, Handley, and Eagle Mountain—were placed in a separate generating division of TU Electric. The division also will operate the Comanche Peak nuclear power plant located 45 miles southwest of Fort Worth near the town of Glen Rose.

TU Electric's power plant at Eagle Mountain Lake is one of three such plants in the Fort Worth area.

TU Electric's employees are active volunteers, participating in many area repair projects. Here, some volunteers repair a Fort Worth youth center.

Fort Worth will be one of the beneficiaries of electricity from Comanche Peak in the 1990s and beyond. TU Electric, the principal owner of Comanche Peak, is building two nuclear-fueled generating units at the station, each of which is designed to produce 1,150 megawatts of energy. The plant's first generating unit is expected to begin commercial operation in 1990, and the second unit is scheduled to begin operating in 1993.

TU Electric envisions the two nuclear units will provide about 29 percent of the additional capability it will need for the next 10 years. In addition to nuclear power, the electric company has diversified its power plant fuels by building facilities that convert native Texas lignite coal to electricity, reducing dependence on natural gas. In recent years about 44 percent of the energy produced came from lignite, 42 percent from gas and oil, and 14 percent was purchased from outside sources. TU Electric's rates are among the nation's lowest compared with residential rates charged by other major electric utilities. The company ranked sixth-lowest of the suppliers serving the 25 largest cities in the United States in 1988. TU Electric's commercial and industrial rates also ranked second-lowest in a national comparison of 23 electric utilities.

Current rates are set by the Texas Public Utility Commission. Aggressive efforts to take advantage of falling natural-gas prices have resulted in two rate decreases in recent years. As a result TU Electric's rates are at about the same level as in 1984.

Electric power has played a major role in the development of Fort Worth, and TU Electric is continuing that legacy. Electric trolleys began operating in 1889, ushering in a new transportation era for the city. During the 1920s and 1930s electric service was extended to many isolated rural communities.

The electric company's influence also touched the arts. In 1936, in observance of Fort Worth's Frontier Centennial, the original Casa Manana theater was built on University Drive. TESCO crews installed electric lines, transformers, and other facilities to handle the power load for lighting and turning Casa Manana's huge revolving stage—a service it still provides today.

During World War II Fort Worth's heavy industry increased production for the war effort and TESCO strengthened and extended service to several major plants, including the new Consolidated Aircraft Company's bomber assembly plant. The facility is now the Fort Worth Division of General Dynamics Corp. and is the city's largest employer.

TU Electric and its predecessor companies have been strong supporters of economic development in the cities they serve. In the 1950s then-company president J.B. Thomas commissioned a study for a future Fort Worth that its creators envisioned would become a model for many of the world's cities. Although it was never adopted, the plan pointed out impending urban problems and alerted the company to factors affecting development of electric power facilities.

Volunteerism is a priority for TU Electric employees. In 1988 then-President Ronald Reagan presented the company a presidential award for the Texas Electric Service division's work on a senior-citizen center in Fort Worth. Employees also received the governor's Volunteer Award for more than 100 Paint the Town projects in Fort Worth and other cities. Employees painted, repaired, and made other improvements to homes of elderly or disadvantaged people. TU Electric Co. employees are involved in many community activities, including the United Way, the Boy Scouts of America, Camp Fire Girls, YMCA, and YWCA.

A TU Electric workman restores residential electrical service after a storm.

Burlington Northern

The railroad was a symbol of growth in the 1800s to frontier towns such as Fort Worth. When tracks were laid and the iron horse arrived, it meant more jobs and business for the town's stores and access to new markets.

Fort Worth welcomed the railroad in 1984, when Burlington Northern, the nation's largest railroad company, moved its headquarters from St. Paul, Minnesota, to Fort Worth. Burlington Northern employs more than 800 workers in Fort Worth, most of them in the headquarters that oversees an international company with annual revenues approaching $5 billion. The company has a local annual payroll of about $32 million and has contributed one million dollars to a variety of city charities.

In moving to Fort Worth, Burlington Northern renewed a historical connection with the city. The old Fort Worth & Denver Railway, which began operating in 1882, was merged into the Burlington Northern system in 1983. In fact, Burlington Northern evolved from more than 300 railroads during 140 years. Its colorful history is intertwined with the history and development of the American West.

The company traces its roots back to the Aurora Branch Railroad, which began operating in 1850 in the Chicago area; it became the second railroad to serve Chicago. By 1864 the railroad had

400 miles of track and adopted the name Chicago, Burlington & Quincy Railroad Co.—the track extended to Burlington, Iowa, from Quincy, Illinois, on the Mississippi River. The name lasted 106 years until its merger into Burlington Northern in 1970.

Through the late 1800s, the Burlington expanded and swallowed up literally hundreds of smaller railroads. Two were notable for their lines: the Hannibal & St. Joseph Railroad Co. (Missouri) and the Burlington and Missouri River Railroad Co. (Iowa).

The Hannibal & St. Joseph brought mail across Missouri to connect with the Pony Express and introduced the first railroad car equipped for sorting U.S. mail en route. During the Civil War it was constantly harassed by Confederate raiders and later became an occasional target of Jesse James and other train robbers.

The Burlington rails pushed farther westward in the late 1880s. The Burlington eventually completed a main line from St. Louis and Kansas City to Billings, Montana. During the same period, the Burlington either built or acquired a network of branch lines over the rich agricultural regions of northern Illinois, southern Iowa, northern

Missouri, and southeastern Nebraska.

Meanwhile, one of the railroads that contributed the "Northern" in Burlington Northern also was edging westward. In 1857 the Minnesota Legislature granted a charter to the Minnesota & Pacific Railroad Co. to construct a westward railroad. The St. Paul & Pacific Railroad Co. acquired the rights after the Minnesota & Pacific had financial problems.

In 1862 a locomotive ran the 10 miles of rail from St. Paul to the village of St. Anthony, now Minneapolis. In 1878 James Jerome Hill, the so-called railroad "Empire Builder," persuaded three other men to join him in acquiring the St. Paul & Pacific. A year later the properties were reorganized as the St. Paul, Minneapolis & Manitoba Railway Co., with Hill as general manager. In the 1880s the railroad expanded farther into Minnesota, and by 1886 the main line extended westward to Minot, Dakota Territory.

Then one of the great periods of railroad construction began. Between April and mid-October 1887, about 545 con-

Burlington Northern trains, operating around the clock, haul millions of tons of coal annually to electric utilities' generating plants.

tinuous miles of line were laid, reaching across mostly unsettled wilderness from Minot to Great Falls, Montana Territory. The logistics of a such a project, far from sources of supply, with 8,000 men working and living in the wilderness, were staggering. Photographs show teams of men laying track across virgin prairie stretching to the horizon.

Hill was determined to press all the way to the Pacific. In 1881 he had acquired Minneapolis & St. Cloud Railway for its charter rights. The Minneapolis & St. Cloud remained a company only on paper until 1889, when Hill changed the name to Great Northern Railway Co. A year later it took over the properties of the St. Paul, Minneapolis & Manitoba.

Construction of Great Northern's extension to the Pacific began in 1890 in Montana. Three years later, after construction in mostly wild and rugged mountain land, the final spike was driven near Scenic, Washington. Regular service between Seattle and the East

over the new transcontinental line began in the middle of 1893.

But Hill did not stop at the Pacific. In 1896 he negotiated an agreement with Nippon Yusen Kaisha, the largest steamship line in the Pacific, to establish service between Seattle and Asian ports—so began Seattle's rise as a world port.

By the end of 1900 Great Northern had more than 5,000 miles of railway. But the building of a railroad never ends, and Great Northern constantly

upgraded and relocated its lines. The weakest link in Great Northern's route to the coast was its line across the Cascade mountain range, which was costly to operate and difficult to maintain. In 1925 the railroad began building an eight-mile tunnel through the Cascades. When it was completed in 1929, it was the longest tunnel in the Western Hemisphere.

Great Northern's second major project of the 1920s was its California extension. With this addition, Great Northern served 10 states and two Canadian provinces.

Burlington Northern's other predecessor companies—Northern Pacific; the Spokane, Portland & Seattle Railway Co.; and the St. Louis/San Francisco Railway Co., known as the Frisco—also each

Railroads cooperate with trucking companies and shippers' agents to provide intermodal services such as BN AMERICA. Intermodal business is one of the fastest-growing segments of railroad service.

brought a rich history and strategically located lines to the railroad.

The Northern Pacific was the first of the northern transcontinentals. Created by an act of Congress that was signed by President Abraham Lincoln, the railroad was to have its eastern terminus at Lake Superior and its western terminus at Puget Sound. Much of its route followed the trail blazed by Lewis and Clark on their expedition across the uncharted West in 1804 to 1806.

The railroad hit some major obstacles along the way. The Panic of 1873 brought financial failure to the bank handling the company's finances, and the railroad sank into bankruptcy. After a reorganization, the western march began again.

General George Custer was assigned to protect the crews in the Montana Territory. Under the leadership of Henry Villard, who became president of Northern Pacific in 1881, the railroad joined the lines from the East and the West in 1883 at Gold Creek, Montana Territory. President Ulysses S. Grant drove the last spike in the track.

In 1901 Northern Pacific and Great Northern jointly purchased nearly all the outstanding stock of the Chicago, Burlington & Quincy Railroad, providing the two lines with direct access to Chicago and the markets of the Midwest and South.

Historians called the Spokane, Portland & Seattle Railway Co. the "newest line in the West." Its heritage dated back to the 1880s, but it was Great Northern that planned to help in the development of Oregon by building a railroad from Spokane to Portland. Great Northern and Northern Pacific jointly controlled and financed the project.

Rivers shaped the railroad's route through the treacherous mountainous country. The SP&S hugs the north bank of the scenic Columbia and Snake rivers for 290 of the 380 miles between Portland and Spokane. The line is now part of Burlington Northern's Pacific division.

The last major line to join Burlington Northern was the Frisco. The railway was the only one of Burlington Northern's predecessor lines with a

BN's intermodal hub center at Irving, Texas, where trains and trucks meet to exchange loads, can accommodate hundreds of truck trailers and serves the area within a 250-mile radius.

major presence in Texas. The Frisco completed a line to the Dallas/Fort Worth area in 1901 and purchased a 58-mile line from Sherman to Carrollton, now a Dallas suburb. It also added a 146-mile railroad south from Fort Worth to Brownwood. The Frisco's tracks eventually branched south into Tennessee, Alabama, and reaching the Gulf of Mexico at Pensacola, Florida.

With routes established throughout the United States, Burlington Northern's predecessor railroads turned their attention to the new streamlined, diesel-powered locomotives in the 1930s and 1940s. Burlington's best-known achievement occurred in 1934, shortly after the railroad introduced the Pioneer Zephyr, the nation's first diesel-powered streamlined passenger train and the first of Burlington's famous family of Zephyrs.

Burlington Northern Railroad is the nation's leading transporter of grain. This is a grain train being loaded at an elevator.

That year Burlington staged a 1,000-mile, record-breaking nonstop run from Denver to the World's Fair on Chicago's lakefront, arriving on stage as the climax of the fair's transportation pageant. The fuel cost for the trip was $14.64, and the train's highest speed was 112.5 miles per hour.

The Chicago, Burlington & Quincy; Great Northern; Northern Pacific; and the SP&S merged to form Burlington Northern in 1970. The Frisco was added in 1980.

Burlington Northern, like most railroad companies, eventually discontinued passenger service, concentrating on transporting freight throughout the United States and to international destinations. Today Burlington Northern serves more than 4,000 communities in 25 states and two Canadian provinces. The company operates 700 trains a day.

Burlington Northern ranks at the top of the industry in almost all operating categories. The company is first in revenue-ton miles (223.6 billion); first in miles of road operated (23,391 miles); first in length of average haul per loaded car (761.0 miles); yet fifth in number of freight cars owned (47,268); fourth in number of freight cars leased (8,849); third in number of locomotives in service (2,324); second in number of carloads carried (more than 4.0 million); and second in number of carloads originated (3.5 million).

The company's largest business segments are transporting agricultural products and coal. Burlington Northern hauls more grain than any other railroad in the nation and transports more low-sulphur coal than any other carrier. The railroad also ships more than one million domestic and foreign cars annually. In addition, Burlington ships food and consumer products and forest and industrial products, including raw materials for industrial production.

As deregulation and growing competition from motor carriers cut into U.S. railroads' business in recent decades, Burlington Northern reassessed its business mission. While its principal goal used to be to run its trains on time, and customers designed their transportation requirements to meet the railroad's schedule, Burlington Northern has become a more customer-sensitive, market-driven company.

The company was the first in the railroad business to organize into business units around each of its main customer product categories. The railroad also established an intermodal business unit in which trucks and trains work together in partnership. Burlington Northern also was the first railroad to incorporate sales and marketing people into the product and service development cycle.

After reorganizing to become more responsive to customers, the company also introduced new products and services to make it easier for customers to transport by rail.

One such service, the Certificates of Transportation program, allows grain shippers to lock in a rate, guarantee car supply, and guarantee a shipment period. The product has been so successful that BN is exploring how to expand the service, hoping to eventually offer a network that covers the nation and Mexico.

Another new offering is BN Lynx™, the first PC software package that allows customers to trace shipments on virtually every major North American rail carrier. Prior to BN Lynx, customers had to rely on each carrier's individual software package, often spending more time switching software than tracing shipments.

Burlington Northern also developed a personal computer program called ShipSmart® that allows customers to quickly compare the cost of transportation alternatives. The program can compare different transportation options at one time, analyzing transportation costs, inventory carrying costs, transit time, and safety stock.

Burlington Northern's domestic container network, BN AMERICA, offers a high-quality door-to-door service that offers customers many of the benefits they expect from a high-service truckload carrier—a damage-free ride, dependable pickup and delivery times, and advance notice of shipment arrival—all on a single bill of lading and available with a single phone call.

The slack-free ride of BN's double-stack cars are representative of the vital role technology is playing in BN's service. BN is in the midst of the most ambitious program in North America to replace wood ties with longer-lasting concrete ties on the most heavily used portions of its system. BN also leads the industry in research and development spending and has established the industry's most sophisticated technical training center, all of which is designed to improve BN's ability to deliver better service to its customers, a better work environment for employees, and a better return for shareholders.

Dallas/Fort Worth International Airport

Dallas/Fort Worth International Airport has probably done more to shape the economy and future growth of Fort Worth, Dallas, and northern Texas than any other single project.

Since it opened in 1974 the airport has become one of the strongest magnets for attracting new industry and visitors to the cities of Fort Worth and Dallas. Millions of tourists and business travelers pour into the state through DFW each year. And in a landlocked area without a seaport to encourage international trade and commerce, the airport is the region's gateway to the world.

The airport is "exceeding the original planners' expectations," says Oris W. Dunham, Jr., DFW executive director. "It has become a driving force of the north Texas economy, helping to bring unsurpassed growth and economic development to the region."

DFW is one of the world's largest airport and the second busiest, behind Chicago's O'Hare. Dallas/Fort Worth

Airport officials estimate that by 2010, DFW will accommodate nearly 100 million passengers on nearly 1.2 million takeoffs and landings annually.

International had more than 47 million passengers in 1989 and handled more than 81,000 tons of mail and 209,500 tons of cargo. Almost 699,000 operations occurred at DFW, most of them air carrier departures and arrivals.

The airport property encompasses 18,177 acres, only about half of which is developed. Locals like to point out that DFW is larger in square mileage than Manhattan.

DFW ranks highly in safety comparisons with other airports in part because of its location. Pilots and aviation safety experts say the airport's size and wide open spaces, plus the mild Texas weather, make flying in and out of DFW safer than at many other airports.

The cast of carriers at DFW has changed and grown in international stature since the airport's early years. American Airlines, which moved its corporate headquarters from New York to Fort Worth in 1979, is the airport's biggest carrier. American operates its largest hub at DFW and controls more than half of the air traffic. Atlanta-based Delta Air Lines operates its second-busiest hub at DFW.

In 1974 Mexicana was the only airline serving foreign cities from DFW. Today the list includes Thai Airways International Ltd., Lufthansa German Airlines, China Airlines, and British Airways PLC. In addition, Delta offers nonstop service to Europe and Mexico from DFW. American in recent years has expanded its direct international service from DFW to Europe, Japan, Mexico, Canada, and most recently, Australia and New Zealand.

Business officials often cite the airport as one of the key reasons companies relocate or expand in Fort Worth/Dallas and the north Texas area. Located in the geographic heart of the United States, the airport offers easy access to both coasts. Since 1985, the airport has been a major factor in attracting nearly 260 corporate relocations and company expansions to the area.

The airport also acts as a kind of international ambassador for the cities of Fort Worth and Dallas, attracting import and export business and foreign-owned companies to establish U.S. headquarters offices in the cities. The airport has spurred new development; the largest project is Las Colinas, a huge office, retail, and residential complex located only minutes east of DFW.

DFW is an economic entity in itself. The airport employs about 25,000 airline and support employees, as well as 35,000 people indirectly. In 1989 DFW contributed about $6.2 billion to the region's economy, airport officials estimate.

In retrospect, civic leaders say it is remarkable such a large, modern airport could have been built in a short five years and for $700 million—a bargain by today's standards.

A number of factors worked in DFW's favor. One of them was Erik Jonsson, Dallas' former mayor who shepherded the approval, design, and construction of the airport. He was convinced the cities must have the facilities to serve the big jumbo jets that were on the drawing boards at that time.

DFW also brought Dal-

las and Fort Worth together physically as well as psychologically, helping to heal a long-standing rivalry between the cities and their leadership. The cities began an unprecedented level of cooperation, established an airport board in 1965, selected the site where the airport is located today, and developed a master plan.

Not everything went smoothly. The first bond proposal to pay for DFW was defeated by voters. But eventually the proposals passed and ground was broken on the site in late 1968.

Two events spurred DFW's growth in the late 1970s. One was the corporate relocation of American Airlines. The other was the passage of the Airline Deregulation Act, which introduced competition into the airline industry. Airlines adopted new routes and established lower fare structures to entice people to fly. Deregulation brought in new passengers and the need for more capacity. Since its opening, the airport has been expanded every year. The im-

provements total $900 million so far, and more expansions are planned.

"Clearly, airport capacity at DFW is one of the major aviation issues of today and the future," Dunham says. "DFW not only has to continue to compete in a nation of airline hubs, but today it must compete in a world of hubs."

Airport officials estimate that by 2010, DFW will accomodate nearly 100 million passengers on nearly 1.2 million takeoffs and landings annually. As part of a long-range plan, DFW has been working with the Federal Aviation Administration, community leaders, and the airlines on an ambitious $3.5-billion airport development plan that could double the airport's capacity over the next 20 years and strengthen DFW's position as a world aviation center.

The plan proposes building two new air carrier runways, developing terminals, enlarging the taxiway system, acquiring an estimated 800 additional acres of land, building a new east-west connector "highway" across the airport,

Dallas/Fort Worth International Airport is the world's second-busiest airport.

and completing Airfield Drive to encircle the airfield. In addition, DFW is extending two of its four north-south parallel runways by 2,000 feet to meet increased capacity and exceed safety margins for the heavy jumbo jets flying directly to international destinations.

The DFW board has been conducting public meetings and hearings with citizens from nearby communities, many of whom are concerned about increased traffic and noise levels.

In addition to those plans, Dallas/Fort Worth International Airport, in conjunction with American Airlines, is studying a new $1.2-billion terminal complex on the airport's west side. Delta, which added a new nine-gate expansion to its terminal in 1988, also needs additional capacity and is considering a $100-million expansion.

Fort Worth Star-Telegram

It began, appropriately enough for Fort Worth, in a stray corner of that lingering western antique patch of cattle pens, the stockyards. The year was 1905. The exact day has been lost, but it was early winter because a biting northern wind had blown in, chilling the men trying to warm themselves around an open fire.

Three of the men, including Amon Carter, a young advertising salesman, began a casual conversation and impulsively decided to publish a newspaper in competition with the *Fort Worth Telegram*. Carter bragged that he could sell ads. He could; and as history proved, Amon Carter could sell almost anything.

So the newspaper, given the grandiose name of the *Star*, was born February 1, 1906, at Sixth and Rusk streets in a tiny room behind a saloon named the Senate Bar. Carter sold more advertising than the fledgling newspaper could publish; it was an auspicious beginning.

Though struggling financially, within three years the *Star* absorbed the *Telegram*. Within two decades the *Star-Telegram* was Texas' largest newspaper; it soon was the largest in the southern half of the United States (between Atlanta and Los Angeles and south of St. Louis). In time the newspaper would emerge as a $100-million communications empire, with its own radio station, WBAP, and the South's first television station, Channel 5.

The newspaper empire and Carter became the driving force for building Fort Worth and western Texas. Carter, as the city's chief benefactor, also became internationally famous for his civic contributions and his folksy philosophy. "You cannot live off a community, you must live with it," he would say, often adding, "When the lake rises, the boat will rise too." Help Fort Worth and the entire region grow, and the newspaper would grow, too, he believed. The philosophy of public service was successful then and now.

In its first 60 years the *Star-Telegram's* readership was mostly in western Texas, a harsh place of sparse population and scant future prospects. Fort Worth was a rustic western town. The paper's masthead bragged that Fort Worth was

The *Star-Telegram's* $75-million printing and distribution center uses the latest electronic equipment to produce the newspaper.

"Where the West Begins;" it became a nationally known slogan. The newspaper covered 82 counties and spread over 350,000 square miles, making it the largest print media news distribution at the time.

The newspaper lobbied for paved roads, public libraries, and utilities in Fort Worth and western Texas. The newspaper and Carter also helped establish Big Bend National Park and Texas Tech University. It stumped for new businesses, raised money in times of disaster, and explained new cattle-breeding methods for ranchers and planting schedules for farmers. The newspaper also helped establish a zoo in Fort Worth and founded a Christmas

charity, the Goodfellows, as well as chartered trains to football and baseball games and political conventions.

The newspaper's reporters rode with Pancho Villa's troops in Mexico's civil war and helped impeach a Texas governor, "Pa" Ferguson. When the Japanese surrendered aboard the USS *Missouri* to end World War II, there were three reporters from the *Star-Telegram* to cover the event—more than from any other news-gathering organization. The newspaper also was first on the streets with

The **Fort Worth Star-Telegram** once delivered to its 30,000-paper constituency by horse and wagon.

New offset presses at the *Star-Telegram*'s printing and distribution center ensure top-quality printing and faithful reproduction.

reports of President John F. Kennedy's assassination and was the first Texas news organization to send reporters to cover fighting in Vietnam.

In 1954, when Carter's WBAP-TV became the first all-color television station west of the Mississippi River, a group of investors, including author and broadcast journalist Lowell Thomas, bought a small UHF television station in Albany, New York, founding a company called Capital Cities. It would be two decades later that the *Star-Telegram* and Cap Cities would merge.

When Amon Carter died in 1955, his son, Amon Carter, Jr., became publisher of the newspaper. By then Capital Cities had become the second-largest television company not owned by a network, and it had moved into the print media with the purchase of Fairchild Publications and several daily newspapers in Michigan, Illinois, and Pennsylvania. In 1974 Cap Cities purchased the *Star-Telegram* with a promise to "further the community welfare."

Cap Cities merged in 1986 with ABC Television to create a world communications giant. The company will bring the *Star-Telegram* into the twenty-first century with a $75-million investment in a new printing plant for the newspaper, which operates on fiber optics, robots, and electronics undreamed of when Amon Carter's little *Star* was being delivered by horse and wagon.

Under Cap Cities ownership the *Star-Telegram* has won numerous awards, including two Pulitzer prizes, journalism's highest honor. In 1981 photographer Larry Price won the award for his news pictures of revolution in Liberia, Africa. Four years later reporter Mark Thompson's stories on helicopter design flaws made national headlines, winning the prize for meritorious public service.

Amon Carter would have liked that. Carter's legend was not his fame nor his riches, nor even the mechanical and business trappings of his communications empire. The legend was, and still is, public service.

American Airlines

American Airlines planted its roots in the Fort Worth area at the dawn of aviation history, when a few business leaders formed a small company that eventually grew into the nation's largest airline. But American's growth over the past decade has overshadowed the growth of the previous half century.

In 1989 American celebrated the 10th anniversary of the return of its corporate headquarters from New York City to a Tarrant County campus adjoining Dallas/Fort Worth International Airport. The celebration commemorated a decade during which American substantially increased its employment, payroll, facilities, and operations in the Fort Worth area.

"We have grown dramatically since we moved to Texas," says Robert L. Crandall, American's chairman and president. "The central location, good weather, and cooperative attitude have all helped."

American has achieved that growth without sacrificing either its financial stability (it is the nation's most consistently profitable air carrier) or its reputation for quality customer service.

During the 10-year period, American's service from DFW Airport—its largest and busiest hub—has surged from 120 departures per day in 1979 to more than 400 in 1989. The carrier now serves 100 destinations from its home base, tripling the 1979 schedule.

American boarded approximately 14.4 million travelers at DFW in 1989, nearly four times the 3.5 million it boarded in 1979. Cargo also grew over that period, from 177 million pounds 10 years ago to 205 million currently.

The number of AA employees in Texas has expanded from 4,500 people in 1979 to nearly 27,000 today, with more than 25,000 in the Dallas/ Fort Worth Metroplex area. American's Texas payroll has climbed from $95 million, when the airline moved, to $750 million now. With American's aggressive expansion, the company's local employment is expected to reach 40,000 people by 1995.

American celebrated its 10th anniversary with an advertising campaign built around the slogan, "Based here. Best here." Buttons and bumper stickers touted the occasion, and the airline sponsored the ice show at the Texas State Fair.

Despite the focus on the past

Late in 1989 American Airlines broke ground for a maintenance base at Alliance Airport, a new industrial airport north of Fort Worth.

decade, American's history in Fort Worth reaches back more than 60 years. The airline's operations in Texas date to 1927, when Fort Worth businessman Temple Bowen established a pioneer air carrier called Texas Air Transport. Bowen, who operated a bus line in Fort Worth, began air-mail service early in 1928 from Fort Worth along two routes—one to Houston and Galveston, and the other to Waco, Austin, and San Antonio. The company introduced the first passenger service in Texas one year later.

Texas Air Transport was acquired in 1928 by A.P. Barrett, who sought help from Fort Worth's Amon Carter, who served on the board of American Airlines until his death in 1955. His son, Amon Carter, Jr., served as a director until 1982.

In the late 1920s Barrett combined Texas Air Transport with another fledgling airline, Gulf Coast Airways, to form Southern Air Transport. Southern Air Transport was combined with several other carriers in 1930 to create American Airways, the direct forerunner of American Airlines. The company opened its Fort Worth headquarters at Meacham Field officially in 1934 and

American Airlines' corporate headquarters is located adjacent to Dallas/Fort Worth International Airport.

The American Airlines hub of Dallas/Fort Worth International Airport averages more than 400 departures a day and serves 100 destinations.

operated there until the mid-1950s.

In 1957 the carrier opened a flight-attendant school on a Tarrant County site that would become the nucleus of its headquarters complex. That school —now tripled in size and known as the Learning Center—was so successful that American built a flight academy for training pilots on an adjacent tract in 1971. The southern reservations office was added to the growing campus in 1975.

Then, four years later, American relocated its corporate headquarters from Manhattan to a wooded site just south of the flight-attendant and pilot training complex. It has since developed a major complex in the Centreport office park. The complex is also the headquarters for American's SABRE system. SABRE, the world's largest privately owned real-time computer system, handles the airline's own computer requirements and generates revenues from other travel industry subscribers.

American's move to Fort Worth, which coincided with the government's deregulation of U.S. domestic airlines, was influenced by the size and potential of DFW Airport, a Texas-scale facility created through the cooperation of community leaders in Fort Worth and Dallas. That airport soon became a cornerstone of a growth plan that continues today.

Over the past six years, American has virtually doubled its size to become the largest airline outside the Soviet Union. In that period, American has expanded to more than 500 aircraft, giving it one of the most modern fleets in the world, with hundreds of additional jetliners on order. It added thousands of new employees and now counts about 90,000 on the staff of the airline and other subsidiaries of the parent AMR Corp. AA also expanded its DFW and Chicago hubs and created new hubs in Nashville, Tennessee; Raleigh/Durham, North Carolina; San Juan, Puerto Rico; San Jose, California; and Miami, Florida, to serve a total route network of some 185 cities. The airline extended operations across the Atlantic and the Pacific, and now counts about 150 flights every week to European destinations alone.

American's global expansion has helped transform the Metroplex into an international business center. The carrier, which has flown between DFW and both Canada and Mexico for decades, has added service to European capitals. It began service to Australia and New Zealand, as well as Costa Rica and Guatemala, early in 1990.

Vigorous growth has taxed the airline's facilities at DFW Airport and challenged its experts to blueprint a new passenger terminal on the underused west side of the airport. Plans call for a giant terminal with 53 gates in the initial phase, with the potential to board more than 20 million passengers annually—about as many as the entire airport handles today. The cost of that facility is more than one billion dollars. In the meantime, American is moving ahead with a $276-million upgrade of its existing terminal facilities, including the addition of several gates and a parking garage.

Another big American Airlines project will add still more jobs in Tarrant County. Late in 1989 the airline broke ground for a $500-million maintenance base at Alliance Airport, a new industrial airport being built near DFW Airport. The base will be fully operational by 1995.

Explaining why American chose the local site, Bob Crandall told reporters, "Texas offers many advantages, including a positive business climate, a reputation for leadership and achievement, and the operational benefit of being in the center of the nation."

The new facility eventually will create nearly 17,000 jobs and pump more than one billion dollars into the local economy—contributing further to American Airlines' stature as a leader among Fort Worth corporations.

American's air cargo service supplements the airline's passenger business.

CHAPTER
TEN

PROFESSIONS

Fort Worth's professional community brings a wealth of ability and insight to the area.

ONE WAY
ONE WAY
ONE WAY
ONE WAY
E 7th
E 4th
FORD

Coopers & Lybrand

Coopers & Lybrand, one of the nation's Big Six accounting firms, has contributed to the success of Fort Worth area businesses for more than 40 years. The firm emphasizes professional excellence, dedication, and responsiveness to its clients and also is active in community affairs.

The Fort Worth office of Coopers & Lybrand has a staff of more than 90 people, making it one of Fort Worth's largest accounting and business-consulting firms. The local office is one of eight Coopers & Lybrand locations in Texas and one of 98 in the United States, the District of Columbia, and Puerto Rico. The firm also has offices in more than 104 foreign countries, and has worldwide revenues of $3.8 billion.

The Fort Worth office serves a large geographic area centered around Tarrant County and extending to clients throughout north-central Texas.

The firm's list of clients in the Fort Worth area is diverse, including financial institutions, oil and gas companies, manufacturers, and transportation concerns. In addition, the office handles most of Coopers & Lybrand's health care clients in the state, including some in southern Texas. The office provides consulting and a range of other services to the state's growing health care indus-

Maribess Miller, general practice partner, conducts a training program to ensure that technically proficient personnel serve each Coopers & Lybrand client.

Managing partner Ronald Clinkscale demonstrates Coopers & Lybrand's computer research capabilities to South Hi Mount Elementary School students Ramon Guajardo and Leigha Mitchell.

try. Although it is known as a certified public accounting firm, Coopers & Lybrand delivers more than professional auditing and tax services to established and emerging local businesses.

"We have been their business advisers," says Ronald Clinkscale, managing partner of the office. "Our expertise and personalized service have played a key role in helping such companies and their owners succeed."

Clinkscale says the firm places top priority on competent, professional people and makes a considerable investment in developing technical skills that will contribute to the success of its clients. "Our goal is to be the best resource for solving the business problems

of our clients," Clinkscale says. "Our professionals integrate client needs with solid business practices to achieve our common goals of growth, stability, and profitability."

Coopers & Lybrand supports the performing arts and nonprofit organizations in the Fort Worth area. The firm has adopted a theme of promoting education and is active in cooperative education projects such as the Fort Worth Independent School District's Adopt-a-School program.

Clinkscale estimates the Fort Worth office's professional staff has spent more than 1,000 hours in the past year working with students in various capacities such as tutoring. Coopers & Lybrand also is involved in programs that foster business and education alliances and encourage students to stay in school.

Everage Consultants, Inc.

Everage Consultants, Inc., is the latest evolution of a company originally established in 1973 to provide planning, engineering, and management services to the development community and municipal governments. Geared to continue its leadership into the 1990s, the company features civil engineering, master planning, and surveying services for the greater Fort Worth area. In its two decades of business, Everage Consultants has designed single family and multifamily residential subdivisions, major arterial roads, bridges, shopping centers and industrial parks, floodplain and hydrology studies, wastewater treatment systems, parks, schools, recreational facilities, and intermodal facilities.

The work of Everage Consultants is visible throughout Fort Worth. Some of the firm's projects include Crowley Road (FM 731), the Hulen Towers office complex, Meadows West Addition, parking facilities at Billy Bob's Texas in the historic Fort Worth stockyards area, John T. White Road, Westpoint Addition, Ederville Road, and the relocation of Commerce Street around the Tarrant County Convention Center.

Many of Everage Consultants' projects are in the public sector, giving the firm a direct role in improving the city's quality of life. The firm's public sector clients include the the City of Fort Worth, the Fort Worth Parks & Recreation Department, and the Fort Worth Independent School District. Members of the firm also serve as city engineers for several local municipalities, giving the firm direct input into the development of communities.

Engineering firms such as Everage Consultants have been in the forefront of Fort Worth's outstanding period of growth. The company has forged long-term business relationships and cultivated new clients that relocated to the area, in addition to working with many long-established firms.

Everage Consultants sees selective expansion and upgrading of facilities and infrastructure as major areas of concentration for the firm in the next several years. One such opportunity is a project that would assist expansion plans of Dallas/Fort Worth International Airport by adding more fuel pipelines to serve major carriers based there. Everage Consultants performed the construction survey in Tarrant County.

Everage Consultants provides a full complement of engineering, planning, and surveying services. In engineering the firm's services include design, computer modeling and simulation, construction cost estimates, and project management and inspection. In the planning area Everage Consultants offers city master planning, feasibility investigations, transportation studies, landscape design, and environmental impact and assessment studies. Platting, boundary, construction layout, topographic mapping, aerial control, and as-built title surveys are among the many surveying services offered. In addition, Everage Consultants also provides professional consulting in design disciplines and specialties. Everage Consultants attributes the quality of its services to the firm's knowledge of Fort Worth and surrounding communities.

Everage Consultants encourages its employees to participate actively in professional and community organizations. Various members of the firm have served in a variety of offices in different organizations, including serving as presidents of professional engineering society local chapters. Everage Consultants, Inc., employees also serve as guest lecturers at colleges, participate in minority organizations that promote professional development, and publish a number of articles in technical journals.

The firm also donates its time and manpower to further new business opportunities in the community through the Oriental trade missions sponsored by the City of Fort Worth and the Fort Worth Chamber of Commerce.

Everage Consultants is a firm that prides itself on its professional approach to all engineering, planning, and surveying projects. Prospective clients can take comfort from the fact that, while Everage Consultants is large enough to handle any size job, it is small enough to provide personalized service to every client.

Gandy Michener Swindle Whitaker & Pratt

Since its founding in 1978, Gandy Michener Swindle Whitaker & Pratt has built a reputation for representing clients in business and commercial transactions and in litigation. The law firm attempts to serve every legal need an executive or business might have.

In 1978 John W. Michener, Jr., an established tax lawyer, merged his practice with Mack Ed Swindle, an experienced trial lawyer; Wayne M. Whitaker, formerly a lawyer practicing in the Securities and Exchange Commission's enforcement division; and Donald O. Pratt, a construction and government contract specialist. The merger was completed in a time of economic boom in Fort Worth, when real estate and oil activity was very strong. The firm had grown to 15 members by April 1, 1983, the date the firm merged with Taylor Gandy, a former two-term Fort Worth city council member.

Gandy Michener is divided into six sections: tax and business planning, corporate and securities, litigation, construction and government contracts, banking and insurance, and real estate and probate.

The tax section, chaired by Michener, includes attorneys who also are certified public accountants. Most of the attorneys also have public accounting experience, and Michener and John Howard are board certified in tax law by the Texas Board of Legal Specialization. All members of the section have extensive income and estate tax planning and have assisted individual and corporate taxpayers whose annual tax liabilities range from a few thousand dollars to more than $10 million. They also have special expertise in representing insiders in publicly held companies.

Gandy Michener's tax practice has evolved to include business planning and financial restructuring, Michener says. The firm analyzes the financial condition of clients and recommends alternative financial restructures to permit clients to accomplish their goals.

The corporate and securities section, chaired by Whitaker, has expertise in representing New York Stock Exchange and over-the-counter trade clients. This section represents corporations in negotiating and drafting bank credit, acquisition, and divestiture agreements, as well as providing necessary documents for various types of securities. The group has worked on a wide variety of transactions from clients of small size up to companies with annual sales in excess of $250 million. "We help clients fund their capital projects and help entrepreneurs locate their initial seed capital," Michener says.

The litigation section handles trials, litigation, and dispute resolution in a broad range of industries and has a number of lawyers who are board certified in civil trial law by the Texas Board of Legal Specialization. The trial lawyers in this section are involved in commercial litigation; personal injury, medical malpractice, and insurance cases; business, contracts, and real estate disputes; computer litigation; trademark, copyright, and trade secret lawsuits; disputes affecting corporate officers, directors, and shareholders; and a broad spectrum of diverse litigation.

In the construction and government contracts section chaired by Pratt, Gandy Michener represents owners and contractors in the construction industry as well as government contractors. The section gets involved in a variety of areas, including contract preparation and negotiation, bid disputes, and design and operational disputes over such

The City Center Towers are home to Gandy Michener Swindle Whitaker & Pratt.

**Mack Ed Swindle (left) and
John W. Michener, Jr.**

matters as changes, delays, disruption, acceleration, and terminations. In addition, lawyers in the section provide labor law advice and frequently participate in arbitration hearings. "This is a unique specialty," Michener says.

"Of all our lawyers, these are the most regional in scope. They do a lot of work outside the state of Texas."

The banking and insurance section chaired by Bruce W. McGee represents both borrowers and lenders in real estate transactions, bankruptcy proceedings, litigation in state and federal courts on financial questions, and commercial lending transactions. The group also represents clients in various areas of the insurance industry.

The real estate and probate group, headed by Gandy, who is board certified in estate planning and probate matters, features attorneys board certified in both commercial and residential real estate law by the Texas Board of Legal Specialization. The section has handled real estate transactions of up to $75 million, large commercial lease transactions representing both landlords and tenants, and financing for large real estate transactions. It has also represented mortgage lenders. Among its clients is Stewart Title Co., one of the area's major title companies. The section also has handled probate work of medium- and large-size estates.

Michener says the firm expects to grow 10 to 20 percent annually in

billings over the next five years. Gandy Michener employs more than 100 people, including 35 attorneys. Michener says the firm has a unique planning process that stresses individual goal setting, and adds that every year except 1982 the firm has exceeded its forecast for collected fees.

"We report progress to every lawyer in the firm," he says. "The youngest lawyer knows what the senior lawyers are doing and vice versa." In 1989 the firm made a commitment to office automation. There are no typewriters in Gandy Michener's offices. Attorneys, paralegals, and secretaries do their work using computers and laser printers. In addition, the firm has access to the Lexis and Westlaw legal data bases on each lawyer's desk. "Lawyers who do not learn to use hardware and software will be like the lawyers who did not learn to use dictating machines years ago," Michener says.

Gandy Michener also emphasizes awards and annually gives bronzes to lawyers in recognition of their individual accomplishments. The firm has adopted a bronze lion as its corporate symbol, which is presented to partners on their 10th anniversary with the firm. In describing the lion, Michener enjoys quoting Proverbs 30:30, "the lion, a hero among beasts, which will not turn tail for anyone."

Gandy Michener Swindle Whitaker & Pratt's daily goal is to be accessible to clients. This is a goal that all employees adopt, from the receptionist to the senior lawyers. Each lawyer strives to complete each transaction in a manner that will encourage the clients to return to the firm for their next transaction.

From the comfort of its reception room to the friendliness of its senior lawyers, Gandy Michener fulfills its promise of accessibility to clients.

Shannon, Gracey, Ratliff & Miller

Shannon, Gracey, Ratliff & Miller is one of Fort Worth's oldest and largest law firms, with a diverse practice and several notable specialties. The firm strives to represent clients vigorously and ethically, stressing responsiveness and flexibility.

Primary areas of practice are litigation, financial institutions, corporate and securities law, construction law, taxes, bankruptcy and reorganization, real estate, and estate planning and probate. However, Shannon Gracey lawyers practice in several legal disciplines, trying whenever possible to use the team approach for solving larger legal problems.

Litigation is the firm's largest practice area and includes commercial, oil and gas, insurance defense, health care, product liability, corporate, and security matters. Shannon Gracey litigation attorneys practice in federal and state courts, as well as in commercial arbitration proceedings.

The firm represents numerous banks and other financial institutions. Shannon Gracey attorneys have represented institutions and borrowers, including major money-center banks in Chicago and New York, in all types of financial transactions.

Shannon Gracey's corporate and securities lawyers have worked with corporations in a variety of transactions, including mergers and acquisitions, leveraged buyouts, public offerings, private placements, and nationwide franchising. The firm also has represented issuers, underwriters, and investors. The firm is experienced in representing clients before the Securities and Exchange Commission and state securities boards.

In its construction law practice Shannon Gracey's clients include architects, engineers, contractors, and owners in almost all types of construction matters, including litigation.

The firm's tax practice includes business transactions planning, the integration of tax and securities laws, tax aspects of corporate reorganizations, acquisitions, partnership formations, syndications, and venture capital projects. In addition, the firm represents both individuals and corporations in civil and criminal tax litigation.

In bankruptcy and reorganization matters Shannon Gracey attorneys are experienced in representing debtors, creditors, committees, and potential investors involved in out-of-court or bankruptcy proceedings.

In real estate law, Shannon Gracey has represented clients relating to the acquisition, improvement, lease, operation, sale, and financing of real estate. The firm also represents clients in the negotiation and drafting of contracts, acquisition and development loans, and financing arrangements.

The estate planning and probate

Earl Harcrow and D. Michael Wallach (right to left) are primary partners in the firm's health care practice. They are pictured at the client facilities of Huguley Memorial Hospital with Bill Robertson, the hospital's chief financial officer, and Gena Rabuka, the hospital's administrative director of case and risk management.

practice involves all aspects of estate and gift tax planning, guardianships, dependent and independent estate administrations, and trust administration.

Health care is an important and growing practice area of the firm, encompassing representation of physicians, clinics, and hospitals. The practice deals with issues related to the business aspects of health law and the defense of liability claims through insurers and self-insured clients.

In addition to those areas of expertise, the firm is one of only a handful of

firms nationally with an equine law practice. Fort Worth is a natural location for such a specialty because of the area's concentration of horse breeders, owners, associations, and other groups which have established themselves in

B. Frank Cain practices in the growing area of equine law.

the city, a longtime center of livestock-related events and activities.

Shannon Gracey represents several associations in the equine industry, including the National Cutting Horse Association and the American Paint Horse Association. The firm also represents individual owners and breeders in a broad range of equine-related areas, including taxation, syndications, and litigation.

Since its founding Shannon Gracey has gradually expanded and prospered, resulting from several mergers. In 1968 the firm of Thompson, Walker, Smith, and Shannon merged with Simon, Crowley, Wright, Ratliff and Miller. The current firm—named Shannon, Gracey, Ratliff and Miller—is the result of that merger.

A number of Shannon Gracey attorneys are certified in their areas of practice, including estate planning and probate law, civil appellate law, civil trial law, personal injury trial law, and tax law.

In addition to their legal practices, Shannon, Gracey, Ratliff & Miller attorneys are active in civic and charitable work, as well as state and national professional associations. Several partners also serve on the board of directors for the Texas Association of Banking Counsel, including one serving as president-elect. Others are active with the American College of Trial Lawyers, the Texas Association of Defense Counsel, and the American College of Probate Counsel.

Peat Marwick

KPMG Peat Marwick is one of the world's leading professional service firms. The firm offers accounting, auditing, tax, and management consulting services to thousands of governmental, institutional, financial, industrial, and commercial clients. Peat Marwick provides these services through the KPMG network of offices, with more than 5,000 partners and 58,000 professional staff operating in 117 countries.

The firm today is the result of an evolutionary process that began in 1897 with two Scotsmen, James Marwick and Roger Mitchell, and has involved a number of mergers over the years. In 1911, seeking a presence in Europe, Marwick Mitchell & Co. merged with the English practice of Sir William Peat to form Peat Marwick Mitchell & Co. In 1987, as a result of a worldwide merger with Klynveld Main Goerdler, the firm became KPMG Peat Marwick in the United States and KPMG around the world.

The establishment of the Fort Worth office in 1959 gave Peat Marwick a foothold in one of the fastest-growing areas in the United States. The Fort Worth office has 70 professionals, led by nine partners, who provide auditing, accounting, and tax services. The office's client list includes high-wealth individuals, middle-market companies, local government agencies, and educational and financial institutions.

Peat Marwick uses the latest in audit tools to provide quality client services. One example is the development of SEACAS, a computer application that enables auditors to more efficiently complete many time-consuming functions that have traditionally been performed manually.

The firm's computer audit personnel receive more than 200 hours of training that emphasize all aspects of the audit process. In addition, Peat Marwick has a large and diversified group of computer consultants who can supplement the auditors' work, as well as provide a wide range of computer consulting services.

The firm's tax practice encompasses a full range of services, including income-tax planning, tax-return preparation, personal financial planning, and representation before regulatory agencies, both on corporate and individual levels. Supporting the local office in these functions are state tax professionals, the Washington national tax practice, and the international tax division. "Our objective is to ensure that our clients obtain all possible advantages under the current tax laws," says Albert H. Coldewey, managing partner of the Fort Worth office.

"In the past year, the firm has conducted a thorough analysis of the Fort Worth office tax practice that has coincided with Peat Marwick's evolution toward a more technologically advanced tax department," Coldewey says. "As a result we have acquired the ability to provide innovative services to our clients, which makes us most competitive in our market."

One of the strengths of Peat Marwick in Fort Worth lies in its client service teams. Each client is assigned a team comprised of a partner, managers, and professionals who possess experience and knowledge that relate directly to the individual needs of the client. Due to the low turnover rate in the Fort Worth practice, Peat Marwick says it is able to provide continuity from one year to the next.

In 1989 the firm introduced a formal client survey—the first of its kind in the industry—to focus on quality service. The feedback from the program will help the firm allocate resources to provide the greatest benefits to clients.

Peat Marwick sees itself as an integral part of the Fort Worth business community. The firm's partners and management group are active in civic, social, and business organizations. Coldewey says Peat Marwick's sound image also has contributed to client retention and the ability to recruit top people from both local and nationally known universities.

LEFT: Peat Marwick's Fort Worth office partners are (from left) Donald C. Spitzer, Clyde E. Womack, Robert A. Pedersen, Glen E. Smith, Albert H. Coldewey, Donald J. Mason, John E. Anderson, Douglas N. Hughston, and Kenneth W. Sanders.

FACING: Peat Marwick's Fort Worth office is located in the heart of the city's downtown area.

Cantey & Hanger

Fort Worth was in the midst of a transformation in the 1880s, when two attorneys formed a partnership for the practice of law. The rough trail town was becoming civilized, with paved streets, sanitary sewers, churches, permanent homesteads, and a growing populace.

William Capps, an attorney and active real estate developer, and Samuel B. Cantey, a newly licensed attorney from Alabama, opened their law firm, Capps & Cantey, in 1882. More than a century and several name changes later, their business evolved into Cantey & Hanger, the oldest and largest law firm in Fort Worth.

The original partnership brought together a bright legal scholar, Cantey, and a judicious businessman, Capps. The firm handled much of the important litigation in Fort Worth. Capps & Cantey became known as a firm with some of the town's top trial lawyers, a reputation still enjoyed by Cantey & Hanger today.

By the late 1890s Fort Worth was beginning to show signs of becoming a big city. The terminal of the Texas & Pacific Railway had been completed and rail lines extended to western Texas. Two great meat-packing houses

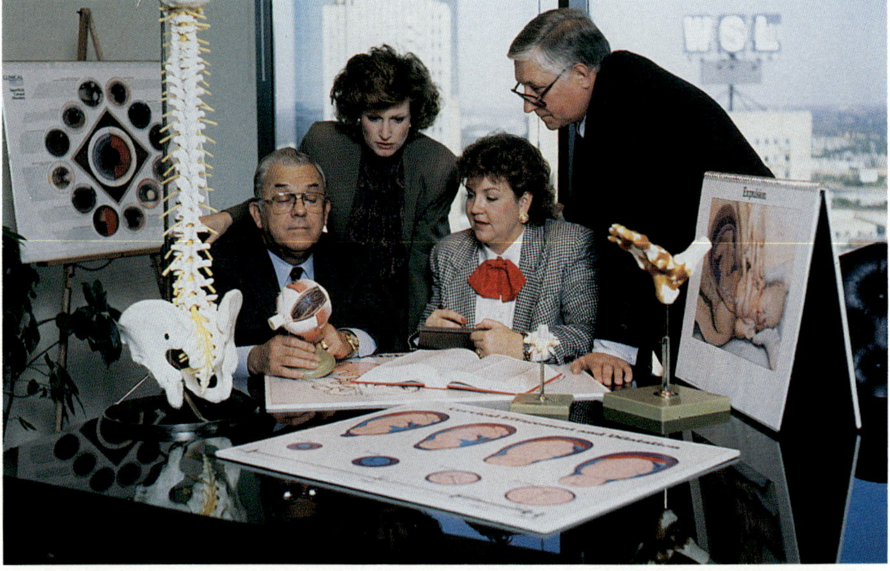

(Left to right) Dr. Dewey Johnston, Carol Traylor, Dorothy Porter, R.N., and partner Richard Griffith review medical charts and models they use in Cantey & Hanger's health law practice.

Partner Lynette Guy Williamson works on a case, helping to keep Cantey & Hanger at the forefront of Fort Worth law firms.

of the Midwest, Armour and Swift, both built plants in Fort Worth, and Capps & Cantey represented them both.

· Cantey established one of the first utilities practices in the legal profession. When the Electric Bond and Share Group of New York linked cities and towns in northern Texas into a single integrated power system, Cantey was largely responsible for the legal methods to create the system. Later, the merging of several small electric generation companies in Fort Worth and western Texas evolved into Texas Electric Service Co., now known as TU Electric. The company remains a client of the firm today.

At the turn of the century, Capps & Cantey added several new lawyers to the firm, including William M. Short, who specialized in damage suits, and William A. Hanger, who later was a state senator for eight years. With the additions, the firm changed its name to Capps, Cantey, Hanger & Short.

By 1920 the firm had nine attorneys, including Cantey's son, S.B. Cantey, Jr. Later Hanger's son, Robert K. Hanger, joined the firm after serving as district attorney for six years.

Over the years the firm grew steadily but not explosively, adding attorneys only as needed. One of the additions was J.A. "Tiny" Gooch, a gentle giant of a man who became a legend in Fort Worth for his civil law skills, civic activities, and his sense of humor. Gooch became especially known for raising funds for the Goodfellows charity. Gooch, who joined the firm in 1930, worked there for more than 50 years, longer than any other Cantey & Hanger partner.

Other well-known attorneys joined the firm over the years, including Gillis Johnson, Warren Scarborough, Carlisle G. Cravens, Jack C. Wessler, Whitfield J. Collins, William B. David, and a third-generation Cantey, the founder's grandson, Emory Cantey.

As the firm's list of clients increased, so did its reach. During the 1950s Cantey & Hanger became one of the leading law firms in western Texas. The firm's trial practice produced several landmark decisions in oil and gas law.

Today Cantey & Hanger still has many of its clients from those early days, including TU Electric and Saint Joseph Hospital. The firm's clients are a diverse group, including manufacturers, transportation companies, financial institutions, utilities, arts organizations, oil companies, governmental agencies, small businesses, and health care organizations, one of the firm's specialties.

Cantey & Hanger's highly diversified clients are mainly in the Fort Worth area, although the firm still represents clients in western Texas, Dallas, and outside the state.

Among the firm's clients are General Motors Corp., American Airlines Inc., Texas-New Mexico Power Co., NCNB Texas National Bank, Arlington Memorial Hospital, Texas Commerce Bank, Union Pacific Resources, Miller Brewing Co., the Kimbell Art Foundation, the Amon Carter Museum, Harris Methodist Health System, CNA, Medical Protective Company, the Hartford In-

Cecil Munn, Cantey & Hanger partner, prepares for trial.

surance Group, Employers Casualty Co., and numerous other insurance companies.

The firm is divided into eight basic sections: appellate, banking and real estate, corporate finance and acquisitions, general litigation, health law, insurance litigation, labor relations, and taxation, estate, and business organizations. Attorneys from several different sections often work together on a single case.

Cantey & Hanger's health law practice, headed by partner Richard Griffith, is unique. The firm has a staff physician and several nurses as medical consultants. The practice represents hospitals and physicians in medical malpractice suits and also has attorneys who specialize in the business, tax, and corporate aspects of health law. For example, Cantey & Hanger attorneys perform general risk management and consulting services for hospitals, nursing homes, and other health care organizations.

"As far as I know we're the only law firm in the area with a full range of health care professionals," says managing partner Allan Howeth. "It's

Tax chairman Harry Bartel (standing) and managing partner Allan Howeth.

brought us a lot of attention."

Many Cantey & Hanger lawyers are board certified in specialized areas of law, such as trial, labor, and estate planning. Cantey & Hanger has more than 75 attorneys and a support staff of more than 100 nonlegal personnel, including paralegals, an administrator, a librarian, and a manager of a computerized bookkeeping and billing system. The firm also has a large law library of about 25,000 volumes and subscribes to computerized legal research systems.

Cantey & Hanger partners and associate attorneys are active in a range of professional organizations, including the state and county bar associations. The firm has produced several judges and elected officials, including Estil Vance, Jr., a Cantey & Hanger trial lawyer who served on the Fort Worth City Council from 1985 to 1989.

The venerable Cantey & Hanger is one of the city's most stable firms, growing gradually instead of through merger.

"The heritage of the firm, its broad client base, and loyal attorneys and staff provide stability," Howeth says. "At the same time we try to remain abreast of ever-changing laws and regulations. Most clients have needs in new and developing areas, which requires us to be progressive and responsive to take care of their needs."

Partner Rory Divin researches a case in the firm's law library.

Kelly, Hart & Hallman

Dee J. Kelly. Photo by Gittings

Kelly, Hart & Hallman is a 78-lawyer firm with offices at 2500 First City Bank Tower, 201 Main Street in downtown Fort Worth, Texas. Representing a diverse range of expertise, education, and geographical background, the firm's attorneys are graduates of more than 20 different law schools and more than 40 undergraduate and graduate schools. Several members of the firm are either licensed or experienced in practice in other states, including Oklahoma, New Mexico, Louisiana, Colorado, and Arkansas.

The firm was formed in 1979, by Dee J. Kelly and a nucleus of attorneys formerly with Vinson & Elkins. Although Kelly, Hart & Hallman has experienced rapid growth, it has maintained continuity and stability, both in its members and its client base, throughout its history. Kelly, Hart & Hallman represents public and closely held companies and individuals in sophisticated commercial transactions throughout the nation in the areas of venture capital, banking, oil and gas, real estate, litigation, workouts, construction, corporations and securities, bankruptcy, labor, public finance, tax, and sports and entertainment.

Kelly, Hart & Hallman is a professional corporation with more than 150 employees. All of the firm's shareholders serve on a board of directors, and Mark L. Hart, Jr., acts as managing director overseeing day-to-day operations. Policy issues and other major issues are dealt with by an eight-member executive committee of the board. A professional staff composed of managers in the areas of accounting, personnel, and operations assist in firm management.

The firm represents a broad range of individuals, public and private companies, financial institutions, foundations, and public agencies. A listing of representative clients are as follows:

GENERAL COUNSEL

Acme Brick Company
The Anne Burnett Tandy and Charles D. Tandy Foundation
Perry R. Bass
Sid R. Bass
Edward R. Bass
Robert M. Bass
Lee M. Bass
Bass Enterprises Production Co.
Burnett Oil Co., Inc.
Burnett Ranches, Inc.
City Center Development Co.
Cook-Fort Worth Children's Medical Center
Cross Timbers Oil Company
Darling-Delaware Company, Inc.
First City, Texas—Dallas (Fort Worth Branch)
Justin Industries, Inc.
Anne Windfohr Marion
Mel Wheeler, Inc.
North Texas Bancshares
Nowlin Savings Association
Pier 1 Imports, Inc.
Sid Richardson Carbon and Gasoline Co.
Sid W. Richardson Foundation
Space Biospheres Venture
Sundance Square
Texas Commerce Bank—Fort Worth, N.A.

REPRESENTING

American Airlines, Inc.
American Savings Bank, F.A.
American Real Estate Group, Inc.
The Airlie Group, L.P.
Arvida Company
Bank of Commerce
Ben E. Keith Co.
Collecting Bank, N.A.
Commerce Financial Corporation
John L. Cox
CRC-Evans Pipeline International, Inc.
Dallas Cowboys Football Club, Ltd.
Drilltec Patents & Technologies Company, Inc.
Equitable Bankshares, Inc.
The First Boston Corporation
Ben J. Fortson
Fortson Oil Company
General Motors Corp.
Harbison-Fischer Manufacturing Co., Inc.
Helen of Troy Corporation
Kawasaki Motors Corp., USA
Lake Worth National Bank
Mitsubishi Aircraft International, Inc.
Mitsubishi Heavy Industries
W.A. Moncrief, Jr.
NCNB Texas National Bank
The Pep Boys
Shoe Gallery Holdings, Inc.
Tarrant County Hospital District
Tarrant County Housing Finance Corporation
Tarrant County Industrial Development Corporation
Team Bank, N.A.
Texas Commerce Bank—Arlington, N.A.
Texas Health Facilities Development Corporation
Texas Stadium Corporation

OPPOSITE: (Left to right) William Hallman, Jr., Dee J. Kelly, and Mark Hart, Jr.

THE MARKETPLACE

Fort Worth's retail establishments and accommodations are enjoyed by residents and visitors alike.

Pier 1 Imports Inc.
134

Tandy Corp.
136

Hyatt Regency Fort Worth
138

Photo by Bob Rowan/Progressive Image Photography

Pier 1 Imports Inc.

When customers go shopping at a Pier 1 Imports store, they literally have a world of choices: Dhurrie rugs from India; wicker and rattan furniture from Indonesia, Hong Kong, China, and the Philippines; folk-art sweaters from Peru; and pillows, linens, and dinnerware in a range of colors and patterns from India, the Far East, and Europe. And those are just some of the decorative home furnishings, housewares and kitchen goods, specialty gifts, and casual, contemporary clothing available at one of Pier 1's more than 560 stores in the United States and Canada.

Considered the leading specialty retailer of decorative home furnishings and related items in North America, Pier 1 also holds the title of the fastest growing. The company has captured the industry's attention in recent years with a string of record sales gains and profits.

By the end of 1990, Pier 1 expects its sales to reach about $620 million, more than double the amount just four years earlier. Retail analysts say the company is poised for many years of continued impressive growth.

The key to Pier 1's success has been a combination of unique merchandise, a strategy to upgrade all aspects of the company's operation, and an affluent, maturing customer base that is devoting more discretionary spending to the home.

"Our goal is to become more fashionable and continue to move up in the quality and style of the merchandise," says Clark A. Johnson, chairman and chief executive officer.

In 1985, after Johnson assumed leadership of the company, Pier 1 went through a major strategic refocus that targeted the maturing baby-boom market—the 79 million Americans born between 1946 and 1964 who make up a powerful buying group.

During the late 1960s and 1970s, Pier 1 was in step with that market during the so-called youth "counterculture" movement. The company's stores offered Indian print bedspreads, throw pillows, beaded curtains, and tie-dyed items. Most of the items were inexpensive, and they became popular with students for decorating their rooms at home and at college.

As baby boomers matured and began wanting more sophisticated furnishings and accessories for their homes, Pier 1 saw the need to update its approach while retaining its focus on unique and unusual merchandise. Through customer research, the company identified the merchandise and shopping experience potential customers wanted. Then it upgraded every aspect of the company—the quality of the merchandise, quality of service, store size, store locations, and number of stores.

"We have basically remodeled all our stores," Johnson says. "Out of 560 stores, all either were remodeled or are brand new within the past 42 months."

Pier 1 also is continuing an aggressive expansion that envisions opening its 1,000th store by 1998. Since Johnson and his management team took the helm, Pier 1 has stepped up the pace of new store openings and increased the average size of stores to about 8,500 square feet. New stores are predominantly freestanding units located in key demographic settings, often in point positions in upscale shopping centers.

Several Pier 1 stores are located in Tarrant County, including locations in

At Pier 1 Imports stores dramatic displays attract the customers' attention to a wide variety of merchandise. Thousands of items are imported from countries around the world, and selections change with the arrival of every shipment.

From six company-owned and -operated distribution centers like this one in Rancho Cucamonga, California, Pier 1 trucks deliver merchandise to more than 500 stores across North America.

The distinctive design of Pier 1's freestanding store at The Parks in Arlington is evidence of the company's success in upgrading its visual image.

downtown Fort Worth, the west side, and in fast-growing suburban areas.

Customers seem to like the changes Pier 1 has made. They spent an average $23.53 per sales ticket in 1989, compared with $17.46 in 1985. Store's sales averaged more than one million dollars in 1989, compared with $662,000 in 1985.

Pier 1 has built its business base with imported merchandise not generally available for purchase in North America. More than 90 percent of the items the company markets are handmade, representing the efforts of thousands of artisans throughout the 44 major countries that supply Pier 1.

The company's buyers annually visit Italy, Germany, France, and other European fashion centers to develop a vision of the texture, color, and style trends that will be prevalent in the U.S. in later years. Then they secure the merchandise that matches these trends. A Pier 1 store typically carries 4,500 individual items, 40 percent of which are new each year.

Home furnishings account for the largest percentage—about one-third—of Pier 1's sales. Apparel is Pier 1's

This boat load of rattan, a stout vine harvested from the floor of Asian jungles, makes its way to the workshops of Chinese craftsmen, who will hand shape it into furniture for Pier 1's renowned wicker collection.

newest merchandise and a fast-growing category. When the company began offering clothing several years ago, most of it was imported from India and most of it was cotton. Although the company's private-label "Passport" line still obtains about 40 percent of its clothing from India, Pier 1 also is buying from the Mediterranean and South America. A wider variety of styles and fabrics is now available, including silks and wools.

Pier 1 has gone to great lengths to make a customer's shopping experience a pleasant, relaxing one. The colorful, airy stores invite browsing and mentally transport the shopper to romantic, faraway places. One retail analyst compared the experience of shopping at Pier 1 with a "treasure hunt," offering something unusual and interesting around every corner.

"Pier 1's unique merchandise and pleasant shopping experience contrasts with the merchandise sameness of many retailers," Johnson says.

The trend of larger stores allow a better display of the merchandise. Pier 1 uses a collection approach in displaying merchandise, grouping furnishings and items together so customers can see how they would look in the home.

The store merchandise also encourages self-expression and promotes the trend of combining different styles of home furnishings to create a highly individualized look.

"There's been an eclectic acceptance in terms of home furnishings where it is legitimate to put many different styles together," Johnson says. "The ethnic look also has been widely accepted. Ninety percent of what we buy are handmade items from around the world."

Pier 1 has chosen Unicef as its major charity because it works with countries worldwide. The company is the largest corporate contributor to this international organization, which aids needy children.

Although its reach is global, Pier 1's roots are firmly planted in Fort Worth. The company is one of the "Tandy babies"—one of several Fort Worth retailers that was spun off from Tandy Corp., owner of Radio Shack. Pier 1 Imports Inc. became an independent company in 1962 and employs about 10,000 people.

In Fort Worth the company participates in Junior Achievement, International Sister Cities, the United Way of Metropolitan Tarrant County, and the Tarrant County Arts Council.

Tandy Corp.

A Fort Worth family leather business and a Boston electronics store chain seem an unlikely business combination. But in 1963 the Fort Worth leather business, Tandy Corp., acquired a nine-store Boston electronics chain and built it into the world's largest network of electronics specialty outlets in the world—Radio Shack.

Today Tandy's Radio Shack chain has more than 7,000 stores, computer centers, and dealer/franchise outlets supplying more than 30 million U.S. households, businesses, and schools. Every year Radio Shack sells to one in every three U.S. households.

Radio Shack contributes about three-quarters of Tandy's annual sales, which are more than $4 billion. Radio Shack sells the latest in high-technology products, including telephones and telephone systems, cellular mobile telephones, radio pagers, satellite television systems, audio and video equipment, electronic parts, and personal computer systems. But as the name suggests, the chain's roots were in radio.

Radio Shack was founded in Boston in 1921 as a retail mail-order company selling to ham radio operators and electronics buffs. The company got its name during World War I from the wooden structures that housed wireless equipment on the decks of ships. The shelter became affectionately known as the "radio shack." Ham radio operators still refer to the room where they keep radio gear as the "shack."

In 1918 in Fort Worth, David L. Tandy and a friend, Norton Hinckley, pooled their resources to start a leather company that sold shoe-sole leather to shoe-repair dealers in the state. Later Tandy's son, Charles Tandy, convinced his father there was a market in leather-craft kits. By the 1950s Tandy Leather Co. was selling do-it-yourself leather kits for making saddles, belts, and other

western leather goods through a successful formula of retail mail order, direct mail advertising, and a chain of 150 leather-craft stores. That business approach was applied to all of the company's specialty retailing operations and remains one of Tandy's key business strategies. In 1962 supersalesman Charles Tandy became intrigued with the potential for rapid growth in the electronics retail industry. The company acquired Electronics Crafts in Fort Worth and, prodded by the success of the pilot electronics operation, began looking for another electronics business. Tandy found Radio Shack in Boston, which was in poor operating and financial condition with annual sales of about $18 million.

The legendary merchandiser Charles Tandy used some of the techniques he had learned in the leather company to revive Radio Shack. He reduced inventories through an aggressive marketing campaign, concentrating on items with fast turnover and broad consumer appeal. He reduced sharply the number of stockkeeping units. He insisted that buyers and salespeople work together to develop new ideas for exclusive yet competitive products. Above all he insisted on higher gross margins.

Two years after Tandy took over the company, Radio Shack had turned a $4-million loss into a profit, had sales approaching $20 million, and operated

In 1986 the company began an $80-million remodeling of its retail outlets to emphasize Radio Shack as "The Technology Store."

more than 300 Radio Shack stores from coast to coast.

By the 1970s the company had become a mini-conglomerate with department stores, an import business, a women's apparel store, nurseries, and a tile company. In 1974 Charles Tandy and the board of directors decided to divest everything but the consumer electronics part of the business. The spin-offs became known as the "Tandy babies" and include some major retailers in their own right: Tandy Brands Inc., Tandycrafts Inc., Pier 1 Imports Inc., Wolfe Nursery, and Color Tile. A more recent spin-off, InterTan Inc., handles Tandy's foreign operations.

Today Tandy employs more than 7,200 people in the Fort Worth/Dallas area. Tandy's downtown headquarters, the twin-tower Tandy Center with its connecting shopping mall and ice skating rink, has become a landmark with its name spelled in lights on the sides of the towers. The lights are reconfigured several times a year to promote special events.

Although the company is primarily a retailer, Tandy is involved in the design and quality control of everything it

ABOVE: Tandy's headquarters, the landmark twin-tower Tandy Center, which features a connecting shopping mall and ice skating rink, lights up downtown Fort Worth.

RIGHT: The company operates more than 30 manufacturing plants worldwide.

sells. The company operates more than 30 manufacturing plants worldwide and has research and product development at seven locations in four countries.

As a result of its manufacturing capabilities, Tandy products sold in Radio Shack outlets depend very little on outside vendors except for components. That ability to build its own circuit boards and power supplies and to control its distribution channel allows Tandy/Radio Shack to keep costs down and maintain its quality control.

Tandy owns Memtek Products, manufacturers of Memorex magnetic audiotapes and videotapes; Lika Corp., manufacturer of printed circuit boards; and O'Sullivan Industries, maker of electronic racks and cabinets. The three operations make up Tandy Marketing Cos., one of two major operating groups in addition to Radio Shack.

The other operating unit is the Tandy Name Brand Retail Group, comprised of McDuff Electronics, Scott Appliances, and VideoConcepts. Tandy acquired these retailers in the mid-1980s to expand its distribution channels for consumer electronics. Tandy also owns GRiD Systems Corp., a maker of lap-top computers for *Fortune* 1,000 companies and federal government accounts.

Victor Technologies, acquired in fiscal 1990, provides Tandy with an established European distribution channel, with sales subsidiaries in 11 countries serving approximately 2,700 dealers and distributors.

As the company looks to the future, chairman John V. Roach envisions a friendly, functional computer in every home, school desk, and office; a cellular telephone in every pocket or purse for convenience and security; and a Tandy THOR-CD—the company's new recordable, erasable compact disc technology—for quality audio recordings, high-capacity information storage, and possibly new video applications.

"We believe our technology base is unique for an American-owned consumer electronics company," Roach says.

Maintaining Radio Shack's position as the premier consumer electronics retailer is the centerpiece of Tandy's plans to expand Radio Shack internally through remodeling and other productivity enhancing programs and externally through expanding channels of distribution and acquisitions.

In 1986 Radio Shack began a five-year, $80-million remodeling of its retail stores around the theme of "The Technology Store." The renovation features a modern decor that resulted in increased sales.

Although Radio Shack's roots are in consumer electronics, Tandy also aggressively pursues the business customer. A separate business products division works with businesses through the company's Radio Shack Computer Centers.

Radio Shack has national procurement agreements with more than half of the *Fortune* 750 companies, in addition to contracts with many government agencies. In the education market, Radio Shack has contractual agreements with states, municipalities, and school systems across the nation.

To promote education Tandy Corp. in 1988 began the Tandy Technology Scholars, a recognition and awards program for academic excellence in public and private high schools with emphasis on math, science, and computer science.

Hyatt Regency Fort Worth

Fort Worth's past and present come together in the Hyatt Regency Fort Worth, a hotel that is both a historic landmark and a luxurious, contemporary creation in the tradition of Hyatt hotels worldwide.

Located on Main Street one block north of the Tarrant County Convention Center, the 520-room hotel is the oldest and largest in Fort Worth—oldest in the sense that the structure was born within the walls of the 1921 vintage Hotel Texas, although much of the hotel has been renovated or added to in the past 20 years.

The Hotel Texas was one of the most famous buildings in Fort Worth history. It was the dream of Winfield Scott, an influential Fort Worth cattleman, banker, and builder who believed a first-class hotel for the city would be his crowning achievement. But Scott's death in 1911 and the discovery of oil 80 miles to the west in the town of Ranger in 1917 delayed action on the hotel.

After the oil discovery Fort Worth became a center for oil operators and transactions. Oil-rich ranchers moved to the city and lived in luxury. Fort Worth's payrolls, population, and affluence grew. Wealth and the steadily increasing number of residents, both permanent and temporary, called for new and more elegant hotels.

In 1919 a group of prominent city leaders gathered to consider building a first-class hotel for the city. They formed the Citizens Hotel Co., raised $1.2 million, and began to solicit outside investors. Soon nearly 800 Fort Worth citizens contributed an additional $1.8 million to the venture, and in January 1920 construction began on the new hotel.

At first the hotel was to be named The Winfield in Winfield Scott's honor. However, as the hotel's opening approached, its builders decided the structure should be known as the Hotel Texas to reflect the city's pride in its Texas heritage. After opening in September 1921, the hotel became known as the "Home of the Cattle Barons."

The original 15-story building was constructed of red brick and featured arched windows and terra cotta ornamentation at the street level and at the crest. The structure incorporated several architectural influences, including Chicago, Georgian, and Renaissance styles. The result was a classical, stately building with a Texas twist.

The hotel quickly became the hub of the city's social, cultural, and business life. Many decisions and plans shaping the city's future were made at the hotel. For example, in 1925 the fund-raising drive to establish the Fort Worth Symphony Orchestra was initiated at a luncheon in the Hotel Texas' Crystal Ballroom.

In 1936 Texas marked its 100-year anniversary of independence from Mexico with a statewide celebration. Fort Worth hired the well-known Broadway promoter Billy Rose to come to the city and stage the Fort Worth Frontier Centennial, an entertainment extravaganza that would attract thousands of visitors. Rose set up his command center in the hotel's Crystal Ballroom, where he auditioned local beauties. He overlooked one woman who had come from nearby Weatherford to audition—Mary Martin, who later became famous for her role of Peter Pan and as mother of Larry Hagman, who plays villainous oil tycoon

The Hyatt Regency Fort Worth, the city's largest hotel and a historic landmark, captures the spirit of Texas' past and future.

The Crystal Cactus restaurant and lounge offers the finest in Southwestern cuisine and is really alive at happy hour.

J.R. Ewing on the television show "Dallas."

Many other famous people stayed at the Hotel Texas during its history, but perhaps the best-known guest was the late President John F. Kennedy. Kennedy spent his last night at the hotel before his fateful trip to Dallas the next day, where he was assassinated. The hotel's Will Rogers Suite had been specially decorated for the president's visit, but secret service officers chose a smaller room for Kennedy because they could better protect him in the more compact room with only one door.

By the late 1970s the grand old hotel had seen much of Fort Worth's history and had gone through several different operators and renovations. It needed a total restoration to continue serving guests in the hotel's traditional grand style.

When the building was offered for sale in 1978, Woodbine Development Corp., a Dallas-based real estate development company that built the Continental Plaza office building in downtown Fort Worth, joined forces with Hyatt Hotels Corp. to create the Hyatt Regency Fort Worth. With the help of JPJ Architects Inc. and interior designers Singer-Christianson & Co., the companies completely renovated the interior and altered the exterior. While the Hotel Texas originally had more than 800 rooms, the new hotel was redesigned to have an additional 520 spacious rooms.

In 1979 the building was named to the National Register of Historic Places, ensuring protection for its familiar facade. The arch, the hotel's most important architectural feature, also became the theme inside the hotel, linking the building's historic exterior and contemporary interior.

While the building's exterior was changed, painstaking reproductions of the terra cotta ornamentation was made with molds of the original designs. The terra cotta design features steer heads as a reminder of Fort Worth's debt to the cattle industry.

Mechanical equipment on top of the building was hidden with a 20-foot-high wall dotted with bright lights, adding to the city's nighttime skyline.

A second building, the east tower, was built immediately east of the historic structure. The tower and main structure are linked with a skybridge across Commerce Street. The east tower houses the swimming pool, sun deck, health club, an American Airlines and Avis car rental office, and a beauty salon. The total cost of the new Hyatt Regency Fort Worth was $32 million.

With the renovations, guests now can enjoy the charm of the old hotel and the conveniences and modern style expected from a Hyatt. Hotel guests arriving by car now pass through gate-

The living room of the hotel's Presidential Suite is the epitome of elegance. It has been judged the best hotel suite in North America.

way columns onto red-brick pavement and stop under two huge barrel-vaulted canopies of brilliant copper. The red brick motif continues into the hotel foyer and ends at the steps leading upward into an elevated lobby.

A 350-car parking garage located under a landscaped plaza linking the hotel with the convention center provides plenty of space for guests and the general public. Guests entering the first floor see an expansive space furnished in colors found outdoors—the deep red of the building and pavement, forest green, teal blue, brown, and gray. The colors are complemented by natural materials such as granite and marble to continue the sense of history.

A major feature throughout the public spaces is the extensive use of Texas granite. More than 739 custom-cut granite pieces form the sculptured walls, flooring, steps, and displays within the hotel.

Public spaces in the hotel have been given names of persons, places, or events relating to the history of Fort Worth or the Hotel Texas. Plaques explaining the significance of the names are located in or near each space.

A 26-foot waterfall beginning in the atrium lobby above gently flows down to a series of reflecting pools in the center of the lobby. The sedate colors and textures within the public spaces are accented with polished brass trim and softly twinkling tivoli lighting.

The hotel features two restaurants and an atrium cocktail bar; the Café Centennial, an informal restaurant in the hotel's lobby; the Crystal Cactus, a fine gourmet restaurant and cocktail lounge featuring glass panels etched with contemporary cactus designs; and the Skylight Court cocktail bar, located under the waterfall and a six-story sloping skylight. Also located on the first floor is W.H. Smith, a gift and sundry shop.

Art also is displayed prominently in the hotel. Rising 24 feet from the atrium is John Reistetter's geode sculpture, with a star-burst shape and extensive use of brass, bronze, geode-formed amethyst, and gem-quality crystals. Each guest room features original lithograph prints by California artists Karla Davison and Marcus Uzilevsky.

Convention attendees, business travelers, and tourists are the three major types of guests served by the hotel. Since the building is across the street from the convention center, the hotel is a natural place for meetings, large receptions, and other events. The hotel also is located near many downtown tourist attractions, such as the Water Gardens, historic Main Street, and Sundance Square.

To accommodate conventions, conferences, and meetings, the hotel has two ballrooms, a pavilion exhibit hall, and more than 20 meeting and banquet rooms totaling 62,500 square feet.

On the mezzanine is the Grand Crystal Ballroom, the largest ballroom in the city, with 14,000 square feet. The ballroom is decorated in varying shades of burgundy and features a ceiling completely covered by chandeliers. The ballroom can be divided into as many as four separate rooms by soundproof partitions. Thus, it can accommodate gatherings of 1,500 guests or intimate parties of 12 people. On the hotel's third floor is the smaller Texas Ballroom, with a capacity of 320, and a series of conference rooms.

The Hyatt Regency Fort Worth's most prestigious accommodations are located on the 15th floor. Each suite has its own distinctive decor. The grandest is the Presidential Suite, which has housed many celebrities and VIPs. The suite offers the ultimate in luxury and features 18-foot ceilings, four bedrooms, six bathrooms, a living room, dining room, wet bar, and Jacuzzi.

Designers Singer-Christianson set out to design a suite with Texas flavor but tempered in tone, combining rustic Texas elements with sophisticated, contemporary furnishings. In 1983 the suite was judged Best Suite in a prestigious lodging design competition that drew 160 entries representing 80 hotels in North America.

The Presidential Suite's intimate dining room is perfect for private receptions.

Photo by Bob Rowan/Progressive
Image Photography
PUBLIC MARKET

CHAPTER TWELVE

QUALITY OF LIFE

Medical, educational, and service institutions contribute to the quality of life of Fort Worth area residents.

Photo by Bob Rowan/Progressive Image Photography

City of Fort Worth

Fort Worth's melding of past and present, of western heritage with modern urban life, is one of the attractions that keeps people coming to—and staying in—the city. Much of the responsibility for maintaining that balance lies with the City of Fort Worth.

With an annual operating budget of more than $325 million, the city is a major enterprise in its own right. More than 5,000 city employees work behind the scenes providing basic services as well as recreational and cultural facilities and programs that enrich the lives of Fort Worth's 452,000 residents.

A nine-member city council, elected by single-member districts (except the office of mayor), acts as the board of directors of the city organization. The city manager is its chief executive officer, overseeing day-to-day operations.

The largest chunk of the city budget, 41 percent, is spent on public safety.

Although Fort Worth's overall crime rate has decreased in recent years, fighting drugs is a top police-department priority as the production and sale of drugs is linked to other crimes. Fort Worth municipal services are a key element in the quality of life, which residents rank as important. Just as the city offers a wide array of services, it has a wide range of revenue sources, from the traditional property tax to user fees and, one of Fort Worth's strongest sources, private/public partnerships.

Recent national press coverage credited Fort Worth's network of parks, museums, and other amenities. The city maintains 171 parks with more than 9,000 acres, second only to Chicago in total acreage. The city also operates 10 libraries with 1.6 million volumes, five

Downtown Fort Worth

municipal golf courses, and 25 recreation and multipurpose centers and is in the process of expanding the Fort Worth Zoo and the central library. The city places a high priority on preserving Fort Worth's western flavor land heritage and has worked with the private sector to restore historic buildings, particularly in the downtown area. Since 1988 the city has operated the Cowtown Coliseum, a focal point for rodeos and other western entertainment located in the historic stockyards area. Two years ago the city also opened the Will Rogers Equestrian Center, one of the largest and most modern livestock facilities in the world. The 12-acre complex has become host of many national and international equestrian events.

Because its central location in the United States attracts many businesses to relocate or expand in Fort Worth,

LEFT: Fort Worth's Village Creek Wastewater Treatment Plant earned the EPA's National Operations and Maintenance Excellence Award in 1988. The award recognized the plant as the best-operated in the country. Village Creek treats 120 million gallons of wastewater per day with expansion plans which will allow a 144-million-gallon treatment capacity per day by 1992.

BELOW: The City of Fort Worth's Cowtown Coliseum, located in the Stockyards, was built in 1908 for the National Feeders' and Breeders' Show, now known as the Southwestern Exposition and Fat Stock Show. In 1918 the world's first indoor rodeo was held in the coliseum, and today the city still sponsors weekly rodeos in the coliseum with an average attendance of 2,100 spectators.

access to airports is critical. The city operates three airports, including Spinks Airport in south Fort Worth and Fort Worth Alliance Airport in far north Fort Worth; Alliance is a unique industrial airport specifically designed to serve the needs of businesses. A city economic development office now works to bring industry not only to the airports but to all the city of Fort Worth.

Saint Joseph Hospital

Saint Joseph Hospital stands out as Fort Worth's first health care provider. The hospital has tended to the medical needs of local residents since the 1880s, when Fort Worth was a rowdy cattle and railroad town.

In 1885 the closest thing Fort Worth had to a hospital was the small wooden infirmary south of town operated by the Missouri-Pacific railroad company. But the city was growing and so was the demand for better medical care. So the Sisters of Charity of the Incarnate Word, a Catholic order based in San Antonio, was asked to take charge of the infirmary.

Eleven Sisters made the long wagon journey from San Antonio to Fort Worth in 1885. Later that year a fire destroyed the infirmary, but not before the Sisters had carried out and rescued all the patients. The women resumed their duties in a temporary building and purchased a 15-acre tract of land on top of a hill with dreams of building a new infirmary.

In 1889 the Sisters moved into a new 60-bed facility. Christened Saint

Saint Joseph Hospital's Surgical Services project (foreground) was completed in 1988 and gave the hospital a new look.

Saint Joseph Infirmary's 60-bed facility, shown here as it was in 1904, was the city's first hospital.

Joseph's Infirmary, it was the city's first hospital.

More than 100 years later Saint Joseph Hospital now has a capacity of 475 beds, but its mission is still the same as it was when the Sisters founded the hospital—to provide quality health care and preserve human dignity.

The Sisters of Charity still sponsor Saint Joseph Hospital, one of 10 members of the Incarnate Word Health Services system based in San Antonio. Affiliate organizations include a foundation, a pharmacy, a diagnostic joint venture, and a for-profit preferred-

provider organization.

Reflecting the changing times, the Sisters of Charity have donned new, modified versions of the floor-length habits they wore in the 1800s. They remain the backbone of the hospital, working in various departments. The department of patient representatives, which promotes patient welfare and good relationships with patients, families, and hospital personnel, was created in the 1970s especially for the Sisters to administer.

Saint Joseph Hospital's areas of excellence include cardiovascular services, orthopedics, ophthalmology, rehabilitation, substance abuse services, weight management, a community hospice, physician referral services, and adult psychiatry.

In 1987 Saint Joseph opened a cardiac catheterization laboratory as one of the first steps toward providing complete cardiovascular services. The lab is equipped to perform diagnostic procedures such as angioplasty, in which a catheter is inserted through a vein into a blocked artery and a balloon is inflated, opening up the artery to allow more blood flow to the heart. Coronary surgery was implemented in 1987, and now surgical teams can prepare for emergency coronary surgery in 15 minutes if necessary. A specially equipped, 600-square-foot surgical suite is used mainly for heart patients.

The Saint Joseph Hospital Guild, with more than 150 members, works year-round raising funds for the hospital, operating a gift shop, and donating their time as volunteers. The guild has contributed more than one million dollars to Saint Joseph Hospital.

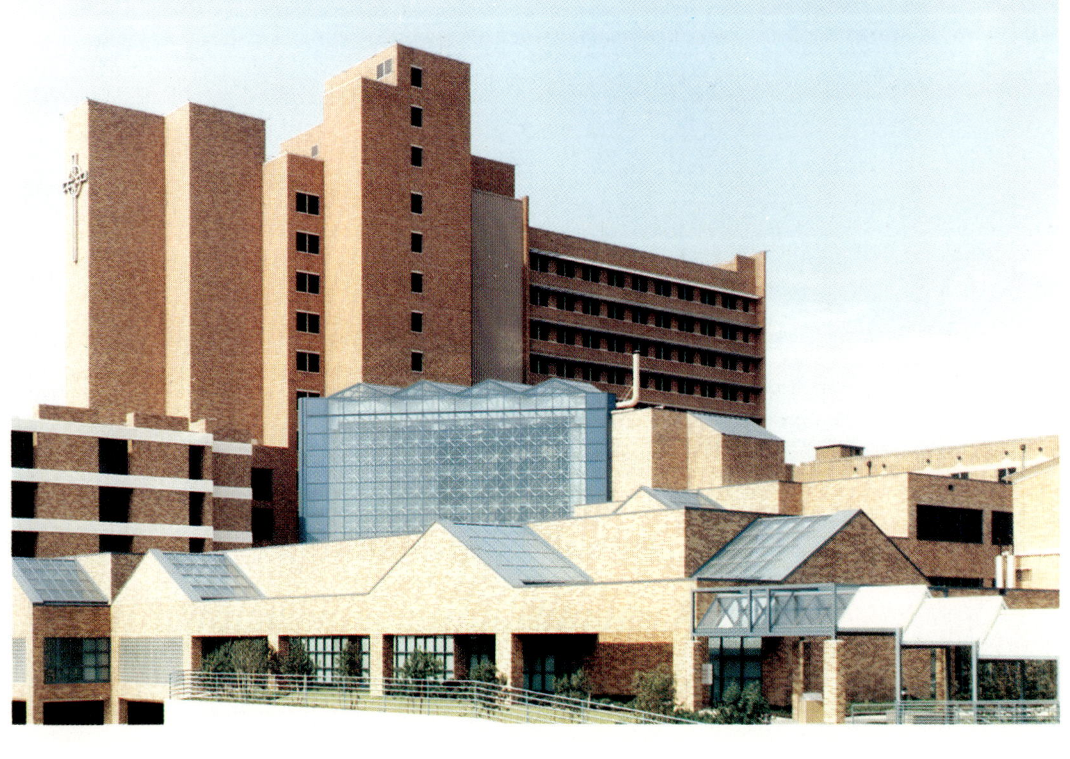

Harris Methodist Fort Worth

In the past 70 years Harris Methodist Fort Worth rose from the vision of prominent physician Dr. Charles Houston Harris to become the city's largest hospital and the centerpiece of the area's major health care organization.

Dr. Harris first proposed the idea of a new hospital to a group of Methodist leaders in 1919. In 1930 the new facility, initially called Methodist Hospital, formally opened.

The hospital grew rapidly, but charitable medical facilities suffered financially during the Depression. In 1937 the hospital could not meet payments and interest on a $25,000 loan, and the hospital was sold to the bondholder.

One month later hospital trustees purchased the facility for $253,000, made possible by a $53,000 gift from Dr. Harris and his personal guarantee on the $200,000 balance. That same year, the hospital merged with Dr. Harris' clinic and was renamed Harris Memorial Methodist Hospital in honor of the doctor's father.

After weathering those early turbulent years, Harris Methodist Fort first kidney transplant in the county and achieved the first in-vitro fertilization pregnancy and birth in 1986.

During the baby boom years the hospital's birth rate hit a record 452 babies born in the month of August 1956. Harris Methodist Fort Worth still provides one of the largest obstetrical services in the county, delivering about 5,000 babies each year.

CareFlite, the helicopter ambulance service based at Harris Methodist Fort Worth took flight in 1979. The helicopters provide residents within a 150-mile radius of Fort Worth immediate access to Harris' emergency medicine and trauma services. The helicopter also serves other major medical facilities in the service area.

Today Harris Methodist Fort Worth is part of the Harris Methodist Health System, a health care organization that operates eight other hospitals, including Harris Methodist H-E-B, Harris Methodist Northwest, and Harris Methodist Southwest. The system also operates a health maintenance organization (HMO) and provides services such as WellCall, a free physician referral and health information line.

In the mid-1970s Harris officials approved a long-range master plan for the hospital that included the Harris Center, a nine-story professional office building completed in 1985. A $4-million gift from the Sid W. Richardson Foundation provided major initial funding for the Sid W. Richardson Pavilion, a 114-bed facility with features such as new surgery suites, an expanded rehabilitation unit, private rooms, a concierge to assist families and patients with a variety of needs, and an open-space interior design utilizing light, greenery, and flowing water. The Mabee Physical Medicine and Rehabilitation Center and the Harris Fitness Center also are located in the pavilion.

Harris Methodist Fort Worth was founded in 1930 (BELOW), and today it is the city's largest hospital (ABOVE).

Worth gradually expanded and built a reputation in specialties including heart care, emergency medicine, orthopedics, rehabilitation, cancer care, and women's services. The 628-bed hospital located just south of downtown Fort Worth is recognized as the heart center of Tarrant County.

In 1959 Harris Methodist Fort Worth became the first hospital in the county to perform open-heart surgery. The hospital also performed the

Southwestern Exposition and Livestock Show

In 1896 a group of Texas ranchers joined forces with the operators of the Fort Worth Stock Yards and officials of railway and meat-packing companies to hold the city's first livestock show. Almost a century later, that one-day event with cattle tethered under shady trees has grown into the 17-day Southwestern Exposition and Livestock Show, one of the country's largest livestock and rodeo extravaganzas and the oldest continuously held annual livestock show.

The exposition at the Will Rogers Memorial Center is the city's most-attended annual event, drawing an average 800,000 visitors that come from every state and 45 foreign countries. In addition to contributing more than $100 million in economic benefits, the Stock Show also preserves Fort Worth's western heritage.

Judges make their selections from more than 18,000 head of livestock in divisions for horses, donkeys, mules, beef and dairy cattle, sheep, swine, dairy goats, poultry, pigeons, rabbits, sheepdogs, and llamas—a category

---

RIGHT: More than 7,000 FFA and 4-H Club members from across Texas participate annually in the Stock Show's junior division.

BELOW: Bronc riding is one of the Fort Worth Rodeo's most exciting and popular events.

added in recent years due to its growing popularity. Judges awarded more than $600,000 to winners in livestock show and rodeo events in recent years.

The exposition features a competitive Junior Division for youngsters, educational exhibits, and special national shows for Hereford, Polled Hereford, Chiangus/Chianina, Red Angus, and Shorthorn breeds. Livestock auctions offer quality cattle and horses as well as a sale for prize-winning animals from the junior division.

One of the biggest attractions is the indoor rodeo. In 1908 the North Side Coliseum, now called the Cowtown Coliseum, was erected as the show's

headquarters. When the show decided to begin staging competitive cowboy events in 1918, the coliseum was the only arena large enough to hold them.

The initial Fort Worth Rodeo featured men and women contestants vying for a purse of $3,000. Contests included bucking bronco, steer riding, and a wild-horse race. In 1920 the rodeo introduced Brahma bull riding, one of the most popular events today.

The first live radio broadcast of a rodeo took place at the Fort Worth show in 1923, and ABC-TV broadcast the rodeo's first live national television coverage in 1958.

Stock Show organizers say entertainment is the key to the rodeo's success. To enhance the quality of the rodeo production in the 28 performances scheduled during the show's run, the rough stock, calves, and steers used in Fort Worth are provided by a syndicate of the nation's top rodeo contracting firms.

The Stock Show remained on the north side until 1942. After a one-year hiatus during World War II, the show opened in 1944 at the Will Rogers Memorial Center. At first the center included the Will Rogers Coliseum, Tower, and Auditorium, and one horse-exhibit barn.

Over the years the Stock Show paid for more than $5.2 million in improvements, helping to add 10 all-weather livestock barns, three multipurpose commercial exhibit areas, dormitory accommodations for almost 400 exhibitors, and the Round Up Inn cafeteria.

In addition to a continuous campaign by the nonprofit organization to provide improvements to the Will Rogers Memorial Center, the Stock Show is an avid supporter of programs relating to education. The show awards annual scholarships and has made significant contributions and endowments to the Ranch Management Program at Texas Christian University in Fort Worth.

Stock Show officials also helped raise private-sector funds for construction of the world-class equestrian center at the Will Rogers Memorial complex. The center is used during the Stock Show's run and for other equine and livestock-related events the rest of the year.

Cook-Fort Worth Children's Medical Center

What child would not be enchanted by a magical kingdom of towers and spires under a rippling skylight sky? That is the sight greeting young patients at Cook-Fort Worth Children's Medical Center.

Opened in May 1989, the new $53-million, six-story facility was designed especially for children, with a pleasing, nonthreatening atmosphere. The most striking architectural feature is the central atrium space. It resembles what one might see in a castle courtyard—windows, balconies, piers, columns, and pediments rising to towers in each corner.

Patient rooms look like they belong in a hotel or home, with calming pastels, accommodations for parents who want to stay overnight with their child, and private bathrooms. Even the necessary medical gases in patients' rooms are covered with panels so they will not frighten children.

Behind the friendly appeal, though, is the serious business of caring for children, many of them critically ill. The medical center is a tertiary referral hospital with a full complement of pediatricians, family practitioners, and pediatric subspecialists, since very ill children often require the collaboration of several specialists. The hospital is especially well known for its expertise in anesthesiology, pulmonology, emergency medicine, blood and cancer diseases, pediatric intensive care, and complications of premature birth.

The center's hematology/oncology department has performed more than three-dozen bone marrow transplants since its transplant program began in 1986. In 1988 Cook-Fort Worth Children's was the first medical center in the state to open a bone marrow purging lab. The lab, which rids the patient's bone marrow of dangerous cancer cells, is one of only three in the United States.

Another unique feature is "Teddy Bear Air," a fixed-wing aircraft intensive care unit that transports critically ill and injured infants and children to the medical center 24 hours a day, within 45 minutes of receiving a call.

Although the building is new, the story behind Cook-Fort Worth Children's Medical Center dates back to 1918, when Ida Turner, concerned

ABOVE: Opened in May 1989, the six-story Cook-Fort Worth Children's Medical Center was not designed to look or feel like a typical hospital. It has a beautiful and comfortable atmosphere to put young patients at ease.

LEFT: The hospital takes its care of the children very seriously. It offers a full complement of pediatricians, family practitioners, and pediatric subspecialists.

about the lack of pediatric hospitals in the area, established the Fort Worth Free Baby Hospital. Through her efforts and the Fort Worth Federation of Woman's Clubs, land was donated, labor unions supplied skilled labor, and lumberyards, concrete dealers, and merchants contributed materials and furnishings. The hospital later moved to a new building in 1961 under the name of Fort Worth Children's Hospital. Meanwhile, when oil was discovered on her family's ranch, Mrs. W.I. Cook, the widow of a Texas rancher, set up a trust for a hospital in memory of her husband and only daughter. Originally the facility was both a 30-bed private hospital and a doctor's clinic. The hospital was converted to a specialized pediatric facility for crippled children in 1952 and was later renamed Cook Children's Hospital.

Community leaders long wanted to combine the two children's hospitals, an idea that won approval in 1985. A board of trustees was formed and set about planning the new medical center facilities.

Throughout its history, the philosophy of Cook-Fort Worth Children's has been to treat the whole child, physically and emotionally, regardless of the parents' ability to pay. As a result, the medical center provides more than $15 million in uncompensated care to patients in north-central and western Texas each year.

Part of the cost of caring for indigent children is provided by the annual Jewel Charity Ball, which has raised more than $7 million to provide quality medical care for children who otherwise could not afford it.

Texas and Southwestern Cattle Raisers Association

A life-size bronze statue of a rider on horseback, a clump of prickly pear cactus, and a longhorn steer all loom in front of the Texas and Southwestern Cattle Raisers Association headquarters on West Seventh Street, often causing cars to slow and fingers to point. *The Brand Inspector,* by sculptor Jim Reno, is a city landmark and tourist attraction, but it is also an apt tribute to the people and organization that have helped the Texas cattle industry flourish for more than a century.

The Cattle Raisers Association was founded in 1877 to fight cattle theft in the region with an aggressive branding and inspection program. And although cattle theft still is a major source of loss to cattle raisers, the association's role has expanded in size and clout.

With 14,000 members in Texas, Oklahoma, and other surrounding states, the association has emerged as an advocate for the region's cattle industry on legislation, animal health issues, regulatory matters, and other subjects affecting cattle raisers. For more than 75 years the association also has published *The Cattleman,* a respected and widely quoted livestock trade magazine.

The Texas and Southwestern Cattle Raisers Foundation, a nonprofit organization created in 1979 by descendants of pioneer ranchers, also strives to edu-

The Brand Inspector is a life-size bronze sculpture by Jim Reno that stands in front of the Texas and Southwestern Cattle Raisers Association headquarters.

cate the public about the industry. The Cattleman's Museum and Memorial Hall was established on the first floor of the foundation's building at 1301 West Seventh Street. The museum, open free to the public from 8:30 a.m. to 4:30 p.m., Monday through Friday, traces the history of Texas' colorful cattle industry with artifacts, photographs, and special displays.

The foundation also supports the Waggoner Library, a collection of rare and general interest books about cattle-related subjects, and it provides seminars for ranchers, tours of livestock operations for young people and the news media, and research grants and scholarships for outstanding students.

But inspection remains the backbone of the Cattle Raisers Association, which first hired six brand inspectors in 1883. Cattle theft was rampant as the price of beef increased, and inspectors were deputized by sheriffs and, in 1893, even made special Texas Rangers. The range detectives carried Colt .45 "Peacemakers" to defend cattlemen's property rights.

Today the association has a staff of 32 field inspectors stationed in multiple-county districts throughout Texas and Oklahoma. The inspectors, all

certified peace officers, are commissioned as special rangers by the Texas Department of Public Safety and the Oklahoma State Bureau of Investigation. Their main responsibility is investigating livestock thefts and other ranch losses, but they also serve as members' agents in claiming and determining ownership of stray cattle, and they will inspect cattle shipments at individual ranches on request.

Texas field inspectors supervise more than 80 brand inspectors who examine millions of heads of cattle at Texas' 160 auction markets and terminals. Brands and descriptive information about animals is recorded on a computerized form that is sent to headquarters, microfilmed, and entered into the association's main computer. The Texas and Southwestern Cattle Raisers Association also publishes a missing and stolen livestock bulletin twice a month and maintains a complete file of more than 100,000 recorded brands in Texas.

In 1989 field inspectors worked closely with other law-enforcement officers to explore 103 theft cases. Their investigations recovered or accounted for more than 3,800 heads of cattle, 614 horses, 216 saddles, 23 trailers, and other ranch-related property valued at nearly $3.6 million.

Schoolchildren enjoy the Cattleman's Museum's entrance diorama.

Brown Gause-Ware, Owens & Brumley

Brown Gause-Ware, Owens & Brumley is the city's oldest provider of funeral services and one of the few remaining family-owned firms in the business. The firm stresses personalized service, catering to family wishes and needs before and after the funeral.

Joe Brown, the firm's owner, and his son operate the business, which is now more than 100 years old. The original firm, Gause-Ware Funeral Home, started in 1879. It was one of the state's first funeral businesses to form its own insurance company and sell pre-need funeral contracts—contracts made while people are still living so they can choose the kind of funeral they want and pay for it in advance. Meanwhile, the Owens & Brumley Funeral Home began operating in 1923. The third business that merged to form the current firm was Meissner-Brown Funeral Home, founded in 1936.

In 1979 the Gause-Ware building burned to the ground. The Ware family bought Owens & Brumley and combined the two businesses. After the last member of the family retired, Joe Brown, owner of Meissner-Brown, bought Gause-Ware, Owens & Brumley and, in 1988, merged the firms to form the current business.

Brown Gause-Ware, Owens & Brumley is located in the stone building on South Henderson Street, south of

downtown, where Owens & Brumley set up shop in 1923. The four-story building has one of the city's largest chapels and has tastefully decorated interiors. The firm has three other locations, two in Fort Worth and one in Grand Prairie.

Brown and his son are the only remaining family members operating the business, bucking a trend of large, national chains of funeral homes, cemeteries, and flower shops.

"We feel there's room for a personalized, family-run funeral business because death is such a personal thing," Brown says.

In addition to providing caskets, vaults, cremation, and embalming services, Brown Gause-Ware, Owens & Brumley also offers family assistance programs as a standard part of its

services. The firm has engaged a local retired clergyman as its family assistance director to provide in-home counseling to family members after a funeral.

The firm provides families with literature advising them on everything from Social Security benefits to how to collect insurance to how to avoid being victimized by con artists who prey on survivors. The company also sponsors grief seminars and will go to families' homes to show films on how to cope after a loved one has died.

Brown Gause-Ware, Owens & Brumley's lawyer donates one hour of free consultation to advise family members on legal matters. The law firm does

Brown Gause-Ware, Owens & Brumley prides itself on its intimate, personalized services.

charge to probate a will or perform additional legal services.

The funeral home offers a special program for law-enforcement employees and fire fighters in Tarrant County. If an officer or fire fighter is killed in the line of duty, the firm will furnish the casket and vault, flowers, and pay for service charges. Brown Gause-Ware, Owens & Brumley also offers law-enforcement officers, fire fighters, and their families a discounted pre-need program.

In addition to funeral services, Brown Gause-Ware, Owens & Brumley also offers a variety of pre-need packages and burial insurance. The firm is licensed by the state and is a member of the National Funeral Director's Association and the Texas Funeral Director's Association.

All Saints Health Care Inc.

When All Saints Health Care Inc. began providing medical care in Fort Worth more than 80 years ago, its first administrator was a nurse, and the hospital was staffed primarily with nursing students. Today All Saints is a diversified health care corporation with four subsidiaries: a hospital corporation that operates a 533-bed facility south of downtown on its main campus and a new 72-bed facility in southwest Fort Worth; a not-for-profit public foundation that acts as the giving link to the entire All Saints family; the Bishop Davies Center Inc. nursing home; and a for-profit subsidiary that holds joint ventures, real estate, and ancillary lines of business.

Fifteen women from Trinity Episcopal Church founded All Saints in 1900, believing the growing city needed more medical facilities. The hospital building was completed and dedicated on All Saints Day, November 1, 1906.

Since then All Saints has expanded and upgraded its facilities and services to become the city's second-largest health care provider. Although the hospital focuses on Tarrant County and surrounding counties, it receives referrals from all over the Southwest

Dr. Robert Murchison (left) and Dr. Charles Langham III are among the pioneers in All Saints laser technology.

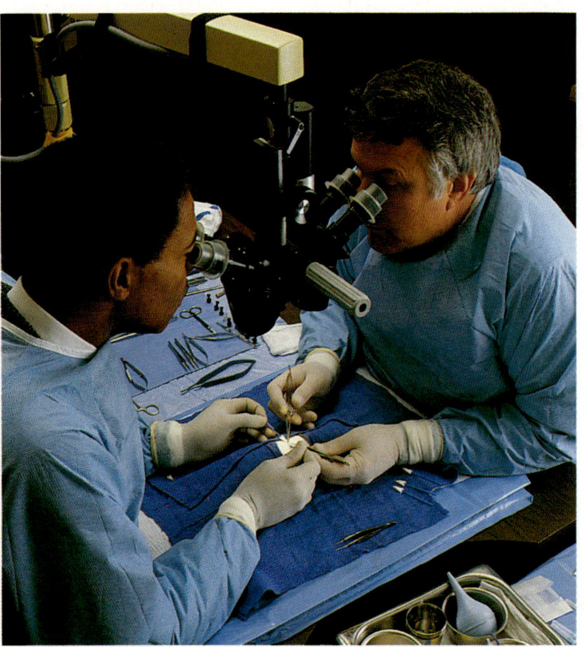

for specific procedures such as laser microsurgery.

"The area in which we enjoy the widest reputation for clinical excellence is laser microsurgery," says James P. Schuessler, president of All Saints Health Care. Other areas of excellence Schuessler mentions are women's services on both of its hospital campuses and outpatient procedures through its Moncrief Ambulatory Care Center.

All Saints was the first health care organization in Fort Worth to purchase a YAG laser. Laser technology is used in procedures in gynecology, urology, plastic surgery, podiatry, ophthalmology, otolaryngology, oral surgery, gastroenterology, neurosurgery, orthopedic surgery, hand surgery, and pulmonary, cardiovascular, and thoracic surgery.

One innovative adaptation of laser technology at All Saints is laser welding, which makes possible the fusion of nerves, blood vessels, or other tissue too small to suture or repair with conventional surgical techniques. Dr. Robert J. Murchison, president of the All Saints medical staff, was the first staff member to perform laser welding in urology to reverse vasectomies. Dr.

All Saints-Cityview hospital filled a need for more sophisticated and convenient health care services in this rapidly growing area in southwest Fort Worth.

Murchison currently has a 100 percent success rate with the reversals, compared with a national average of 85 percent.

The 1980s represented a decade of sweeping change at All Saints as the organization added new services and facilities to keep pace with medical technology and patients' changing medical needs and life-styles. The hospital established an accredited school of radiology, one of the nation's few sleep-disorder centers, and gave the lobby of its main campus a face-lift.

The organization's most recent expansion was the opening of a 72-bed, full-service community hospital in the Cityview area in southwest Fort Worth. Located on Oakmont Boulevard just off Hulen, All Saints-Cityview features private rooms, a five-bed emergency center, two medical/surgical units—each containing 28 private rooms—four operating rooms, nine obstetrical beds, and one traditional delivery room. A two-story professional building was built adjacent to the hospital, and a second professional building is planned.

Schuessler says the hospital chose to expand in the Cityview area because of

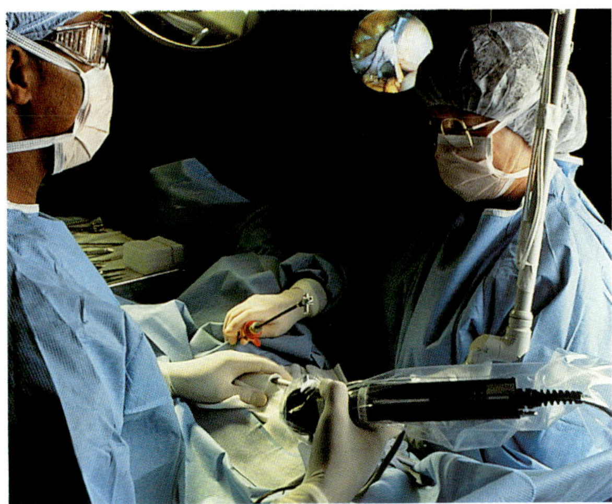

ABOVE: Dr. Charles Langham III's use of a narrated videotape of laser procedures allows patients to better understand their condition as well as the measures that are necessary to correct it.

RIGHT: All Saints' Magnetic Resonance Imaging Center offers the latest advances in diagnostic procedures.

the strong demographics and residential growth in that part of Fort Worth. Many physicians have relocated to Cityview or opened second offices in the area.

All Saints-Cityview allows physicians to consolidate their health care services in one spot. Physicians with offices in the professional building can use hospital services such as laboratories and X rays in the adjacent hospital.

"The facility was designed to be very flexible," Schuessler says. "It's not unusual to have 20 to 25 different physicians with patients there at a given time."

The Cityview facility emphasizes women's services, offering an obstetrical program that Schuessler believes is unique in the city. "It's the only place in Fort Worth that has all the facilities to offer all the choices for a pregnant patient and her family—birthing facilities in addition to traditional labor and delivery suites, supplemented by the ability to support the newborn in the room or in a traditional nursery

All Saints Episcopal Hospital's main campus.

facility," he says.

In 1985 the Moncrief Ambulatory Care Center was built to offer outpatient surgery, an option many patients prefer to traditional hospital stays. Ear, nose, and throat surgery, ophthalmic microsurgery, and plastic surgery are procedures regularly performed at the center. The facility also is used for gastrointestinal procedures, bronchoscopies, thoracentese, phlebotomies, chemotherapy and other intravenous therapy, blood transfusions, and some dental surgery.

In the early 1980s All Saints began a wellness program for its employees, called Wellstyle, that eventually expanded into a complete education and

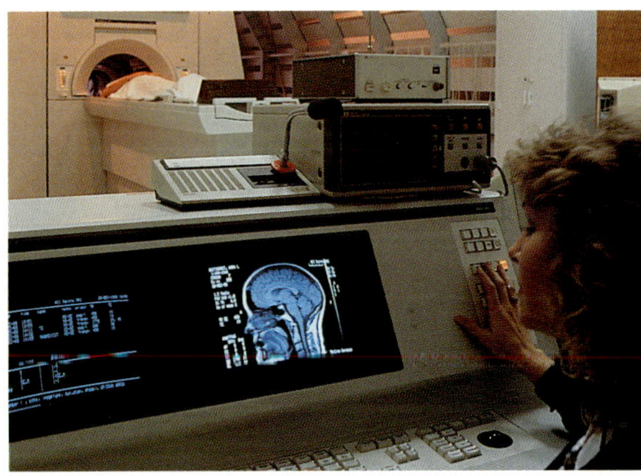

fitness series available to the community. A variety of membership options are available, ranging from a onetime enrollment in a single class to a full membership with unlimited use of All Saints' Carter Rehabilitation and Fitness Center. The center features an indoor track, heated indoor swimming pool, exercise gym, complete electrocardiograph monitoring capabilities, a stress-test laboratory, examination room, education classroom, and locker and shower facilities. The center also offers a Quality of Life program that tailors presentations to companies and other groups on subjects such as stress management and cholesterol screening and control.

One of the latest trends in health care is joint ventures, and All Saints and Huguley Hospital have formed such a partnership with the Ask-a-Nurse education and referral service. People seeking health information or referrals call a number and talk to nurses who can answer their questions.

All Saints Health Care Inc. also is active in a variety of community programs, including the Countdown USA cholesterol-screening program held every spring, the Main Street Arts Festival, and the annual Cowtown Marathon and 10K run.

Moncrief Radiation Center

The Moncrief Radiation Center is the oldest freestanding radiation treatment facility in the Southwest and one of the largest freestanding centers in the nation for the treatment of cancer. Since its founding in 1958, the center has cared for more than 40,000 patients.

Planning for the center began shortly after World War II and spanned a decade. Dr. Thomas B. Bond was the catalyst of the group that originated the idea for the first community radiation center in the Southwest. Many influential Fort Worth citizens—including Amon G. Carter, Gillis A. Johnson, Marvin Leonard, Webb Maddox, and Katrine Deakins—envisioned a special healing environment that would emphasize a positive, caring attitude. Representatives from local hospitals, the American Cancer Society, and the Fort Worth Cancer Society created a local tax-exempt foundation, the Radiation and Medical Research Foundation of the Southwest, to provide support for

The comfortable, home-like furnishings found in the center's treatment rooms help alleviate the cold, clinical environment typical of most health care facilities.

the facility.

The center initially began operating in 1958 with a 2-million-volt Van de Graff X-ray generator and a Cobalt 60 unit. At that time the building covered approximately 5,000 square feet and could treat 40 patients a day. Originally called the Radiation Center of Fort Worth, the facility was renamed in 1980 after William A. and Elizabeth B. Moncrief in recognition of their generous contributions and support.

Today the 34,000-square-foot facility treats 200 patients a day with the help of advanced technology that has enhanced precise treatment for more patients. The original treatment units have been replaced by six linear accelerators of various energy levels, a Superficial unit, and a newer Cobalt 60. The center also houses three simulators for pretreatment planning, a treatment planning computer system, and two nuclear medicine imaging units. An on-site engineer and physics staff maintain, monitor, and calibrate the highly precise equipment.

To further its ability to provide quality care for patients, the center is undergoing an expansion

The Moncrief Radiation Center has provided treatment to more than 40,000 cancer patients since it opened in 1958.

and renovation that will add 5,600 square feet of lobby, examination rooms, support service area, and office space. The center's renovated lobby will be more spacious and comfortable for patients, their families, and guests.

In addition to the treatment staff of radiation oncologists, radiation therapy technologists, nuclear medicine specialists, and dosimetrists (specialists who calculate radiation dosages), the center provides personnel for counseling and information services. A staff social worker is available to help patients and families with emotional and social concerns by providing counseling, information and referrals on financial resources, transportation, housing, home care services, home equipment, cancer education materials, and support groups.

Nutritional counseling also is provided since cancer patients may be deprived of important nutrients due to their illness. A registered dietician is available to help patients adjust their diets while undergoing radiation treatment. A financial counselor assists patients with insurance and Medicaid matters, in addition to providing a cost estimate of their radiation therapy. The Moncrief Radiation Center continues to provide treatment to all patients regardless of age, race, or ability to pay.

Photo by Brad Crooks

BUSINESS AND FINANCE

Fort Worth's solid financial base has provided a dynamic environment for the economic growth and opportunity of both individuals and businesses in the community.

Photo by Brad Crooks

National Farm Life Insurance Co.

In 1946 William C. "Brigham" Young started a life insurance company in Fort Worth for farmers and other agricultural workers. He set up the office of National Farm Life Insurance Co. in the old bank building on Fort Worth's north side, next to the historical stockyards.

Later, in the early 1950s, the insurance company realized that many people in the traditionally rural agriculture industry were getting out of the agriculture business and moving to towns. So the company broadened its life insurance sales to include all Texas residents in both rural and metropolitan areas. But the word "Farm" is still in the company's name.

National Farm Life has more than $1.1 billion worth of life insurance in force throughout the state and more than 900 statewide representatives. National Farm Life is the largest life insurance company based in Texas that only markets life insurance in Texas.

National Farm Life moved its home office to a larger building atop a hill on the city's east side and uses the latest computer technology to keep track of policyholders and process claims. Company officials continue to stress personal service. And even though the company now markets life insurance products to metropolitan areas, its rural roots remain strong. Many of National

Farm Life's policyholders still live in rural areas.

The image the company wants to portray is one of safety. Young founded the company based on two basic business philosophies: People buy life insurance to transfer risk, not take on new ones, and life insurance companies must be perceived as safe. National Farm Life's structure enhances that image of safety.

The company was chartered a stock life insurance company. Its payment of dividends to shareholders is limited to 10 percent of the original purchase price of the stock, or a maximum of $14,000 a year. All additional earnings must be used to provide for its policyholders in the form of financial safety and payment of policyholder dividends. The company has paid more than $1.2 million in policyholder dividends in 1989.

National Farm Life has more than $75 million in diverse assets, including blue-chip investment grade instruments. The company's investment portfolio consists of bonds and first-lien mortgages

RIGHT: Donald L. Jones, Jr., National Farm Life's president and treasurer, poses with a bronze bust of the late founder William C. "Brigham" Young. Photo by Jack W. Dickerson

BELOW: National Farm Life's home office stands atop a hill on 20 acres of land on the city's east side. Photo by Cary L. Wright

The holiday season is a special time of year for National Farm Life. People in the yuletide spirit gather to enjoy the Eastside Business Association's annual Christmas tree lighting on the National Farm Life hilltop (right), and the company's headquarters is creatively decorated (above). Photo by Jack W. Dickerson

with treasury notes and other short-term instruments to meet short-term obligations.

A.M. Best Co., a respected independent analyst of the insurance industry, gives National Farm Life an "A," or excellent, rating for its overall financial condition.

National Farm Life is managed by president and treasurer Donald L. Jones, Jr., and his management team of J.D. "Chip" Davis, Jr., senior vice president/finance, and Ron Downing, senior vice president/marketing. The company's board is comprised of Dr. Noel R. Bailey, vice president and medical director; William F. Bennett, Ph.D; J. Fred Davis; John E. Hutchison, Ph.D; Donald L. Jones, Jr.; Stephen G. Richards; Bob G. Walker; and William M. Young, son of the founder.

Running the life insurance company has become a family affair for Jones, who has associated with National Farm Life since childhood. His father, Donald L. Jones, Sr., was president from 1946 to 1973.

National Farm Life continues to grow. The company attracted a tremendous influx of new business in 1983, when it introduced a new product portfolio that recognized policyholders were living longer. National Farm Life became one of the first life insurance companies to begin using the 1980 mortality table. Basically, it gave the company a competitive edge needed to offer a new life insurance product and lower the premiums in its life portfolio.

Fort Worth residents and visitors who are not familiar with National Farm Life's operations probably know the company's building well. It stands alone on the highest hill in Tarrant County on Bridge Street just north of Interstate 30. For many east side residents, the building symbolizes the Christmas spirit. When National Farm Life celebrated its open house at the new location in 1968, it held a ribbon-cutting ceremony, draping the building with a red bow and streaming red ribbons, giving it the appearance of a giant gift-wrapped package.

The ribbon became a tradition and the building became a landmark for commuters and travelers along the interstate linking Fort Worth with Dallas. Every year during the holiday season, National Farm Life meticulously drapes six vinyl red ribbons 54 feet long and 4 feet wide over the building and hoists a giant, 350-pound, 22-foot red bow above the front entrance. It gets so windy on the hill that the ribbons have to be weighted with sandbags on the roof and checked daily to make sure they are secured. The tradition has evolved into an even larger celebration. The Eastside Business Association planted a 20-foot-tall Austrian pine on a high point on the company's rolling 20-acre property. The Christmas tree lighting has become an annual event on National Farm Life's grounds.

National Farm Life Insurance Co. also is involved in the Boy Scouts of America, the YMCA, and the Adopt-a-School program. The company is a member in the industry's Texas Life Insurance Association and American Council of Life Insurance.

Woodbine Development Corporation

Woodbine Development Corporation's presence in Fort Worth dates back to 1979, when the real estate company renovated a downtown landmark into one of the city's most luxurious hotels. Having just completed development of the Hyatt Regency Dallas hotel and Reunion Tower, now Dallas' most prominent skyline signature, Woodbine was approached to renovate the 1921-vintage Hotel Texas in downtown Fort Worth. The Hotel Texas was a grand old hotel that had played host to presidents and oil barons. But having gone through several operators and partial renovations, the hotel was in need of a complete restoration.

Woodbine completely renovated the property and restored it to a position of importance in the Fort Worth community. Hyatt Hotels Corporation manages the 530-room luxury hotel across from the Tarrant County Convention Center.

The Hyatt Regency Fort Worth marked the first of several high-profile projects by Woodbine in Fort Worth. Continental National Bank (formerly MBank and now BankOne) was planning to build a bank building on land that it owned one block north of the Hyatt Regency. Bank officials recognized the benefit of building a skywalk to access the bank building with the Hyatt Regency Fort Worth and contacted John Scovell, Woodbine's president.

Thereafter, Woodbine agreed to develop the bank building with Continental National Bank as the lead tenant. In 1982 the 40-story, emerald-glass Continental Plaza office tower was completed by Woodbine, including the skywalk to the hotel. Continental Plaza became the tallest building downtown and reshaped the city's skyline. It remains one of the largest downtown office towers, with such prominent tenants as Burlington Northern Railroad, the Petroleum Club of Fort Worth, National Foundation Life Insurance Co., and BankOne.

Woodbine's relationship with Hyatt Corporation continued in 1987, when, together, the two companies purchased Amfac Corporation's twin hotel towers at the center of Dallas/Fort Worth In-

ABOVE: In 1982 the 40-story emerald-glass Continental Plaza office tower, at the time the tallest building in downtown Fort Worth, was completed by Woodbine.

BELOW: The Continental Plaza office tower (background) is connected by a skywalk to the Hyatt Regency Fort Worth (foreground).

ternational Airport, including a 36-hole championship golf facility. Woodbine renovated the hotel and resort into the Hyatt Regency DFW and Hyatt Bear Creek Golf and Racquet Club. The complex is the world's largest airport hotel, with 1,390 rooms in two towers that straddle the airport's main artery. The accompanying Bear Creek golf resort is recognized by *Golf Digest* as one of the top 25 public courses in the country.

Woodbine's other projects in Fort Worth were two master-planned, mixed-use communities that combine residential, office, and commercial development: Fossil Creek in northeast Fort Worth at the intersection of Interstate Loop 820 and Interstate 35-W, and Team Ranch in southwest Fort Worth at the intersection of Interstate Loop 820 and Interstate 20.

Both developments are in the fast-growing areas of the city. The Interstate 35-W corridor in North Tarrant County is becoming one of the nation's hottest spots thanks to the new Fort Worth Alliance Airport. And the southwest sector is booming with new hospitals, shopping centers, and residential development.

Fossil Creek is a 1,150-acre community notable for the way it conforms to the land and maximizes its natural assets of rolling hills, open meadows, and wooded creeks. Fossil Creek preserves a wide corridor of natural greenbelt, yet offers a championship golf course designed by golf legend Arnold Palmer. The Golf Club at Fossil Creek represents Palmer's first golf course in northern Texas. Marriott Corp. manages The Golf Club for Woodbine and plans a resort hotel adjacent to the golf course.

In addition to the golf course, Fossil Creek has an extensive hiking and bicycle trail system through the golf course and wooded creek areas. A private park, picnic areas, playground, and fishing pier on the lake have all been provided as recreation amenities for Fossil Creek residents.

Fossil Creek's central design theme is reminiscent of the quaint towns in the Texas Hill Country. Many of the buildings, including the information center and The Golf Club, are constructed of

ABOVE: The Hyatt Regency DFW resort complex, conveniently located within the Dallas/Fort Worth International Airport, is the world's largest airport hotel.

BELOW: The Golf Club at Fossil Creek offers an 18-hole championship course designed by golf legend Arnold Palmer and managed by Marriott Corp.

the cream-colored Austin stone found in the Hill Country and sport slanting metal roofs. Tall oak trees surround The Golf Club and have been preserved throughout the residential areas.

The 425-acre Fossil Creek Business Park has attracted a range of industries, including manufacturing, distribution, electronics, architects, builders, and publishing firms. Motorola Inc. became the first tenant purchasing a 100-acre site off Loop 820 for a new communications-equipment manufacturing plant. Woodbine used Motorola as the anchor to create a master plan for the business park. Coca-Cola Bottling Co. of Fort Worth next purchased 45 acres to become the second tenant and co-anchor of the business park.

Other Fossil Creek Business Park tenants include Albert H. Halff Associates Inc. Engineers, Trammell Crow Co., American Association of Petroleum Landmen, Sweet Publishing Co. Inc., NCR Corp., State Farm Insurance Co., Tandy Brands, and Novatel Cellular.

On the city's southwest side, Woodbine is developing the first phase of Team Ranch, an 1,800-acre mixed-use

development, at the intersection of Interstate Loop 820 and the new Interstate 20 extension. The 170-acre first phase will offer extensive commercial freeway frontage and sites for single-family and multifamily residences. The project is master planned to include pedestrian paths, private parks, and greenbelts to provide residents and tenants the feel of wide-open ranch-like spaces.

Dallas oilman Ray L. Hunt formed Woodbine Development Corporation in 1973 to manage the commercial real estate activities of his Hunt Consolidated Inc., Hunt Oil Co., and other Woodbine subsidiaries and affiliates. Although these parent companies are based in Dallas, Woodbine's total assets are split evenly between Tarrant and Dallas counties. Woodbine locates its Fort Worth development office in Fossil Creek.

Since its formation, Woodbine has quietly become a major developer in the Fort Worth and Dallas areas, and it is known for being extremely selective about the projects it undertakes. The company has developed office, hotel, and warehouse properties, industrial and office parks, golf courses, and master-planned, mixed-use communities throughout the area. Indeed, Woodbine's list of projects is not notable for quantity but rather for quality, including several area landmarks and well-known buildings and developments. While some developers have tended to tear down old buildings, Woodbine developed a reputation for its restoration work, beginning with its renovation of the Hyatt Regency Fort Worth. The company has renovated more than one million square feet of historical buildings in Fort Worth and Dallas, including two other notable projects: the restored Union Station railroad terminal and Founders Square office building in downtown Dallas.

Westbridge Capital Corp.

With the cost of health care ever rising, employers and individuals are more aggressively shopping around for quality insurance coverage at affordable prices.

Westbridge Capital Corp. has positioned itself in that increasingly competitive insurance market as a specialty provider. The Fort Worth-based holding company's operating units serve niche markets with innovative individual and small-group accident and health insurance policies.

Westbridge underwrites and sells accident and health insurance products mainly through its wholly owned subsidiary, National Foundation Life Insurance Co., and its 40 percent interest in Freedom Holding Co. of Louisville, Kentucky. National Foundation Life, with its home office in Fort Worth, does business in 32 states. Freedom Holding owns Freedom Life Insurance Co. of America, a Mississippi insurer licensed in 34 states.

The operating companies' main products are medical expense and supplemental hospital income insurance. The policies are sold largely by independent agents in the southern and western United States.

The medical expense products include policies providing reimbursement for various medical and hospital care, policies supplementing the federal Medicare program, and catastrophic nursing-care policies and home health care. Supplemental hospital income products include policies designed to provide daily indemnity for hospital confinement and convalescent care for treatment of specified diseases, confinement in an intensive care unit, and policies that provide a fixed benefit in the case of accidental death.

Neither product competes directly with programs offered by major medical programs to employer-sponsored groups. The supplemental hospital-income product complements major medical insurance products. The medical expense product provides coverage similar to major medical insurance programs but is sold to people not covered in an employer-sponsored group.

Westbridge also receives fee income through its 51 percent ownership position in an insurance agency organiza-

tion called LifeStyles Marketing Group Inc. and its wholly owned Foundation Financial Services Inc. (FFS) subsidiary.

LifeStyles has more than 150 agents in 15 branch offices who sell National Foundation Life's medical expense and term life policies as well as the products of other insurers not offered by National Foundation Life. LifeStyles' FFS subsidiary administers flexible compensation plans and is also a third-party administrator of benefit programs for self-insured employers. Westbridge believes its subsidiaries have the ability as specialists to deliver products at affordable prices while preserving the consumer's freedom to select his or her own doctor and hospital.

In recent years Westbridge has taken a new approach to marketing its subsidiaries' health insurance products. Before 1987 National Foundation Life delivered its products through a network of independent agents with whom the company had little contact and control. Today Westbridge's marketing

Westbridge Capital Corp. offers innovative individual and small-group accident and health insurance coverage at affordable prices.

is conducted mainly by sales organizations in which the company is a significant owner.

Westbridge also plans an expansion of its telemarketing operation and expects to improve its ability to target specific markets, generate significantly more leads, and control sales costs.

Westbridge employs more than 150 people. National Foundation Life's home office in Fort Worth includes an underwriting staff that reviews and approves policy applications and standards, a policyholder service and agency departments that respond to policyholder and agent requests for information and service, and a claims department that reviews, analyzes, and processes policyholder benefit claims.

Texas Livestock Marketing Association

In its 60 years of existence, the Texas Livestock Marketing Association has been one of the driving forces behind the state's world-famous cattle industry. The association is a full-service organization that provides livestock producers with a new electronic video auction marketing system, "private treaty" livestock marketing, a futures hedging service, forward contracting, live auction marketing, and livestock production loans.

Although the Texas Livestock Marketing Association did not start until 1930, its heritage dates back to Texas' early statehood in the 1850s and 1860s. Grazing land was Texas' first great natural resource, and thousands of unbranded cattle roamed the state after the Civil War. Although southern Texas and coastal areas had a long

The Texas Livestock Marketing Association's office is located in a historic building on East Weatherford Street in downtown Fort Worth, previously occupied by the Texas and Southwestern Cattle Raisers Association.

tradition of cattle raising, dating back to the Spanish colonial period, other parts of the state also began raising livestock. These animals became Texas' first profitable industry during the Reconstruction years after the Civil War.

Hundreds of thousands of head of cattle were driven to railheads for shipment to the East. Americans liked the taste of beef, and the Texas beef industry began to emerge.

In the 1900s producers saw a need to broaden their marketing from regional or statewide emphasis, and increased the potential for profit by offering livestock to national buyers through competitive bidding.

So in 1930 ranchers organized a cooperative in Fort Worth called the

The Texas Livestock Marketing Association's latest marketing tool is the electronic video auction.

Texas Livestock Marketing Association. Its sole purpose was and is to market livestock "with efficiency and integrity."

Every producer who sells livestock through the association automatically becomes a member and has a voice in the organization. The present officers and directors come from throughout Texas and New Mexico.

The association has grown to an institution that serves many needs of today's livestock producers—from marketing to financing to management. National Finance Credit Corp., a subsidiary of the association, also organized in 1930, provides financing for ranching and other livestock operations. In recent years, National Finance loaned more than $85 million to ranchers.

Another affiliate is the Texas Livestock Commodities Inc., a commodity brokerage service for association customers. Through the service, producers can use the futures market to moderate price risk and to reduce complications in marketing decisions.

The association's marketing program centers around forward contracting, order buying, and private treaty services. The association's newest marketing tool is electronic video auctions, designed to seek the highest market value for livestock through competitive bidding on a national level. In the auctions, the actual sale is conducted in Fort Worth and beamed via satellite to locations throughout the United States. Prospective buyers, equipped with a television screen, can bid on the animals as in a live auction. The electronic video auction gives the livestock more exposure to broader markets.

David J. Simons, Texas Livestock Marketing Association executive vice president, says the electronic video auctions have been very successful in the two years they have been held. "They're certain to gain momentum," Simons says.

MANUFACTURING

Producing goods for individuals and industry, manufacturing firms provide employment for many Fort Worth area residents.

Photo by Bob Rowan/Progressive Image Photography

Motorola Inc.

When electronics giant Motorola Inc. chose Fort Worth as the home of its Mobile Products Division in 1974, the decision propelled the city's burgeoning communications industry into a period of new growth.

The Motorola division began producing its two-way radios, pagers, and other communications systems in lease facilities in the Richland Hills Plaza. Not long after, construction began on a headquarters complex in Fossil Creek, a mixed-use development located at Interstate 35 and Loop 820 on the city's north side. In 1978 Motorola opened its 346,000-square-foot facility on 100 landscaped, rolling acres. The company was the first major industrial tenant in the Fossil Creek complex and is credited with helping to fuel the north side's growth. The Fort Worth operation is responsible for the development, manufacturing, and sales of all Motorola two-way communications products not only in the United States, but also throughout the world. Motorola also has other two-way communications manufacturing operations worldwide, but most are feeder facilities that make partially completed products for final manufacturing in Fort Worth.

The market for Motorola's two-way communications products is large and growing. Key market segments include agriculture, commercial business, state, local, and federal government, industrial, and small business. Many police departments, for example, use the company's two-way communications equipment for receiving dispatches and transmitting information back to headquarters.

Motorola's roots go back to 1928, when Paul V. Galvin founded the company as the Galvin Manufacturing Corp. Its first product was a "battery eliminator," a device that allowed consumers to operate radios from household electrical current instead of using the batteries supplied with the early models.

In the early 1930s the company successfully commercialized car radios under the brand name "Motorola," a word suggesting sound in motion. During this period the company also established home radio and police radio departments and in the late 1940s entered government work and opened a research laboratory to explore solid-state electronics.

After Paul Galvin died in 1959, his son Robert W. Galvin led the company's expansion into international markets in the 1960s. Motorola began shifting its focus away from consumer electronics and, in the mid-1970s, sold its color television receiver business.

In the past decade Motorola continued its growth and investment in Europe and Asia, particularly Japan, where the company established a wholly owned manufacturing and marketing subsidiary, Nippon Motorola Ltd., and a joint venture with Toshiba Corp. for manufacturing semiconductor products.

In addition to two-way communications systems, Motorola's product line today includes cellular telephones, integrated circuits, defense and aerospace electronics, automotive and industrial electronics, and data communications and information processing and handling equipment.

Ranked among the United States' 100 largest industrial companies, Motorola has about 105,000 employees worldwide, including more than 1,000 in Fort Worth. The Schaumburg, Illinois-based company's operations are highly decentralized, with business operations structured as sectors, groups, or divisions, depending on size.

The Fort Worth plant is part of the communications sector, based in Schaumburg. Other units include the semiconductor products sector, head-

Motorola Inc. produces two-way communication systems, cellular telephones, integrated circuits, defense and aerospace electronics, automotive and industrial electronics, and data communication on a global level to keep us all in touch.

quartered in Phoenix; the general systems group, also based in Schaumburg; the information systems group in Canton, Massachusetts; the government electronics group in Scottsdale, Arizona; the automotive and industrial electronics group in Northbrook, Illinois; and the new enterprises organization based in Schaumburg that manages the company's entry into new, high-growth businesses.

In addition to Fort Worth, Motorola also has semiconductor plants in Austin and Seguin in central Texas. Many of their products are used in the communications equipment and other Motorola systems.

Motorola credits its standing as one of the top electronics companies with a combination of aggressive product innovation, strategic long-range planning, and a philosophy that allows employers to contribute ideas on quality standards. This philosophy is evident in the company's participative management program, or PMP.

All employees that are not executives are part of a PMP team. On each team are employees who work in the same area or who share the responsibility of meeting a specific goal. PMP teams meet often to identify goals, assess progress, and work on problems. Periodically the company evaluates PMP objectives and directions and rewards successes with cash bonuses. Over the past several years, about 3 percent of Motorola's payroll has gone toward PMP bonuses.

The program helped Motorola win the first Malcolm Baldrige National Quality Award in 1988. The award was named after the late U.S. Department of Commerce secretary who believed that the quality of U.S. goods and services is central to the nation's market position, competitiveness, and standard of living. It is the highest level of national recognition of quality for a U.S. company.

Motorola's submission for the award represented all of its businesses, including the Fort Worth operation, and covered seven categories: leadership, information and analysis, planning, human resources, quality assurance, quality assurance results, and customer satisfaction.

In addition to its facility complex, Motorola has 200 acres of lakefront recreational property on the west side of Eagle Mountain Lake north of the city. All Motorola employees in the Dallas/Fort Worth area can use the property.

Motorola Inc. employees are active in many Fort Worth organizations, community activities, and charities, including the United Way, the March of Dimes Walkathon, Junior Achievement sponsorship, community blood drives, the University of Texas at Arlington Robotics Center, and industry trade and business groups. The company also has underwritten special programs on public television.

ElectroCom Automation L.P.

Few people give much thought about what happens to a letter after it is mailed. But that simple action sets in motion a complex, carefully mechanized reaction that requires sophisticated equipment to transport, electronically scan, and sort billions of pieces of mail for the U.S. Postal Service each year.

ElectroCom Automation L.P. is the leading supplier of such high-speed document-processing equipment with more than 3,500 machines delivered or on order. The U.S. Postal Service is the company's largest single customer, and other users include financial institutions and government agencies.

ElectroCom also designs and manufactures land mobile radio systems and markets voice- and data-transmission telecommunications systems for public-safety agencies, utilities, and other businesses that need to manage fleets of vehicles. The company's communications systems customers include the Fort Worth police and fire departments.

ElectroCom is relatively young as a separate corporation, although its predecessor companies date back more than 30 years. The company was formed in 1983, after having previously operated as the Commercial Division of E-Systems Inc., a Dallas defense-electronics developer.

Since then the privately held company has won a series of Postal Service contracts, helping push ElectroCom's annual sales to about $200 million. ElectroCom's document-handling systems process mail through almost every operation within the U.S. Postal Service. The company's equipment includes optical character readers, bar-code sorters, and mechanized mail-forwarding systems.

The largest postal contract came in 1989, when ElectroCom won a $265-million U.S. Postal Service award to manufacture 346 electronic mail-sorting machines. The system uses optical electronics to read the street address, city, and state on pieces of mail, then applies a nine-digit ZIP code, and prints the code on envelopes for other machines to handle and sort. The contract eventually could be worth up to $400 million if the U.S. Postal Service exercises options to order 300 more

systems. As part of the award, ElectroCom will establish a training center in Arlington, Texas, for postal technicians.

In addition to the U.S. Postal Service, ElectroCom provides equipment for government organizations, such as the U.S. Department of State. Its systems help the department and its agencies process its mail. The equipment will improve processing speed and accuracy as well as provide security features.

The U.S. Navy also purchased ElectroCom equipment to help it keep track of microfiche. The Internal Revenue Service uses the company's Omnisort mail-processing system. Corporate customers include Security Pacific National Bank and Bank of America.

All of ElectroCom's document-processing systems manufacturing takes place in Arlington, where the company employs about 700 people. ElectroCom expects to add several hundred new jobs over the next several years to keep pace with the new contracts.

ElectroCom also offers parcel-sorting warehousing systems produced in part by a Danish company. Typically ElectroCom provides the system design, electronics, controls, and other hardware; the Danish company provides the mechanical parts and devices that make

ElectroCom's main building complex in Arlington, near the intersection of Highway 360 and Interstate 30, includes administrative, research and development, and manufacturing facilities. All of ElectroCom's document-processing systems are made in Arlington.

its sorter unique.

Such warehousing equipment is used by Sears, Roebuck & Co., Target Stores, the Book-of-the-Month Club, catalog companies Lillian Vernon Inc. and Chadwick's of Boston, Consolidated Stores, and Japanese and European retailers.

ElectroCom's telecommunications systems business specializes in land mobile radio systems for both voice and data applications. A California subsidiary, Console Systems Inc., makes a range of consoles for public safety and emergency vehicles. The color monitors can display up to 2,000 characters and feature compact, color-coded keyboards. They also can connect with a radio, computer, or telephone.

ElectroCom also is a leader in simulcast voice radio coverage, a high priority with paramedics, police officers, and fire fighters. The company is under contract with the Los Angeles Sheriff's De-

The Digicom® MDT-870, Electro-Com's mobile data terminal, is used by police and fire departments, emergency medical providers, and other organizations for transmitting and receiving critical information, querying data bases, and dispatching.

partment to provide a communications system consisting of an extensive simulcast radio with 46 channels and mobile data communications within a 4,300-square-mile area. The system is designed to meet the department's requirements for radio channel loading through the year 2000. When fully operational, the system will include almost 9,000 pieces of equipment.

Since 1981 the Los Angeles Police Department also has been using a voice- and digital-communications system installed by ElectroCom. The firm also designed and built mobile data terminals for 850 patrol vehicles. The police department uses the terminals to get information from data bases, for digital dispatching, digital messages from vehicles, and unit identification and status.

ElectroCom used the experience with the Los Angeles project to develop the Fort Worth police and fire communications system. The system provides voice and data communications throughout Tarrant County so fire fighters in the field can communicate with their dispatcher and with other fire fighters in neighborhood cities.

In addition, the company provided consoles and an electronic wall map system for a new fire dispatch center, designed and installed a fire alert system in all fire stations, and enhanced communications with mobile, portable, and desktop radios for fire stations.

The police department's data communications system operates more than 200 mobile data terminals (MDTs) in patrol cars. The system features a message switch that connects to state and national data bases and a new dispatch center incorporating 14 call-taker positions and 10 voice/data dispatch positions. ElectroCom also installed a diagnostic system to monitor the police and fire communications system, which has been in service since 1985. ElectroCom Automation will be a major competitor for the Fort Worth city-wide communications upgrade, which is planned for 1990-1991 implementation.

The company's mobile data communications systems also are in use in Texas by the Houston, Garland, and Mesquite police departments, as well as the mid-cities of Grapevine, Hurst, and Euless. ElectroCom recently completed a major data communications system in Michigan, including more than 1,100 MDTs servicing Detroit's fire, emergency medical, and police departments, as well as neighboring Oakland County law-enforcement agencies. ElectroCom also has large installations in Miami and Pinellas County in Florida.

General Electric Co. also chose ElectroCom Automation Inc. as design contractor to develop simulcast capabilities for its new public-safety trunking system. The system provides simulcast of voice and digital control channels with radio sites linked on microwave networks.

ElectroCom's Optical Character Reader (OCR) systems electronically read information on mail and other documents so they can be sorted.

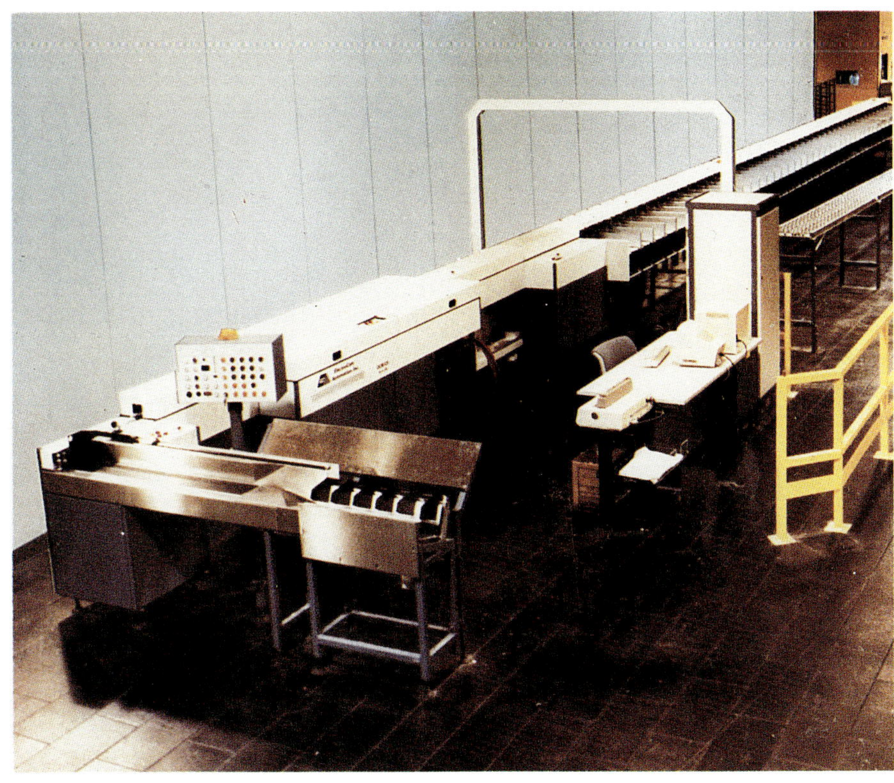

General Dynamics

When war broke out in Europe in 1939, U.S. military officials began to prepare for the strong possibility that the United States would join the fighting. Later that year Army Air Corps Major General Henry "Hap" Arnold asked Consolidated Aircraft in San Diego to design a strategic bomber that could "fly the skin off any rivals."

The resulting aircraft, the XB-24, was in such demand by 1940 that the Department of War planned new facilities to step up production. Fort Worth was chosen for the site of a new government-owned assembly plant.

Fort Worth's major civil leader at the time, the late Amon G. Carter, had lobbied hard for the plant and saw to it the facility was four feet longer than one just built in Oklahoma. Construction workers toiled around the clock to build the massive plant, which has almost 5 million square feet under roof and an assembly bay that stretched for almost one mile.

In less than one year after the ground breaking in April 1941, the "Bomber Plant," as it was called, began churning out B-24 Liberators for the war effort. The plant was the largest air-

An F-16 flies high over Fort Worth.

conditioned building in the world.

Consolidated since has merged with other companies to form General Dynamics Corp., one of the nation's top defense contractors. The Fort Worth plant is now a separate General Dynamics division and the largest employer in Tarrant County, with 30,000 area workers. The division is building the F-16 Fighting Falcon, the U.S. Air Force's frontline fighter.

Through the years, the plant also spawned new defense companies and suppliers, helping to build an industry that has become a major driver of Fort Worth's economy. Many area subcontractors depend on the division for business. General Dynamics estimates it pays more than $150 million annually

to the top 10 area companies that supply it with everything from contract labor to office supplies.

Since the plant opened, more than 7,000 aircraft have rolled down its assembly line. The division sells more than $3 billion worth of military aircraft per year, making it General Dynamics' largest operating unit.

The F-16 has been one of the most successful defense aircraft ever. Originally designed as a low-cost, lightweight fighter, the aircraft is expanding into new roles such as reconnaissance and support of ground activities. The U.S. Navy is using the F-16 to simulate adversary planes at its elite "Top Gun" pilot training school in Miramar, California.

In addition, the F-16 is the United States' leading military export item. More than one dozen foreign air forces fly the plane.

Four countries—Belgium, Denmark, the Netherlands, and Norway—are members of a European consortium that may participate in full-scale development of an upgraded F-16. Turkey, which is manufacturing the F-16 under license, also has asked to join the consortium. Another program that has potential for the division is the so-called FS-X, a Japanese fighter based on the F-16. The United States and Japan have signed a memorandum of understanding to develop the fighter. General Dynamics will share in key elements of the program with prime contractor Mitsubishi Heavy Industries. The division stands to reap about one-third of the estimated $20 billion for up to 130 FS-X planes.

Looking beyond the F-16 program, the division is participating in the design and development of several next-generation aircraft worth potentially billions of dollars in new contracts.

A team of General Dynamics and McDonnell Douglas Corp. won a $4.4-billion contract to develop the Navy's new A-12, an aircraft carrier-based, all-weather aircraft. Scheduled to enter service in the mid-1990s, the A-12 will

F-16 fighter planes on the production line at General Dynamics' mile-long Fort Worth facility.

This automated machine weaves special coverings for cables used in the F-16.

replace the U.S. Navy's 600-aircraft fleet of A-6 Intruders. The team also is studying the adaptability of the A-12 to U.S. Air Force requirements.

The division also has joined with Boeing Co. and Lockheed Corp. to compete against another industry team to develop the air force's advanced tactical fighter. The team has begun detailed design and construction of prototypes.

General Dynamics also is one of five contractors cooperating to build the hypersonic X-30 National Aero-Space Plane, designed to fly in and out of earth's orbit from conventional runways. One of the major benefits of X-30 work is that its technology can be applied to future aircraft designs.

Meanwhile, the division is continuing to upgrade the F-111 aircraft it built in the 1960s and 1970s. The F-111, capable of long-range nuclear and conventional attacks on supply lines, will be part of the air force's inventory through the year 2010.

In addition to aircraft, the division's electronic products organization develops a variety of electronic systems. The division has operated the U.S. Air Force Electronic Warfare Evaluation Simulator laboratory since the mid-1950s. The simulator has been used to develop most electronic countermeasures systems built for the United States and its allies.

In 1967 the division developed the first replica radar system to emulate the electronic signature of many foreign defense radars, including Soviet Union radar.

While defense contractors have experienced shrinking defense budgets and cuts in some programs, the Fort Worth division is in the enviable position of producing and designing some of the Department of Defense's most important systems, such as the F-16. Its work on the A-12 program also virtually assures its future, if funding for the program continues as envisioned.

"Our programs represent the 'heartland' of defense programs," says Charles A. Anderson, vice president and general manager of the Fort Worth division.

Production rates for the F-16 have dropped from 180 a year to 150 a year. "We still believe the F-16 program, because of its capability and price, is the only thing to fill the force structure needs. So that will keep a significant number of Fort Worth employees here."

As work on the F-16 slows down, the A-12 program should keep the division's employment stable. The division's employment mix, however, is shifting as rapid advancements in technology demand a more technically skilled work force.

"We've moved from where we sculpted planes out of metal to where we're sculpting planes out of advanced composites," Anderson says. "Our goal is to keep the maximum number of people employed and do it by keeping the cost of our airplanes down."

The F-16's sophisticated technology undergoes testing in a special chamber free of echoes and reverberations.

Design Foods

When people go out to eat in Texas or anywhere in the United States, chances are they enjoy some of Design Foods' products. Design Foods, a division of the Chicago-based Sara Lee Corporation, covers the spectrum of the food-service industry. Nationwide customers include major chain restaurants, food-service distributors, supermarket delicatessens, convenience stores, schools and universities, hospitals, caterers, vending operations, and independent restaurants.

Design Foods is the leading producer of precooked meat pizza toppings and supplies the major pizza chains throughout the country. Many quick service restaurants and theme restaurants nationwide are supplied a wide range of products from Design Foods. These vast specialty food items include taco meat, chili, burritos, taquitos, portioned precooked meats, sauces, entrées, desserts, soups, stews, and more.

What sets Design Foods apart from its competitors in the food-service business, says president Charles Stacey, is the company's ability to customize products. "We are able to custom manufacture and custom design products for our customers," Stacey says.

Three companies form the Design Foods organization. Standard Meat Company, founded in Fort Worth in 1935 by Ben H. Rosenthal, and Hi-Brand Foods, located near Atlanta in Peachtree City, Georgia, form the Design Foods parent company, whose corporate headquarters is Fort Worth. Cook's Foodservice, headquartered in Ohio, is a subsidiary of Design Foods.

Standard Meat Company was one

ABOVE: Delicious beef for Mexican dishes is one of Design Foods' specialties.

LEFT: Design Foods supplies toppings to major pizza chains throughout the country.

of the nation's largest suppliers of precooked meat pizza toppings, entrées, side dishes, and steaks. Since its founding the company has supplied meat products to customers such as restaurants, hotels, schools, and the military.

Standard Meat reached a turning point in 1965, adopting a new marketing philosophy of developing products tailored to the customers' needs. Standard Meat's research and development staff began working hand in hand with customers' research and development staffs to design custom products.

The company tailored delivery, storage, preparation, menu planning, food cost analysis, new product development, and market forecasting to each customer. The approach led to long associations with customers such as Pizza Hut and Steak & Ale.

Hi-Brand Foods, located in Peachtree City, Georgia, had a broad line of products ranging from Mexican foods, precooked hamburger patties, battered and breaded beef, chicken, pork and veal patties, dessert items, and battered and breaded vegetables.

Cook's Foodservice, located in Sandusky, Ohio, specializes in distribution

Design Foods prepares breaded and battered chicken and vegetables in many styles for a variety of tastes and occasions.

of frozen "center of the plate" items, including bakery products, meats, Mexican foods, potatoes, pizza, seafood, and steaks. Cook's Foodservice serves the midwestern market.

Design Foods employs about 1,200 workers throughout the three companies, with about 465 people in Fort Worth. The division's total sales are about $275 million.

Design Foods' corporate headquarters and largest facility is in Fort Worth, located just east of downtown on East First Street. The state-of-the-art facility is more than 200,000 square feet and is where pizza toppings and precooked taco meat are produced. Other items produced in this facility are sauces, soups, fajitas, and meat components for major manufacturers of retail frozen dinners.

The Fort Worth facility also has a state-of-the-art pilot plant equipped with small-scale production equipment

Design Foods offers a diverse line of products, including soups, stews, sauces, Mexican foods, and even dessert items.

for test product runs. In addition, the facility houses freezers, administrative offices, research and development, and quality-control activities.

In Design Foods' research and development operation, project managers who hold degrees in food science develop new products and test them for ease in handling and consistency in a test kitchen.

The Fort Worth plant also has chemistry and microbiology laboratories to analyze foods for protein, moisture, salt, and fat content, as well as monitoring microbiology activity. This ensures the consistently superior quality for which Design Foods has become known.

The Lampasas plant in central Texas produces tacos, taquitos, burritos, and entrées such as those found in restaurants, convenience stores, and in supermarket delicatessens.

Stacey says the four areas that Design Foods is "fanatical" about are product quality and consistency, customer satisfaction as perceived by the customer, low-cost production, and growth and development of employees. "Design Foods' goal is to be the low-cost producer in all its businesses," Stacey says.

Design Foods became part of the Sara Lee Corporation in 1983, when the Rosenthal family sold Standard Meat Company to what was then called Consolidated Foods Corporation. Consolidated later adopted the name of one of its successful divisions, Sara Lee.

Design Foods is part of Sara Lee's meat group, which includes such well-known brands as Jimmy Dean, Hillshire Farm, Bryan, Sweet Sue, Kahn's, and State Fair.

Sara Lee Corporation encourages community involvement, and Design Foods is active in several civic and charitable organizations, including the Adopt-a-School program and United Way.

Lennox Industries Inc.

Any Fort Worth resident who has survived a hot Texas summer will say it is hard to get along without air conditioning. So it is appropriate that one of the largest manufacturers of air conditioning and heating systems, Lennox Industries Inc., located a major division in a city in the warm Southwest.

Lennox has had a presence in Fort Worth since 1948, when the company acquired a small manufacturing facility and rented warehouse space. Back then the plant manufactured sheet metal fittings, evaporative coolers, floor furnaces, and gravity furnaces.

Several expansions later, the plant has grown from 40,000 square feet to 650,000 square feet of production, warehouse, and office space located off State Highway 121 northeast of downtown. The factory—part of Lennox's Southwest Divison—produces split-system heat pumps and air conditioners, packaged heat pumps and packaged air conditioners, gas heating/electric cooling units, evaporator and condenser coils, "low-side" cooling coils, copper hairpin tubes, and blower-coil units.

Most of the products made in Fort Worth are for the commercial market. The plant's newest product addition also is one of the company's most sophisticated and important systems—the GCS16, a new rooftop residential and commercial unit that features a new design and new technology. Lennox officials expect the next-generation unit to help dramatically increase the company's market share and represent much of the Fort Worth's plant work in the future. The unit uses a rugged, commercial heat exchanger that is compact in design and extremely efficient, says Tom Morton, the plant's vice president and general manager.

Each new generation of technology requires a more sophisticated factory. Lennox has been upgrading the Fort Worth plant almost constantly to keep up with changes in heating and air conditioning technology and product lines. In recent years Lennox has rearranged production lines on the factory floor, installed new computer-controlled equipment for inspection and quality control, and implemented new processes to reduce the amount of scrap generated by the plant and to increase productivity. Any amount of savings is crucial with a plant that annually consumes 12 million pounds of aluminum, 10 million pounds of copper, and 10 million pounds of steel.

In addition to evolutions in system and factory technology, the heating and air conditioning industry also has undergone major changes in the way it sells and distributes products.

"Heating and air conditioning didn't change too much until 10 to 15 years ago, when the energy-efficiency push began," Morton says. "The major market used to be people who were putting it into their houses for the first time."

As utility companies offered incentive programs to consumers who bought energy-efficient systems, and consumers demanded more efficient systems to save on heating and cooling bills, the replacement market started to grow.

Lennox now sells and distributes products from its factories and distribution centers through a network of more than 8,000 independent dealers worldwide. The contractors sell the equipment to consumers, install the systems, and service them.

The Lennox dealer organization is the largest in the United States, and

the company attributes the network for much of the company's success. Lennox spends a lot of time fine-tuning the network and making sure dealers have the training, information, and support they need.

Lennox sales representatives, called territory managers, call on dealers within assigned geographic areas to provide assistance in the dealerships' operations. Territory managers also help dealers by meeting with potential consumers and work closely with Lennox's dealer marketing advisors, who provide specialized marketing support to help dealers increase sales and installations.

Fort Worth is the headquarters for the five-state Southwest region that includes Texas, Oklahoma, Arkansas, Louisiana, and New Mexico. Branch offices and warehouses are located in Fort Worth, Dallas, Houston, Austin, Lubbock, San Antonio, Oklahoma City, Tulsa, Little Rock, and New Orleans.

In addition to manufacturing, division offices, and sales support staff, Lennox also has a training facility in Fort Worth for contractors and a dealer service center that distributes parts and supplies that contractors need to install products. The Southwest Division employs more than 600 in Fort Worth.

The Fort Worth plant is one of five Lennox factories. The others are in Toronto, Ontario; Columbus, Ohio; Stuttgart, Arkansas; and Marshalltown, Iowa, where Lennox was founded in 1895. Lennox also has factories and sales organizations in England and Australia.

Lennox Industries' parent company, Lennox International Inc., based in Dallas, emerged from the original Lennox Machine Shop in Marshall-

town, founded by inventor Dave Lennox. Lennox perfected the steel sheet-metal furnace construction ideas of two other inventors and built a quality product. He sold the furnace business in 1904 to a group led by D.W. Norris.

Norris retained the Lennox name and rode trains from coast to coast to sell the furnace. He stopped in Fort Worth, and a local furnace company became the area's first Lennox product installer.

The Norris family still owns the company, which is one of the largest privately held businesses in the United States. Lennox president and chief executive officer John W. Norris, Jr., is the grandson of D.W. Norris.

Lennox still uses Dave Lennox's name in its advertising, and the firm hired an actor, clad in overalls, to portray the founder and personify the com-

pany's family image.

In 1978 Lennox moved its headquarters to Dallas from Marshalltown. A year earlier the company moved its research and development laboratory to the Dallas suburb of Carrollton from Iowa. The facility is considered one of the top research labs in the heating and air conditioning industry.

The Fort Worth plant keeps in close contact with the research and development facility. A research and development employee is based at the Lennox Fort Worth plant for a year to get a close-up look at the manufacturing process. Conversely, it is not unusual for production workers to suggest design changes they believe would improve product quality or streamline the manufacturing process.

Lennox Industries Inc. instituted a quality-improvement program in recent years to identify and solve problems

ABOVE: A heat exchanger is lowered into a large commercial unit. Residential and commercial systems such as this one are marketed to consumers and business clients by more than 8,000 independent Lennox dealers worldwide.

LEFT: Products from Lennox's 650,000-square-foot factory in Fort Worth and from other Lennox factories in North America and England are recognized throughout the heating and air-conditioning industry for their quality, energy-efficiency, and reliability.

before its systems reach the consumer. Twenty quality teams within the Fort Worth factory meet on a regular basis to work on different issues.

For example, one team came up with an idea to change the copper tubing to improve wiring on the new GCS16 unit. Several teams also devised better ways to run the fabrication presses used to manufacture coils.

"It improves the whole quality of the work life," says Bill Cors, the factory's manager of quality and human resources. "It creates a feeling of more ownership in the bottom line of the business. Employees feel more directly involved. Design and manufacturing work as a team."

Holt, Rinehart and Winston Inc.

Fort Worth's publishing industry took a giant step forward in 1989 when Holt, Rinehart and Winston Inc., one of the nation's leading publishers of college textbooks, completed its corporate relocation to Fort Worth from New York.

The company, wholly owned by publishing giant Harcourt Brace Jovanovich Inc. of Orlando, Florida, has three "imprints" out of the Fort Worth corporate office. Holt, Rinehart and Winston Inc. publishes behavioral, social sciences, foreign language, and humanities textbooks and has editorial offices in Fort Worth. The other imprints are The Dryden Press, a business-book publisher located in Hinsdale, Illinois, and Saunders College Publishing, a science and mathematics book publisher in Philadelphia.

Elementary- and secondary-level textbook publishing is performed by a separate, unrelated unit, Holt, Rinehart and Winston in Austin.

The Fort Worth-based organization has about 5,200 items in print, including about 2,000 textbooks. Most of the books are undergraduate level, although the company also publishes many books for master of business administration programs and books for graduate school. It is one of the leading publishers of textbooks in chemistry, biology, foreign languages, finance, astronomy, physics, anthropology, English, psychology, and marketing.

The company completed its relocation in February 1989 and currently occupies three floors of the downtown City Center. The publisher's lobby is striking for its tall bookcases, their shelves brimming with some of the company's titles. The corporate symbol, the owl, is captured in ceramics and paintings throughout the office.

Acquisition editors—the people who seek out authors—represent about 25 percent of the staff. The company also has a marketing staff for all three imprints and a production department for Holt, Rinehart and Winston Inc., including project editors, production managers, and an art and design staff.

A manufacturing department does the ordering of printing and binding for all three imprints. Holt, Rinehart and Winston Inc. does not do any of the

printing itself, but instead contracts it out to printers nationwide.

Although the company is now part of a publishing empire, it began with the ideas of one man, Henry Holt. In 1866 Holt and another publisher, Frederick Leypoldt, formed a publishing firm to provide American readers with good translations of the best European writers. Leypoldt later sold his share of the company to Holt, and the firm became known as Henry Holt and Co.

The firm's textbooks continued to be the profitable part of the business, but

Holt, Rine hart and Winston's view from high atop downtown Fort Worth's City Center gives the company an excellent perspective on the city.

Holt experimented with several new concepts. In the 1870s Holt conceived the idea of publishing a series of well-written novels in an attractive format and at a relatively low price. In 1872 he issued the first group of novels in his now-famous Leisure Hour Series. Among the writers included in the series were Johann Wolfgang von Goethe, Thomas Hardy, William Shakespeare, Ivan Turgenev, and many other American and European authors. Holt also initiated the American Science Series, which devoted whole volumes to the writings of renowned scientists on subjects such as astronomy and chemistry.

Perhaps the most famous writer closely affiliated with Holt was the poet Robert Frost, who considered himself "Holt's oldest employee." Frost's connection with the Holt firm extended more than 48 years.

Through the years and through various mergers, textbooks remained a central part of the company. In 1966 CBS purchased Holt, Rinehart and Winston, which included trade, school, and college departments. In the late 1960s, the company acquired The Dryden Press and Saunders College Publishing, pulling them all together in CBS Educational and Professional Publishing.

In 1986 CBS sold the school and college publishing groups to Harcourt Brace Jovanovich.

The Southwest and particularly Texas represents a huge market for Holt, Rinehart and Winston Inc.'s textbooks. The area's abundance of junior colleges and universities offers a rich source of new authors, buyers, and students/readers.

Although the number of high school and college students declined during

Janet Wilhite (LEFT) is an acquisitions editor in the humanities, and Meera Dash (ABOVE) is a developmental editor in the social sciences.

BELOW: Gail Blonsky is a financial analyst at the company's new Fort Worth Office.

ABOVE: (From left) John Ritland, Serena Barnet, Annette Wiggins, and Tom Urquhart are members of the company's production and art departments.

the 1980s, rapid growth for the textbook publishing business is expected in the 1990s as enrollments swell again. Third, fourth, fifth, and sixth grade classes already are much larger than those in the past. The company already is planning for the textbook publishing boom when those students begin entering college. That expected growth is one of the reasons the company wanted to relocate to Fort Worth.

Uniden America Corp.

Most buyers of personal communications products probably know the Uniden name from the citizens-band radios and cellular phones and cordless phones the company makes and sells under its own label.

But Fort Worth-based Uniden America Corp., the U.S. headquarters for Uniden of Japan, makes a much wider variety of electronic products than consumers may realize. That is because many of the products Uniden manufactures are sold under the labels of other major companies throughout the United States.

Uniden's diverse product line includes satellite receivers, satellite-based

---

Uniden's U.S. headquarters facility is located in Centreport, near the Dallas/Fort Worth International Airport.

pagers, marine radios, land-based radio equipment, scanners, cellular telephones, standard and cordless phones, radar detectors, and answering machines. The company's two-way commercial radios are standard equipment in many law-enforcement agencies, on school buses, and on farms and ranches.

Uniden ranks first or second in manufacturing in all of its product categories. The company makes about 70 percent of all the CB radios sold in the world, about a third of all the cordless telephones, and about a third of all the satellite receivers.

Uniden sells its products through a large distribution network in the United States. Stores that carry Uniden's brands include national retailing chains such as Sears, Roebuck & Co., Wal-mart, and Service Merchandise. Professional golfer Jack Nicklaus has been associated with

Uniden as their corporate spokesperson since 1981.

Market research firms place Uniden among the top five sellers of such electronic and communications equipment in the United States. Analysts say the company has been able to dominate so many communications markets because of its high-quality, low-cost approach and by quickly offering new features and enhancements once it gains a foothold in a particular niche.

For example, Uniden rapidly capitalized on the growing market for cellular telephones, capturing a major share of the market in its first year. Once firmly established as a cellular telephone provider, Uniden was one of the first suppliers in the industry to offer a voice-recognition system, called VoiceDial. This technology lets Uniden cellular phone users talk, dial, answer, and hang

up—all without using hands. Unlike older technologies, VoiceDial does not have to be programmed to identify specific speech patterns.

In marine electronics the company's products include devices such as navigational aids, VHF radios, fish finders, depth and speed/temperature gauges, transducers, and impellers, or rotors that transmit motion.

Uniden produces and assembles its diverse line of electronic communications products in Fort Worth and around the world.

And in response to U.S. consumers' demand for a wider variety of television programming, Uniden supplies more satellite receivers to more users than any other company. One of the latest receivers incorporates an electronically delivered, constantly updated program guide, Super Guide® gives viewers unprecedented power by providing both current program information and satellite receiver control—all through the hand-held remote control.

One of Uniden's newest offerings on the exploding home VCR market is a network service that allows subscribers to electronically "rent" major motion pictures on videocassette from their homes. To watch a movie, subscribers simply dial a toll-free number. The charges are added to their phone bills.

Uniden is not a newcomer to the United States. Truckers and motorists were the first to communicate with Uniden products in the 1970s. In 1976, in the height of the CB radio boom, Uniden began importing and distributing its President brand of CB radios. Soon, the company also began marketing cordless telephones. Other products followed.

In 1988 the company moved into a new headquarters facility in Centreport, just south of Dallas/Fort Worth International Airport. From the headquarters office Uniden markets its entire product line for North American and South American accounts. More than 420 people work for Uniden in Fort Worth.

The company's 240,000-square-foot facility houses marketing, sales, engineering, quality control, and production operations. Uniden produces some cellular telephones and paging equipment at the site and performs subassembly for two-way radios in Fort Worth.

In addition, Uniden has manufacturing sites throughout the world. The company says its global manufacturing capability allows it to hold down labor costs and keep its products affordably priced.

Engineering is a growing responsibility for the U.S. operation. In past years Uniden had done part or all of its engineering work in Japan. But after opening its new headquarters facility, the company added additional engineers to its staff. Now, engineers in Fort Worth work with the engineering staff in Japan on new technologies and product development. Uniden plans to continue to build its engineering staff in Fort Worth.

The cooperative engineering efforts do not end there. Uniden invests in other businesses that are developing leading-edge communications technologies with the goal of not only advancing new ideas, but also applying them to future Uniden products.

Such investment partners include Magellan Systems Corp., which developed the satellite-based global positioning system used for precise navigation; Voice Control Systems Inc., and By-Word Technologies, codevelopers of the VoiceDial voice-recognition feature Uniden uses on its cellular phones; and TVN Inc. and AT&T, with which Uniden produced the first phone-ordered, electronically delivered movie rental system for the home satellite receiver.

To help develop students' interest in technology and launch careers in communications research, Uniden America Corp. has established a one-million-dollar engineering scholarship endowment at the University of Texas at Austin. Uniden also offers UT engineering graduates internships at the company.

Alliance

Just five years ago, a 17,000-acre parcel of land in north Tarrant County was the only undeveloped area in the Metroplex. Today that same acreage boasts Alliance—a regional development that includes Alliance Center, a 4,800-acre business, aviation, and trade complex built around an industrial airport; Park Glen and Hillwood, two master-planned residential communities totaling 3,500 acres; and Alliance Gateway, a 2,500-acre residential and commercial development anchored by State Highway 170.

Alliance Center, the business complex, is designed to provide a custom-tailored environment for all types of businesses, from small entrepreneurs to large industrial users. "Alliance attracts a variety of users because of its multi-modal transportation hub," says Fort Worth Mayor Bob Bolen. "Manufacturing firms can choose between air, rail, or truck for shipping goods."

This is not idle chatter; all three transportation modes are represented by *Fortune* 500 companies with heavy capital investments at Alliance: American Airlines, Ishida Aerospace Research, the Federal Aviation Administration (FAA), Santa Fe Railway, and Texaco.

Alliance, the brainchild of The Perot Group, is a milestone in public/private cooperation. The project was conceived in 1987, when the FAA asked The Perot Group to donate some of its undeveloped acreage in Tarrant and Denton counties for an airport to relieve congestion at nearby Dallas/Fort Worth International Airport. The Perot Group agreed but offered a different approach.

"Alliance Airport started off as a general aviation airport, with a 6,000-foot runway," recalls Ross Perot, Jr., the project coordinator. "But after discussions with the FAA and potential users, we realized that north Texas did not need another general aviation airport, but an industrial airport."

With the FAA, The Perot Group, and the city of Fort Worth pulling together state and federal assistance, work on the new airport began in record time. Ground was broken by May 1988, and Alliance Airport officially opened 18 months later—significantly ahead of the FAA's proposed 8- to 10-year timetable.

Alliance Airport is the first industrial airport in the nation and is emerging as a prototype for the future. "With Alliance, we are going to be the airport and aviation capital of the nation," declares Mayor Bolen.

The project is well on its way to fulfilling Bolen's prediction. In June 1989 American Airlines announced that the airport would be the site for its new major maintenance facility. Scheduled to begin operations in 1992, the $481-million facility will include a 480,000-square-foot hangar—the world's largest cantilevered structure—a dozen industrial and office buildings, and 42 acres of employee parking lots and roads. Ini-

Alliance Center

tially, 2,500 people will be employed at the maintenance facility, but this number will increase to 4,500 after a second phase of construction is completed.

Experts estimate that American's facility will add $800 million a year to the area's economy. "What attracted us to Alliance is economics, demographics, an airport that is almost unequaled in the world today, and the can-do attitude of the city of Fort Worth and The Perot Group," says Joe Kitching, American's managing director of corporate real estate.

The well-known Japanese technology firm, Ishida Aerospace Research, began construction for a new manufacturing facility at Alliance in 1990. The 65,000-square-foot plant, scheduled to open in September 1991, will be dedicated to designing and producing the revolutionary Ishida TW-68—a new commercial aircraft that takes off and lands like a helicopter, and cruises at high speeds like a conventional turbo-prop aircraft.

"We chose to locate our facility here because we need runway access for bringing in clients, to test and deliver our product, and make sales," says David Kocurek, Ishida president. "Alliance Airport offers everything we need in a turnkey operation."

Already operating at Alliance is the FAA's new flight standards district office. The 5,040-square-foot facility employs 25 people and supervises regulation of aircraft agencies and personnel in 30 Texas counties. The FAA decided on Alliance after exploring several other surrounding airports. "The FAA believes it made a good choice because we think the future is at Alliance," says Bernard Mullins, manager of the office.

The railroads are represented at Alliance by Santa Fe Railway, which operates an auto distribution facility at Alliance for American Honda Motor Company and Ford Motor Company. About 130,000 vehicles a year pass through the railroad's Alliance facility on the way to auto dealers across Texas.

In 1990 construction was begun on a Texaco System 2000 unit. The combination food mart and service station, part of Alliance Center's master-planned retail development, gets Alliance truckers, employees, and residents fueled up and onto the new network of highways and freeway exchanges that is also part of the Alliance development.

The construction of State Highway 170 will provide increased access between Alliance and nearby Dallas/Fort Worth International Airport. "What makes Alliance special is that it is roughly 15 miles northwest of D/FW Airport," says Perot, Jr. "We felt it was very important to link these two airports together." In addition, State Highway 170 opens 2,500 acres of Alliance Gateway for industrial and commercial development.

The Perot Group believes that a large percentage of the region's population growth will be concentrated in and around Alliance during the next 10 to 15 years. "What we have done with Alliance is to go out early, ahead of the growth, and prepare the infrastructure so the growth will be high quality and controlled," says Perot, Jr.

This infrastructure includes a new $10-million power loop system installed by TU Electric, a new transmission line for water service put in by the city of Fort Worth, a new $12.5 million wastewater treatment plant recently completed by Trinity River Authority, and one of the most technically advanced fiber-optic transmission and telecommunication systems in the nation installed by Southwestern Bell.

Also being served by these systems are the two master-planned residential developments—Park Glen and Hillwood—to house Alliance employees. Park Glen, a 1,100-acre community, has been open since January 1989 and was the most active project in Tarrant County in housing starts and new home sales in that year. Hillwood—a 2,500-acre community featuring custom homes and luxury estates—will begin development soon. Both communities have access to a wide range of family-oriented amenities, including a regional shopping mall, landscaped boulevards, and 200 acres of greenbelt and park systems with jogging paths, bicycle trails, and basketball and tennis courts.

"One of the reasons American Airlines selected Alliance is that Alliance provides the houses needed for American's employees," says Perot, Jr. "We have worked closely with the city of Fort Worth to build Park Glen, and it has become a very successful project."

Alliance provides facilities for manufacturing and corporate headquarters; air, rail, and interstate access; and quality residential development—everything that booming north Tarrant County needs.

The runway at Fort Worth Alliance Airport

Miller Brewing Company

When Miller Brewing Company decided 20 years ago to brew beer outside Milwaukee, it chose a rather unusual spot for its newest brewery: Fort Worth. At the time Texas was known for its Old West heritage, and Fort Worth was far removed from the traditional beer-producing states in the north.

But Fort Worth had a brewery for sale, the one-year-old Carling Brewery. The city also had a good water supply, an available labor pool, and a central U.S. location.

Miller purchased the Fort Worth brewery for $5.5 million. However, the plant, with a brewing capacity of 300,000 barrels a year, was much too small for Miller's plans. So the company immediately began expanding the plant to triple production capacity, removing the existing brewing equipment and adding thousands of additional square feet of warehouse and production space.

Three years later, in 1969, the newly expanded and equipped Miller brewery opened in south Fort Worth with a big celebration that brought a slice of Milwaukee beer country to Texas. Miller recreated a German beer garden, complete with an old-fashioned beer tent. As a polka band played, more than 700 guests sipped Miller beer from steins and ate bratwurst cooked in their newest local product. Charles W. Miller, then president of Miller, told the crowd that not only would the new plant produce one million barrels of beer a year, but he also expected that number to double within five years.

The brewery met his expectations and later far exceeded them. By 1974 production was at 2 million barrels annually, as Miller predicted. Today, after four major expansions totaling $200 million, production is eight times original capability, making Miller the largest brewery in Texas.

The Fort Worth operation annually produces nearly 8 million barrels of Miller High Life, Miller Lite, Miller Genuine Draft, Milwaukee's Best, Milwaukee's Best Light, Magnum, Meister Brau, Meister Brau Light, and Lowen-

Miller Lite is the nation's favorite reduced-calorie brand, and it is the best-selling beer in Texas, accounting for nearly one-fourth of all beer sales.

A Miller Brewing Co. chemist performs one of some 170 quality assurance checks made on Miller products.

brau. In 1989 the brewery hit record production of 7.5 million barrels. The plant is one of six Miller breweries.

The brewing process is carefully controlled with emphasis on founder Frederic Miller's motto of "Quality, Uncompromising and Unchanging." Production begins when malted barley is mixed with water and combined with another starch to make a mash. The mash is then cooked at rigidly controlled temperatures to convert the starches into fermentable sugars. After the starch is converted, solid parts of the mash are separated from the liquid. This liquid, called wort, is boiled, and hops are added to provide the characteristic bitter flavor of beer.

Yeast is added to begin the fermentation process. Each brewer's yeast differs slightly, and brew masters take great care to preserve their unique strains. As the yeast ferments it produces carbon dioxide and alcohol in the beer. Next the beer is filtered and aged. Most packaged beers are pasteurized to preserve freshness. Non-pasteurized keg beer is refrigerated throughout storage and shipping.

Quality checks begin with raw ingredients and are maintained throughout the brewing and packaging process. Each batch of beer is sampled before it leaves the brewery by Miller's trained tasters.

Once the beer leaves the Fort Worth brewery, it goes to 200 distributors in 11 states in the South and Southwest. Texas is a particularly important state to Miller; the Lone Star State is second only to California in total industry barrel sales. According to the trade publication *Beverage World*, Miller Lite is the nation's number-two beer brand, and it is the best-selling beer in Texas.

Since its relocation Miller has grown into one of Fort Worth's major employers and taxpayers. The brewery employs about 1,000 workers, covers more than one million square feet, and occupies 145 acres in the Carter Industrial Park adjacent to the city's South Freeway.

In addition, Miller contributes more than $390 million annually to the Texas economy in salaries, wages, benefits, utilities, taxes, and purchases of goods and services from local suppliers. The majority of that amount stays in the Fort Worth area.

In the 1970s Miller entered the can manufacturing business, and, in 1976, opened the Fort Worth Container Plant behind the brewery. The container plant is one of five such facilities Miller operates nationwide, and its only customer is the Fort Worth brewery. The plant supplies about 50 percent of the 12-ounce cans the Fort Worth brewery needs, producing about 2 million aluminum cans a day and 750 million a year. The plant made its 5-billionth can in 1985.

The container operation is unusual because it never has had a seasonal layoff. Because the plant does not supply all of the brewery's cans, the facility avoids the seasonal fluctuations that often beset other can manufacturers, says plant manager Henry A. Ford. As a result, employment is stable for the plant's 140 workers.

The container facility is geared toward efficiency and keeping the cost of each can down to a minimum. Helping control costs is a highly automated manufacturing process employing a network of high-speed conveyor belts that move the cans from the time they are stamped and ironed out of coiled aluminum sheets through trimming, cleaning, inside coating, drying, printing and varnishing, baking, necking, and on to inspection.

With the cost of aluminum increasing, manufacturers are exploring new ways to make cans that are thinner and

In the 1970s Miller entered the can manufacturing business and, in 1976, opened the Fort Worth Container Plant.

thus use less aluminum. Another method Miller uses to save aluminum is to put a smaller neck at the top of the can, which reduces the size of the can lids purchased from an outside vendor.

Miller has made a strong commitment to protecting the environment. The Fort Worth operation has spent more than $5 million on programs to ensure compliance with air-quality standards. The container plant has its own wastewater treatment system. Moreover, all scrap aluminum generated at the plant, as well as imperfect cans that inspectors have rejected, are crushed into large bricks and recycled to aluminum companies.

Through the years Miller has under-

gone changes in ownership. After German immigrant Frederic Miller founded Miller in 1855 in Milwaukee, the company was owned and operated by the Miller family for more than 100 years. Philip Morris Companies Inc. acquired 51 percent of the company's stock in 1969. A year later Philip Morris purchased the remaining shares. Today Miller Brewing Company is a wholly owned subsidiary of Philip Morris Companies Inc., with its headquarters in Milwaukee.

In keeping with Philip Morris' philosophy of corporate citizenship, Miller's Fort Worth operations contribute to many community events and organizations. Miller is the largest single contributor to the annual Main Street Arts Festival and is a major sponsor of the Chisholm Trail Roundup and the Cowtown Marathon and 10K run, among many others. The company also

has received awards for its work with minority organizations and is an industry leader in significant minority programs.

Miller offers several national alcohol-education programs through its government affairs department. These include an alcohol-education program given by distributors, and an alcoholic-beverage server education program to train bartenders, waiters, and waitresses as to how alcohol affects behavior and how to serve alcohol responsibly. The company also has paid for public service announcements that encourage drinking in moderation and caution about the dangers of drinking and driving.

Miller Brewing Company employees celebrated their 20th anniversary in Fort Worth in 1989, and they look with pride to the future and their company's continuing role as a leading corporate citizen.

Photo by Bob Rowan/Progressive Image Photography

Patrons

The following companies and organizations have made a valuable commitment to the quality of this publication. Windsor Publications and the City of Fort Worth gratefully acknowledge their participation in *Fort Worth: New Frontiers in Excellence*.

Alliance*
All Saints Health Care Inc.*
American Airlines*
Brown Gause-Ware, Owens & Brumley*
Burlington Northern*
Cantey & Hanger*
Cook-Fort Worth Children's Medical Center*
Coopers & Lybrand*
Dallas/Fort Worth International Airport*

Design Foods*
ElectroCom Automation L.P.*
Everage Consultants, Inc.*
Fort Worth Star-Telegram*
Gandy Michener Swindle Whitaker & Pratt*
General Dynamics*
Harris Methodist Fort Worth*
Holt, Rinehart and Winston Inc.*
Hyatt Regency Fort Worth*
Kelly, Hart & Hallman*
Lennox Industries, Inc.*
Miller Brewing Company*
Moncrief Radiation Center*
Motorola Inc.*
National Farm Life Insurance Co.*
Peat Marwick*
Pier 1 Imports Inc.*
Saint Joseph Hospital*
Shannon, Gracey, Ratliff & Miller*

Southwestern Exposition and Livestock Show*
Tandy Corp.*
Texas and Southwestern Cattle Raisers Association*
Texas Livestock Marketing Association*
TU Electric Co.*
Uniden America Corp.*
Westbridge Capital Corp.*
Woodbine Development Corporation*

*Participants in Part Two, "Fort Worth's Enterprises." The stories of these companies and organizations appear in chapters 9 through 14, beginning on page 104.

Bibliography

I. BOOKS

Flemmons, Jerry. *Amon, the life of Amon Carter, Sr. of Texas*. Austin: Jenkins Publishing Company, 1978.

Gard, Wayne. *The Chisholm Trail*. Norman: University of Oklahoma Press, 1954.

Garrett, Julia Kathryn. *Fort Worth: A Frontier Triumph*. Austin: Encino Press, 1972.

Givner, Joan. *Katherine Anne Porter, A Life*. New York: Simon and Schuster, 1982.

Knight, Oliver. *Fort Worth: Outpost on the Trinity*. Norman: University of Oklahoma Press, 1953.

McAlester, Virginia and Lee. *Discover Dallas/Fort Worth*. New York: Alfred A. Knopf, 1988.

Pate, J'Nell L. *Livestock Legacy: The Fort Worth Stockyards, 1887-1987*. College Station: Texas A&M University Press, 1988.

Pirtle, Caleb III. *Fort Worth: The Civilized West*. Tulsa: Continental Heritage Press, Inc., 1980.

Sanders, Leonard. *How Fort Worth Became the Texasmost City*. Fort Worth: Amon Carter Museum of Western Art, 1973.

Schmidt, Ruby, ed. *Fort Worth & Tarrant County: A Historical Guide*. Fort Worth: Texas Christian University Press, 1984.

Schmelzer, Janet L. *Where the West Begins: Fort Worth and Tarrant County*. Northridge, California: Windsor Publications, Inc., 1985.

Webb, Missy, editor. *Directory of Texas Foundations*. San Antonio: Funding Information Center of Texas, Inc., 1989.

Williams, Mack. *In Old Fort Worth*. Fort Worth: As published in the *News-Tribune*, 1986.

Worchester, Don. *The Chisholm Trail: High Road of the Cattle Kingdom*. Lincoln: University of Nebraska Press, 1980.

II. NEWSPAPERS

Dallas Morning News
Dallas Times Herald
Fort Worth Star-Telegram
The Business Press

III. MAGAZINES

Fort Worth Magazine
Aura Magazine
Newsweek
Town & Country Magazine

IV. ADDITIONAL RESOURCES

Arts Council of Fort Worth and Tarrant County
City of Fort Worth
Dallas/Fort Worth International Airport
Fort Worth Chamber of Commerce
Fort Worth Convention and Visitors Bureau
Fort Worth Independent School District
Fort Worth Symphony Association
Fort Worth Theatre
Hip Pocket Theatre
Ivory, David. Fort Worth League of Neighborhoods. Central Bank & Trust Co., Fort Worth, Texas. Speech, December 7, 1989.
Shakespeare in the Park
Southwestern Baptist Theological Seminary
Tarrant County Junior College
Texas and Southwestern Cattle Raisers Foundation
Texas Christian University
Texas College of Osteopathic Medicine
Texas Wesleyan University
Van Cliburn Foundation

Index

GENERAL INDEX
Italicized numbers indicate illustrations.